A Far Valley

THE KAN YAMAGUCHI SERIES

Publication of this book was assisted by a generous grant provided by Ms. Kan Yamaguchi of Tsuchiura City, Japan. A select number of interesting works in English on Japan have been given such assistance.

A Far Valley

Four Years in a Japanese Village

Brian Moeran

KODANSHA INTERNATIONAL
Tokyo • New York • London

Acknowledgment

I would like to thank the Japan Foundation, the School of Oriental and African Studies in London, and the Social Science Research Council of Great Britain for helping to fund the fieldwork I did in the Oni valley. I also owe a great deal to my former colleagues at SOAS, particularly to Adrian Mayer and David Parkin. My greatest debt, however, is to a large number of Japanese friends and acquaintances who went out of their way to encourage and support us during our stay.

First published by Stanford University Press in 1985 under the title *Ōkubo Diary: Portrait of a Japanese Valley*.

Distributed in the United States by Kodansha America, Inc., 114 Fifth Avenue, New York, N.Y. 10011, and in the United Kingdom and continental Europe by Kodansha Europe Ltd., 95 Aldwych, London WC2B 4JF. Published by Kodansha International Ltd., 17-14 Otowa 1-chome, Bunkyo-ku, Tokyo 112-8652, and Kodansha America, Inc. Copyright © 1998 by Kodansha International Ltd. All rights reserved. Printed in Japan.
First edition, 1985
First paperback edition, 1998
98 99 00 01 02 10 9 8 7 6 5 4 3 2 1
ISBN 4-7700-2301-4

For Shibby, Mugi, and Superats
with all my love

Contents

Introduction

This is a book about the four years I spent with my family in a remote valley in Kyushu, in southern Japan, back in the late seventies and early eighties. Based on three diaries that I kept at the time, *A Far Valley* is part private journal, part ethnographic record, and part social and moral commentary on everyday life in a Japanese valley. It describes our intrusion into people's lives; our delight at what seemed to us to be their often fascinating and funny ways; and our eventual disillusionment as we became enmeshed in a series of half-truths, deceits, and downright lies after our older son, Alyosha, broke his neck in a diving accident in the local primary school swimming pool.

Both people and places portrayed in *A Far Valley* have been fictionalized—partly to protect the privacy of those with whom we had the pleasure of sharing four years of our lives; partly because when I first wrote the book, the objective "truth" of some of the events described here was being contended in a Japanese court of law; and partly to help me bring some coherence to a rather loosely structured book. In spite of this fictionalization, however, I should perhaps emphasize that everything related here actually happened. All I chose to do when writing *A Far Valley* was to amalgamate two or three living people into single composite characters and to play such havoc with local geography and names that in the end I was forced to draw up a chart on the wall of my study to remind myself of who was who and what was where.

Given that this book is all about country people, and given that fewer than one tenth of Japan's population of 123 million or so now live in the country, people nowadays might justifiably say: "Why write about something that doesn't really exist?" There are several answers to this question. The first is: because of chance. I first went to the Oni valley in order to conduct an ethnographic study of a community of potters who, whether they liked it or not, were closely involved in the Japanese folk art (*mingei*) movement. As I soon found out, *mingei* potters and their work were idolized by people in urban areas precisely because they continued to live and work in "traditional" ways no longer found in Japan's cities. It was not all personal idiosyncrasy, therefore, but the romanticism of Japan's urban intellectuals and aesthetes that took me to study Sarayama Onta and so bring my family to live in the Oni valley nearby.*

A second good reason for writing about rural life is that, in spite of its apparent lack of comparability with what is going on in an urban environment, it provides in the village a coherent unit with which to try to make sense of a particular kind of society's ongoing relationships and ways of thought. As *A Far Valley* clearly shows, until Japan's postwar economic development brought about considerable improvement in communications and employment opportunities, people out in the country tended to be born, to go to school, work, get married and have children in and around the same community. The same can hardly be said of those living in cities, where families are segregated from work and education is divorced from neighborhood affairs. It is thus much more difficult to arrive at a complete understanding of the ways in which an urban society functions and the underlying patterns of behavior that sustain city dwellers' social interaction. It is the overall coherence of rural life, I believe, and the sum of my experiences in a country environment that led me to a clearer understanding of who "the Japanese" might be.

At the same time, it should be recognized that the people encountered in this book are far removed in almost every way from their urban contemporaries. Indeed, one of the pleasures taken by my Japanese friends in Tokyo on my occasional visits to the capital was in having me recount what had gone on at the latest *sake*-drinking session or how a particular dispute had been successfully negotiated to a harmonious conclusion. They found the

---

*A number of people commenting on the original version of this book mistakenly assumed that Oni *is* Sarayama Onta. Let me state here, once and for all, that Sarayama Onta is not located in the Oni valley. Neither the places nor the people living there should be equated with one another.

people of the Oni valley as alien as did I myself and, shaking their heads in disbelief, would exclaim: "They can't be Japanese!"

Now, under such circumstances, it would be easy to see this book as just one more addition to those Orientalist writings about "traditional" Japan and its exotic past that somehow mark out the Japanese as "different" and "unique." Clearly, this would be a mistaken view. Firstly, as we have just seen, there is no such thing as *the* Japanese; if there were, my Japanese friends in Tokyo would never have reacted in the ways they did. Secondly, I have tried to portray my friends and acquaintances as living people rather than as caricatures or stereotypes, so that we can begin to understand the disparate voices that make up "the Japanese." Thirdly, when we read accounts by other anthropologists or historians about rural life in remote places, we often find the same kind of innocence, naiveté, unexpected humor, prejudice, and parochialism encountered here; in this respect, the world of *A Far Valley* is as like that of the African tribe studied by Elénore Smith Bowen in *Return to Laughter* (Harper & Brothers, 1954) as it is of Ronald Blythe's portrayal of rural England in *Akenfield* (Penguin, 1969). When we read about country people in Japan, therefore, we are also reading about other people living in rural areas all over the world. Implicit, then, is a notion of comparison, and it is comparison that is the stuff of anthropology.

Now let me turn from the development of Japanese society to that of this book. Originally published under the title *Ōkubo Diary* back in 1985, *A Far Valley* can be seen as very much part of a transition in writing about Japanese society and culture that began to take place in the mid-1980s, when Alan Booth's *The Roads to Sata* (Weatherhill, 1985) and John David Morley's *Pictures from the Water Trade* (Atlantic Monthly Press, 1985) were first published. Interestingly, these three books were all written and published within a year of one another by authors who had been born in England just after the war (I am now Irish by nationality) before becoming expatriates in Japan in blithe ignorance of each others' existences.* But, while *The Roads to Sata* and *Pic-*

---

*I was later fortunate enough to meet and enjoy the wicked humor and touching kindness of Alan Booth, whose untimely death from cancer has left a great emptiness in the hearts of his many friends.

tures from the Water Trade sold in their tens of thousands and brought their authors appropriate fame, *Ōkubo Diary* remained relatively unknown, except to a small audience of anthropologists and their students (who never could afford to buy the book, of course, and had to content themselves with copies borrowed from their university libraries). Indeed, at one stage—I was informed with an appropriate air of gravity—the book was Stanford University Press's "worst-selling paperback." In my more uncharitable moments, I suspect that this was because nobody at that prestigious academic institution was particularly concerned with marketing, preferring to devote themselves to producing scholarly books that were carefully edited and artistically designed. Let's face it, making money and perceptions of "quality" tend not to make good bedfellows in academia. What sells cannot be good; what is good should not sell; ergo, *Ōkubo Diary* must be a great book!

Since its republication by a commercial publisher now threatens to upset the academic equation, perhaps I should say quite clearly here that I have never seen this book as "academic." Friends and students have found it funny, informative, exasperating, frank, ambivalent, even close to tragic (mainly because of Alyosha's accident). My academic peers, on the other hand, have generally been at a loss as to how to comment on a "scholarly" publication that had neither bibliography nor index. They have found it "refreshing," "evocative," "revealing," but, at the same time, they have felt obliged to criticize it. "The trouble with Moeran," says one, "is that he can't make up his mind whether the Japanese are group-oriented or individualists." Another suggests that the problem with the book is "the quality of the generalizations and the categories of culture in which they are framed." A third complains that the author was "naive to assume that he could 'become' Japanese." They're right, of course. All the same, one of my unstated points in writing *A Far Valley* was to show that Japanese people are never entirely *either* this *or* that; that generalizations and categories of "culture" as such tend to be rather meaningless in the long term; and that a sense of honesty demands that we *should* reveal our own particular naiveté when *all* of us who go to live in Japan are, in one way or another and to a greater or lesser degree, naive.

One final word. The book ends on a rather bitter note—bitter enough for some people to ask me whether I haven't had enough of Japan and the Japanese. The immediate retort to that is: no, definitely not. By chance, it is exactly thirty years to the day since I first rolled off a Russian ship that had braved two typhoons to bring me from Nakhodka and anchor uneasily in Tokyo Bay. Since that fateful evening, an awful lot has happened to Japan, to my Japanese (and other) friends, and to myself. We've grown older; we've lost—one or two of us—our hair, but grown liver spots instead; we have scars physical and psychological on various parts of our bodies. All this can be depressing. But, by all the pantheons of deities throughout the world, let me say how I look forward with relish to thirty more years of contact with Japan and its people.

So, if you're sitting comfortably (as a BBC radio storyteller used to say every afternoon when I was a very small boy), let us begin. . . .

Hong Kong
September 21, 1997

1 The River's Flow

> The flow of the river is ceaseless; its water is never the same.
>
> —*Kamo no Chōmei*

I   *Whole days spent before this* diary, *with nothing better to do than jot down at random whatever comes into my mind.* Tonight is *the* full moon of the year—August 15 by the lunar calendar. Would that I, too, could write such lyrical prose in celebration of the people of this valley.

In the meantime, I have the moon before my eyes, the sweet scent of the mock orange flowers (*mokusei*) in my nostrils, and the sharp taste of *sake* on my tongue. What more can one want of this bridge of dreams?

2   The charm of this dialect that I am finally learning to understand. Its verb forms are old, echoes of classical Japanese. "It won't sting" comes out, not as *sashimasen*, but as *sasu wa sen*; "she's doing it" is *shi oru* rather than *shite iru*; "eat!" is a gentle *tabennai*, instead of standard *tabenasai*. Then there is a whole range of unaccustomed vocabulary. Some of it makes sense—like *sukan*, which replaces the more usual *kirai*, for "dislike" and which turns out to be no more than the negative of the standard word for "like" (*suki*). But a lot of words and phrases make less sense. *Dogē shioru* is a question that had me pondering for days—and worried, too, since it is frequently used as a form of greeting, and greetings are not to be questioned in any society, unless you are out to create confusion and upset the status quo of social interaction. I have now realized that the phrase merely stands for *nani o shiteru*, "what are you up to?" *Horuki* is another word that took me time to work out as *sore kara*, "and then."

Other words I begin to understand through context. A child who falls over and grazes his knees is *muginē*, "poor thing" (*kawaisō* in standard Japanese); an unusual event is *myō na kotsu* (*hen na koto*); and a woman expressing a sense of shame says *ha ga ii* (*hazukashii*). Some of the phrases are more expressive. For example, when people exclaim how surprised they are, they say that their "testicles have gone up" (*tamagatta*). What I find most surprising about this is that it is often women who use the word!

The other day, on our way back from a *shigin* (Chinese poetry) singing session down in the valley, Kajiwara Buntarō began talking about a softball game and a pitcher who had struck out almost every batter he faced with his lob ball. "The trouble is," Buntarō went on, "you can't hit a *shomben-dama* ['piss ball']." He shook his head in exasperation, while I marveled at his elegant simile between the trajectory of a slow lob and that of a man's urine as he stands to relieve himself. Buntarō drove on, unloosening his collar and tie. "Well, there's no more need of this piece of seaweed," he exclaimed with relief and stuffed his tie in his jacket pocket.

I've got to the stage now when I try to practice the dialect I've picked up on the local people—much to their surprise and seeming pleasure. Somehow I doubt, though, that I'll ever be able to master this variety of language fluently. And it is my failure in language as much as anything else that will always set me apart from those among whom I am living.

3 Names are very important here in the valley. When I came to study in Kamayama, the first problem people faced was what they were going to call me.

"What's your name? Moeran?" one of the potters asked. "Well, in that case, we should call you Mōsan. Or Mōshan, as we would pronounce it in our dialect. The trouble is we've already got a Mō-shan in the hamlet, so you'll have to have a different name."

"Well, my first name is Brian. Bu-rai-an in Japanese," I spelled it out to help. "And for some reason, my wife and children have always called me by the diminutive form, Būchan. Why don't you call me that? Or do you have another Būchan?"

"Būchan!" The potter laughed, slightly embarrassed. "But that means 'piglet.' We can't call you that."

"Everybody else does."

There was a pause as the potters looked at one another. Then one of them handed me a *sake* cup.

"I'm pleased to meet you, Būchan," he said. "How about a cup of *sake* to celebrate your coming here to Kamayama."

I soon learned that all members of a country community are on first-name terms with one another, and that these names are frequently abbreviated. Akihito, for example, is called Akichan, Daisuke Daichan, Tatetarō Tatechan. Sometimes the diminutive is more difficult to follow. Tadashi becomes Tadassan or Tadashisan, Chitose Chitossan, Katsuhisa Katchan, and Asao Āchan. Women's names often end in the suffix -*ko*, meaning "child," and it is this that is dropped in the familiar form. Misako is Misachan, Eiko Eichan, and Akiko Akichan. With women, there is a tendency to use the friendlier -*chan*, as in Akemichan or Tsuruchan (for Tsuruyo). For three-syllable men's names, people often just add on the more formal suffix -*san*, as in Osamusan or Takeshisan.

Family pet names are occasionally used, but this is not so common. A man called Nonoshita is known by the familiar Nonchan. In the cities, of course, you never hear anything but family names, even among friends. But here in the Oni valley, a lot of people have the same family name, so that using first names is the best way to distinguish one person from another. I must say, I find it so much more pleasant and friendly, calling people by their first names. It is very much part of the communal nature of valley life, and names become an integral part of each person's social identity.

4   I really must find myself a house of my own. It's not that I'm unhappy at the family inn in Kamayama. Far from it. This past half year has been the happiest time in my life. What is upsetting, though, is that I haven't been able to share my experiences with Kyōko and the children.

The trouble is knowing where to start. There are two or three buildings in Kamayama that might be suitable, but I've made a few inquiries, and it's clear that I'm not going to be able to persuade anybody there to give me accommodation. I shall have to find a place farther down the valley and commute on my 50-cc bike.

The best person to ask for help is Inoshige. Friends in Tokyo first told me about this potter, whose work had already won two or three prizes in national ceramics exhibitions. We met soon after my arrival in Kamayama and found that we got on together very well. It has been Inoshige who has been patiently explaining and teaching me the basic techniques of pottery these past six months. He has lent me the use of his wheel, so that I can throw my own bad pots. He has let me join in the hard grind of preparing clay, drying wood, glazing pots, and loading, firing, and unloading his climbing kiln. He has more or less adopted me into his household, introducing me as his "younger brother" to people all over the valley and down in the town, where he frequently takes me on extended tours of the local bars. When I get pent up and frustrated by the stifling atmosphere in Kamayama, I always have Inoshige to turn to.

He is decorating some slabware dishes when I slide open the door of his workshop.

"Ah! Būchan! You're still alive, then?" he says by way of greeting. Finishing the brushwork he is doing, he switches off the radio. "And what brings you down here at this time of the morning? Have you had enough of tracing genealogies?"

Such a direct question deserves an equally direct answer. With Inoshige, at least, I can say what I please and not worry too much about the local people's art of indirect allusion. "It's time I found somewhere to live. Then Kyōko and the children can join me here. And I thought that maybe you could help."

Inoshige drags over a wooden stool for me, placing it down in the middle of the workshop near the oil stove. It isn't that cold, but it has been raining a lot recently, and pots aren't drying quickly enough. Inoshige has a large order to be filled by the middle of next month, and he has fallen behind schedule.

"I wondered when you were going to ask me that," he says, lighting a cigarette. The workshop door rattles open as Ayako comes in with tea.

"This is a surprise," she says, laying the tray on a third stool set between us and pouring out the hot green liquid into three of Inoshige's delicately made cups. "It's early for you to be down in the valley at this time of the morning, isn't it?"

I repeat what I had said to Inoshige. Ayako glances down at her husband, who remains impassive and thoughtful.

"Well, there's always Fujinori's place up in Kamayama, of course. You know, the old house where they store wood now. They used to live in it until three or four years ago." Ayako must have seen the expression on my face because she adds quickly, "Still, I doubt whether the old man would ever let you stay there."

"There's an empty house up in Ichinotsuru," adds Inoshige. "I've asked Gotō Chitose about it because he's head of the main house and cousin of the man who's gone away. But Chitose is a big land-owner, and you need to be careful with people like that. Anyway, the fact that the people who own the house have moved so far away makes things difficult. You can't talk things over properly."

Inoshige sips his tea and takes a pickled plum from the bowl on the tray. "No. I think the best bet would be for us to look a bit farther down the valley. There's a place in Kodake by the Coordi-nation Office, where they keep records of all the households in the valley, and another one in Ōkubo, up above Inekari. Kodake might be better. The people who own it are nice. And the house is conve-nient, right down by the road. The other one's too isolated, really. And anyway the owner, Yamaguchi Takeshi, is a pretty tricky char-acter. You never know with him what is going on. But he's got a good wife and nice family," Inoshige adds, always careful to present a balanced view of people.

It is interesting how my search for somewhere to live is already being translated into a network of people with whom I will have to communicate. I have already discovered this with pottery in Ka-mayama, where critical appreciation of the folk-craft style by out-siders is interpreted by potters in terms of community relations and a conflict between older and younger men. In a Japanese country valley, objects and actions are almost invariably interpreted as facets of social relations. People are the idiom for time and space.

But what comes as more of a surprise is the fact that Inoshige and Ayako have already been discussing between themselves the possi-bility of my moving into a house outside Kamayama, where I am doing my research. They have even gone so far as to make one or two inquiries on my behalf. A few words with Fujinori had been enough for Inoshige to realize that the people of Kamayama would prefer me to live elsewhere, and he had turned his attention to places outside the small pottery community. In the meantime, firm in the belief that as an anthropologist I had to live with the com-munity I was studying, I had blundered from one possibility to another within Kamayama. When I myself had asked Fujinori about his old house at the top of the community, he had replied that he couldn't help. He had too much wood stacked up inside and the place was too damp, situated as it was right beside the river. Why didn't I ask Shigeomi? He owned the old community house, the one that had been built by the prefectural authorities when they thought that the emperor's sister-in-law was going to visit, and that could easily be converted into suitable accommodation for us.

So I had approached Shigeomi, who had sounded willing enough, but pointed out that he kept all his household farming equipment in the building in question. It was right by the road where the tourist buses parked, and there was no privacy, of course, especially on Sundays. And then there was the fact that the building may have been owned by him, but it had been built by the prefectural authorities. I'd have to get their permission as well. Why didn't I try Masao? He had a nice thatched cottage above his place. It was a bit tumbledown, but it had a lovely view out over the community.

Masao was more helpful. Sure, I could take a look at the house up by the bamboo grove. But the mosquitoes would be a plague in the summer, especially now that the walls had mostly fallen down. The roof was leaking, of course, and there was no floor to speak of. If I wanted to live there, I could, but I'd be wiser to talk to Fujinori. He had a nice old thatched house near the top of the community. It had a bit of wood stacked away in it, perhaps, but it hadn't been empty that long and was just the right size for me and my family. Like a hot potato, I had been passed along from one man to the next. And yet here were Inoshige and Ayako working out how they could incorporate this outsider into their valley community. Perhaps, after all, I would be better living out of Kamayama and commuting there on my bike. I would meet new people, see and hear new things, and so be able to look at the place more objectively. There is something to be said for getting away from informants whose ways of thought could stifle reflection and numb the mind.

"Leave things to me," Inoshige breaks in on my daydream. "We'll see what can be done about a house."

5   A couple of days later, Inoshige phones me to say that he has got permission to look over the house in Kodake. I get on my motorbike and ride the two and a half miles to his house, down the twisting narrow valley, with its cascading stream a muddy brown torrent from the rain that has been pouring down all morning.

Inoshige is waiting inside his workshop. With him is Higuchi Daisuke, a carpenter who lives just up the road in Amagase. Some people's names or faces I've found it hard to remember in the time I've been here. But not Daisuke's. How can you forget a man who tells you over an exchange of *sake* cups that his wife is his mother's younger sister. Being somewhat the worse for a hard evening's drinking, I was convinced at the time that I had discovered a case of incest, and that this would be my single contribution to anthropological knowledge. But the next day Daisuke dampened my excitement by explaining that he wasn't his mother's real son, and that his father was in fact his uncle. He had been adopted into the Higuchi household soon after he had left school, and his uncle-cum-father decided to marry him off to his wife's younger sister. So uncle and nephew, sister and sister, all lived together as a "family," and the younger couple now had two grown boys nearly finishing school themselves.

"Būchan, I've asked Daisuke here to come along with us to look at the house. Yamamura, the man who owns it, said over the phone that the place was pretty run down and would need repairing. In which case, Daisuke here is the man to help. Isn't that right, Dai-chan?"

Daisuke flashes a toothy smile and touches the peak of his gray cap, which is inscribed with the name of the prefectural carpenters' union. "That's right," he says. "Anything I can do to help you settle down. I know what it's like being a newcomer to this valley. You need all the help you can get."

We go out into the rain and get into Daisuke's van, the three of us squashed together on the bench seat. The mist clings tightly to the hillsides; the golden rice ears hang heavy in the fields on the other side of the valley across from the river. We drive down through the tall cedar trees to the Todoroki bridge. The river water is almost up to the parapet.

"This bridge is a joke, if ever there was one," muses Daisuke as he guides the van carefully across. "Todoroki is written with three characters in one, all meaning car [*kuruma*]. And yet here we are, hardly able to drive this small van across without scraping the sides."

"Still, it's better than the old one, isn't it?" says Inoshige. "In rain like this, the suspension bridge would get washed away, and we'd all have to turn out one weekend to build a new one. You see the house across the river there?" He points to a deep thatched roof

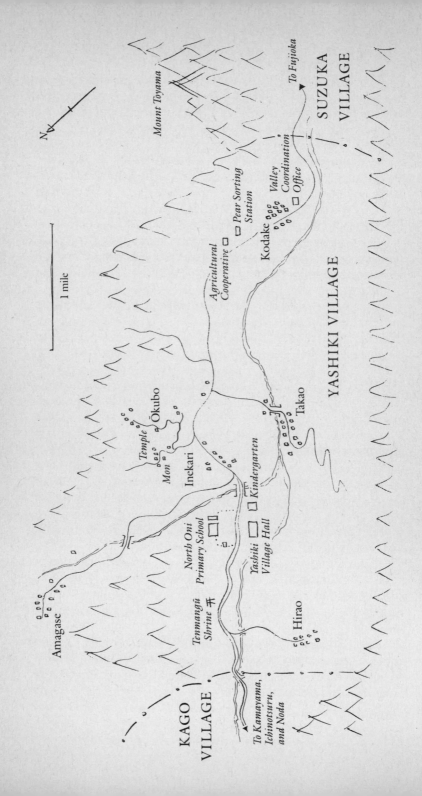

N

1 mile

KAGO VILLAGE

Amagase

Tenmangū Shrine

North Oni Primary School

To Kamayama, Ichinotsuru, and Noda

Temple
Mon
Ōkubo

Inekari

Yashiki Village Hall

Kindergarten

To Hirao

Hirao

Takao

Mount Toyama

Agricultural Cooperative

Pear Sorting Station

Kodake

Valley Coordination Office

To Fujioka

SUZUKA VILLAGE

YASHIKI VILLAGE

rearing up from the terraced rice fields. "That's where the old road used to go. Up by the woods, along the edge of the rice fields there. And now just look at the place. All on its own. The only way you can get there is across a footbridge. Poor Katō Michiya, the man who lives there, has to beg his neighbor to lend him a few square yards of land on this side of the river, so that he has somewhere to park his car by the side of the road."

We drive on down the valley, past the *sake* shop and small shrine. Inoshige motions up above our heads through the tall thick bamboo. "Somewhere up there is the other house I was telling you about. It's funny, really. That used to be on the main road, too. Coming up from Fujioka, at the bottom of the valley, the road was more or less straight enough until it got to this point." We are passing another thatched-roof house and a more recently built house with a tiled entrance and a barber's red-and-white-striped sign outside. "Then it wound off up the hill between Kumao's place and the barber's shop, round past Aso's place, and then back down again through Ōkubo, along the top of Inekari, and on to Katō Michiya's. Yes, in the old days, the road just followed the houses, and it didn't matter much if you did wander along in a series of half-circles. People weren't in that much of a hurry anyhow. Nowadays the road goes in a straight line, and we build our houses beside it."

We pass the Pear Sorting Station. Daisuke slows down and pulls into the side of the road. There is a narrow track running at an angle off behind a row of houses leading to the Valley Coordination Office. There are two or three houses on the left, as we look, backing on to the rice fields. It is at one of these that Inoshige stops.

"Well, here we are," he says and slides open the door.

We go in. There are two fairly large rooms, with a small cubbyhole of a kitchen at the back and an outside toilet to one side, but no bath. Clearly, the place has not been lived in for some time. There are no connecting screens (*fusuma*) between the two rooms, and all the shōji (sliding window-doors) need repairing. The floorboards don't feel too firm underfoot either.

Daisuke sucks in his breath sharply. "We're going to have to do something about these floorboards, of course. And it looks as if one of the shutters will need replacing. But the roof's sound enough. It's lucky we came while it was raining."

"What about sunshine?" I asked. "Which way is the house facing?"

Inoshige pauses to think for a moment. "The wrong way," he answers. "West, not south. What about a bath, Daichan?"

"We can probably fix something up temporarily. After all, Būchan doesn't plan on staying here forever. And there's space in the vegetable patch here for me to rig up some sort of lean-to for a bath. We'll need a plumber as well. There's a lot of work to be done."

"You mean it's going to cost quite a bit," muses Inoshige. "Still, Yamamura's an understanding sort who won't charge much, if anything, in the way of rent. What do you think, Būchan?"

I am not entirely happy. The place is a bit cramped for the four of us. And it is situated so close to the road you can hear the traffic passing up and down the valley. Typical urbanite that I am, I have come to the country expecting peace and quiet. I am pretty certain that Kyōko will feel the same.

I decide to ask about the other house that Inoshige had mentioned the day before yesterday. He and Daisuke exchange glances. "Well, I suppose we could have a peek. But it's really out of the way, you know."

"Which is precisely why I want to have a look at it," I answer quickly.

So we pile back into Daisuke's van and drive back up the valley. Soon after passing the barber's shop, we turn right up a steep slope, drive a couple of hundred yards, and then turn sharp right again, zigzagging up the steep hillside. The road veers left, and Daisuke drives straight on. For a moment I think we are plunging off the road, but then I see a narrow dirt track leading gently down between a bamboo grove on one side and a large pear orchard on the other. We come out into the open and suddenly there is a panoramic view of orchard, cedar forests, and mist-laden hills. In front of us, to the left, is the house, perched right on the edge of a 15-foot precipice.

"There!" says Inoshige. "I told you the place was isolated."

"It's beautiful," I gasp in wonder.

"Beautiful? It's *sabishii*—lonely and isolated," Daisuke insists.

We get out of the van and walk up to the house. There is a second house behind it, hidden from the road and standing back against the hillside.

"That's Aso Masaki's place," explains Inoshige. "It used to be owned by Kumao. You know, the man who lives down next to the barber's shop. But Masaki's house in Ichinotsuru burned down, and Kumao wanted to move down by the roadside, so they made a deal. As for this house, it used to belong to a man called Katō. He's been dead some years now, and his family moved away somewhere. That was when Yamaguchi Takeshi bought up the house and land. It was rice fields then, but he cashed in on a Coop drive and converted them all to pear orchards."

The door is open, so we are free to go in and have a look around. The place is in chaos. There is a quarter-inch of dust on the moldy tatami mats, and the single downstairs room is full of junk and empty bottles. But there is a reasonably good-sized kitchen, the traditional *kotatsu* area with its sunken charcoal-burning hearth, a toilet, and a bathroom with a wood-fired iron tub.

Upstairs is much more spacious, for the house has been built onto, so that both floors now follow the slope from one orchard to the next. Two small rooms are above the downstairs room, adjoined, in the newer section, by two large rooms with a veranda looking out over the valley. The ceiling of the room downstairs may be so low that I have to bend almost double when walking around; there may be gaping holes in the mud-and-wattle walls of the smaller rooms upstairs; the toilet may not have a ceiling or the bathroom a door, but none of these things matter. There is light, there is space, there is a view, and there is quiet. This is the sort of house I have dreamed about—*a cocoon spun by an aged silkworm.*

I ask Daisuke what he thinks.

"What do I think?" he retorts. "I think you foreigners have interesting ideas about housing. There is nothing I can do about these upstairs rooms except to seal them off entirely. The walls need redoing. The window here is a mess. And the floor is partly rotten. It would be quicker to rebuild the place entirely. But the rest of the house will be fine, once you tidy it up a bit. I can give you some ceiling tiles and old floorboards for the bathroom and put a door on it. I can rebuild that cupboard for your bedding and put in a rail here for you to hang your clothes. I'll help you rip that ridiculous sink out, and I've probably got some old piping for drains, which you'll have to run from the bathroom, down the wall, across the track, and out into the orchard. That's what I think," Daisuke finishes with a grin.

"So now all we have to do is talk to Yamaguchi Takeshi," sighs Inoshige. "Persuading him to rent you this place is going to be our biggest problem of all."

6   In the old days the bus that carries people back and forth between the valley and the nearest town used to stay overnight in Ichinotsuru. The bus company considered it uneconomical to have the bus come down empty last thing in the evening and go back up the valley empty first thing in the morning, when it picked up the local commuters. So the driver used to stay with the conductress in the hamlet of Ichinotsuru, at the top of the valley, and the villagers there took turns putting them up for the night.

In a mountain community there was little to do in the evenings before television relieved the monotony of darkness. So almost every evening the driver and his conductress were entertained with *sake*. The story goes that very occasionally everyone got so merry that they would all pile into the bus and drive down to the town for a few more drinks in the bars. Eventually they would head for home with the driver weaving an erratic course up the valley toward Ichinotsuru. Once he strayed too far from the not so straight, but very narrow, and the bus went off the edge of the road into a rice field. Everyone had to scramble about in the mud and somehow managed to push and lever the bus back onto the road.

These are stories about *sake* drinking, told over more *sake* drinking, and embellished for my notebook, no doubt. Another subject that frequently crops up on such occasions is that of *yobai*, or "night crawling." Anyone acquainted with the literary works of the Heian period (794–1185) will know about the way in which sweet-perfumed courtiers would spy through fences in order to catch a glimpse of some beautiful woman. An exchange of poems would follow, and he would hope that she would give him permission to visit her until the dawn. I am assured that here in the country men still make it a practice to visit women at night. Their art of lovemaking has been refined, however, in a manner somewhat less genteel than that practiced by such elegant courtiers as Hikaru Genji. It is said here that certain rules should be adhered to, if a man is to succeed in his venture. First, he should wear but a simple cotton robe (*yukata*) belted with an obi about the hips. Upon arriving at his lover's house, he should urinate upon the wooden shutters, so that they will then slide open soundlessly. Once inside, he should untie his belt and, with a bowling action, unroll it across the tatami mats toward where his lover is lying. By walking on his belt, he successfully masks the noise of his feet, and his robe, of course, is now wide open for the ensuing pleasure.

I am not convinced that this is really how things are done. Those who deem themselves to be experts in night crawling complain, for instance, that modern aluminum-framed sliding doors cannot be lulled to discreet silence by an injection of urine in the appropriate place. Inoshige says that he overslept one morning and ended up having breakfast with the girl's father, who pretended not to notice that he was there. In Ichinotsuru one of the bus conductresses was abducted from her bed and taken off into the night by an ardent young lover. But somebody was awake and heard a noise. The alarm was raised, and people got up to search for the culprit. Nobody knew who it was for days on end, and one or two young men found themselves being accused of a deed that they would like to have done, no doubt, but of which at the time it seemed wiser to feign a certain innocence. Eventually the culprit was found, an unlikely youth by all accounts, who elicited considerable admiration for his choice of venue—a disused charcoal-burning kiln nearby. The bus driver was furious and said that from then on the bus would never stay overnight in Ichinotsuru. The hamlet chief, Gotō Chitose's father, hastily agreed, but said that it would be better for all if the suggestion were made to the bus company by him. After all, the girl's honor was at stake, and there could be no end of trouble between her family and the bus company, trouble that was bound to involve the driver ultimately. No. The suggestion should be seen to have been initiated by Ichinotsuru. The driver, realizing the wisdom of this way of handling things, agreed. But the hamlet chief did nothing. This annoyed the bus driver even more, and he was still looking for a way to let his company know what had happened when a second conductress was molested in the night. The bus company had no alternative but to allow the driver to bring an empty bus home last thing in the evening. This made more sense than a girl's lost virginity and possible pregnancy.

7   If you are looking for a girl with whom to arrange a marriage, for your own or for someone else's family, then the best person to talk to is the postman. He is the only man who knows everybody in the valley.

8   Inoshige has finally managed to arrange a meeting with Yamaguchi Takeshi. "It hasn't been easy," he explains as we drive down to Yamaguchi's house, "because there's a way of doing things that has to be followed. It doesn't matter what you do in this valley—whether you're renting a house, buying some land, or looking for a prospective daughter-in-law—you should never do things on your own. Two people talking is anti-social; it smacks of secrecy and double-dealing. What I mean is, never approach anyone directly, but try to get somebody else to act as a disinterested third party on your behalf. Try to involve as many people as possible. That is the first rule of life in the country. That way, you'll have people to support you if something goes wrong. People are a kind of insurance.

"But you've already worked that out for yourself. At least, I presume so from the way that you have asked me to help you find somewhere to live. But I'm not on any kind of social terms with Yamaguchi, since he doesn't happen to be a man I've come across very much in the past. He may own land in the same village as I do, but he lives in the next village down the valley, and it's not often that people from different villages get together, unless they happen to be related to one another or doing the same sort of work. But he's a pear grower and I'm a potter. About the only time we do meet is at the annual *shigin* singing contest in the Yashiki village hall.

"And that's why I've called on Wada Tatetarō to help. Tatechan, as you know, is a member of the South Oni *shigin* group, even though he does occasionally come up to sing with us in our north group. He is also a man of consequence in the valley. The fact that he is in charge of the Fujioka branch of the Agricultural Cooperative means that people here tend to listen to his opinions. After all, the Coop is an important place for us country people. We can buy our insecticides and farming equipment there. We can buy our gas there and invest our savings there. And the Coop lends us money at a reasonable rate when we need it and gives us advice on how to improve our farming techniques. So you can see how important a man like Tatetarō is. Finally, he is a relative of Yamaguchi's. They're cousins, in fact. So with Tatetarō to help us, things ought to go all right."

He turns the car into a narrow lane that winds up to Yamaguchi's house.

"Tatetarō lives over there on the other side of the river, beyond the water mill. This house here belongs to Wada Hiromi, his and Yamaguchi's uncle. Even so, he's not that much older than either of them. Hiromi is an employee of the city government. He works with the local Education Authority, so he's the one you'll be talking to about putting your children into the North Oni Primary School."

We pull up at Yamaguchi's house and slide open the front door. "*Gomen kudasai!*"

"*Hai!*" comes a voice in answer from the back of the house. There is the quick patter of feet on the corridor floor, and a figure in a kimono appears. It is Yamaguchi's wife, Hanako. She greets us and shows us into the main guest room, but Inoshige asks her not to stand on ceremony. If it wouldn't inconvenience her, we would be quite happy to go to the *kotatsu* room and relax with our feet under the low table, dangling down against the charcoal brazier.

As we take our places, Yamaguchi comes in. We immediately clamber out of the *kotatsu* and kneel to make our formal greetings. Yamaguchi beams at me with one of the toothiest smiles I have ever seen. "Haro," he says in English, with an accent that reminds me at once of where we had met before. About six weeks ago, I ran in a "marathon" at the school. As we trotted out of the playground and down the hill past the barber's shop, a funny-looking, buck-toothed man in his late forties had tagged on beside me. "Let's run together," he had said, and run together we did, down the valley and up again, until the last stretch uphill, when my long legs and competitive nature had drawn me ahead of my partner. Now I wish I hadn't left Yamaguchi Takeshi behind on the last stretch!

At this point Tatetarō comes in through the back door, and once more we get out of the *kotatsu* to exchange greetings. Hanako serves us tea and a dish of quartered persimmons, fresh from the tree outside the house. We make small talk before Inoshige eventually decides that the time is right to broach the matter in hand.

"Yamaguchisan, as you know, Būchan here has come all the way from England to study those potters living up the next valley in Kamayama. He's been there now for more than six months, living on his own at the inn. It's a good place to live, but—as you've probably heard—he has a wife and children, and they're all getting a bit lonely."

"Especially at nighttime," adds Tatetarō, "and with the winter approaching he'll need all the warmth he can get in bed. Isn't that right, Būchan?"

We all laugh as Inoshige continues. "Well anyway, those of us in the *shigin* group feel that Bū ought to live here with his family, rather than on his own as he is now."

"Quite right, too," says Yamaguchi, giving me one of his toothy grins.

"Now in my opinion Būchan is a bit different from all those dirty-looking foreigners we often see wandering around Kamayama. He's got a Japanese wife, and he reads and writes Japanese better than any of us here. He's an anthropologist, too, from the University of London. Now, I don't know much about what an anthropologist is or does, but if it means that he takes part in our valley life and learns to sing *shigin* like us, then I figure it can't be such a bad thing to study after all."

"Quite right," adds Tatetarō, "and he's got a good voice, too. Haven't you, Būchan?"

Fortunately, he doesn't expect a reply, but hurries on. "Būchan here asked Inoshige for help because he's an outsider. For some reason or other, these two have got on rather well ever since Būchan came to the valley. I suspect it's got something to do with drinking *sake*, but it's because we are all members of the *shigin* group that Inoshige has asked me to help."

"You see, Tatetarō mentioned one evening that he thought that you, Takeshisan, had an old house somewhere up in the orchards of Ōkubo. Now I don't know whether this is true, or if it is, what sort of condition the house might be in," Inoshige quickly continues with a slight falsification of reality, "but do you think it might be the sort of place you might like to lend to someone like Būchan?"

Yamaguchi scratches his head thoughtfully, staring into his cup of tea. "Well, it's a kind of, what should I say?" he mumbles somewhat incoherently before getting to the point. "Well, it's not really the sort of house a person like Būchan ought to live in."

"Why not?"

"Well, because it hasn't been lived in for a long time. And it's falling down. And I sometimes use it when I hire a few women to help me put paper bags on the pears in the early summer. I serve them tea there on the veranda."

"Has it got a veranda?" asks Inoshige innocently. "How pleasant!" How well he plays this game.

"Yes. Facing out onto the valley."

"That sounds like the perfect place for me to study," I venture.

"That may be so, but really the place is in too much of a mess."

Yamaguchi begins to enumerate some of the problems that Daisuke the carpenter had already solved. Tatetarō, however, knows that his objections are to some extent for the sake of form.

"Look, Takeshisan. Suppose Būchan here decided that he liked the house, and suppose that he felt he could clean up the place on his own, so that his wife and children could come and live in the valley, would you be prepared to lend him the house?"

"And pay rent, of course," adds Inoshige quickly.

"But Būchan may not like the house."

"Ah! That's a good point," says Tatetarō, looking first at Inoshige, then at me. There is a pause. I glance at Inoshige before blurting out: "Well, actually I do like the house. You see, the other day I was exploring the valley, and I came across your house. And since nobody seemed to be around, I had a look inside. I know it needs to have a lot of work done to it, and I know that it would be very inconvenient for you having us live there. But I also know that your house is just the sort of place we would all like to live in."

"And we could all go and practice *shigin* there one evening, couldn't we, Būchan?" Tatetarō adds quickly.

"Of course," I reply. "And sing 'You Are My Sunshine' the way you did after the marathon race the other day." I do my best to remind him indirectly of our chance meeting earlier.

Yamaguchi breaks into a toothy grin once more and starts to sing the first bars quietly, before trailing off.

"You see," Inoshige pounces on another chance to persuade a reluctant Yamaguchi. "When you start forgetting your English, Būchan, you can go and talk to Takeshisan. Now, that's what I call a real landlord."

But Yamaguchi hasn't quite finished with his objections.

"You'll have to ask Aso Masaki next door whether it's all right with him for you to live in my house," he says.

"Of course we have to, yes."

"And you'll have to get permission from Noda Shōsuke, the village headman. He should be told what is going on."

"That's a point," Tatetarō sucks in through his teeth slightly. "You really are a thoughtful fellow, Takeshisan."

"And you'll have to find out whether your boys are entitled to go to the North Oni Primary School," Takeshi continues, unmoved by his cousin's attempt to flatter him.

"I've already checked that out with the PTA," answers Inoshige, much to my surprise. I am beginning to realize that it's no easy task, renting a house in the country. Three of the most important social relations, involving neighborhood, local authority, and state education, have now been mentioned.

"And once we've done all that," muses Tatetarō, "I suppose we come to the matter of rent for your house." He laughs loudly to cover his embarrassment. Money is not an easy subject to discuss in public.

"Oh, I don't need rent," mumbles Yamaguchi.

"Yes, you do. After all, Būchan will be causing you no end of trouble. He'll be using your track and walking through your orchards. And you won't be able to come and go as freely as you'd like because Bū's family will always be around. And—"

"I've just had a thought," Inoshige interrupts. "What are we going to do about the cesspit?"

"Oh, yes. The cesspit. Now there's a problem."

"Is there?" I ask, secretly hoping that this was where the participant aspect of observation came to an abrupt end.

"Yes, there is. The 'honey wagon' doesn't go up to Ōkubo, so somebody's got to clear out the cesspit from time to time. And you can't do that, Būchan. You're a university anthropologist."

This is the first time that academic life has ever proved useful.

"Quite right, Tatechan. And anyway Būchan's a big fellow. The cesspit would fill up in no time at all. He'd never get any study done."

"And it's a very small cesspit, too." Yamaguchi gives me a quick glance before staring back down at the table top.

"Mmm. That is a problem, isn't it, Takeshisan?" Tatetarō looks inquiringly at his cousin. Then he continues. "You don't think you could help Bū out there, Takeshisan?"

Yamaguchi mumbles something that is taken for assent.

"Now that's what I call a really good man. Someone who is prepared to help out at all times. Thank you very much, Takeshisan. Now, what about the rent?"

"I don't need any rent," repeats Yamaguchi.

"Yes, you do. After all, Būchan will be causing you no end of trouble. Wait a minute," Tatetarō checks himself with a smile, "I've said all that before, haven't I? How about . . ." He pauses to calculate. "How about thirteen thousand yen a month?"

Yamaguchi's eyes seem to brighten a little.

"No. That's much too much. I don't need any rent."

"Yes, you do."

"No, I don't." Yamaguchi seems a great one for saying things according to form.

"Good." exclaims Tatetarō, "That's fixed then. Thirteen thousand yen a month, payable in advance. All right, Būchan?"

"Fine," I reply, aware that Inoshige had told me that I'd probably only have to pay between 3,000 and 5,000 yen a month. Still, 60 dollars a month isn't much to pay for rent.

"Good. Then let's clap hands on it."

"In that case we need some *sake*. Oy! Hanako!"

"Coming," calls Hanako from the kitchen, where she has been pottering around these last few minutes. She slides open the shōji screen and brings in a tray of cups and two *sake* bottles already warmed. Such thoughtful efficiency.

Yamaguchi pours us out some *sake*, and Hanako is asked to stay where she is by the *kotatsu*.

"You stay here and listen, Hanako," explains Tatetarō. "Takeshi here has agreed to lend Būchan that old house of his up in Ōkubo. Even though Takeshi has been very kind and said that he doesn't want any rent, I've said that Būchan ought to pay thirteen thousand yen a month, payable in advance."

Hanako looks embarrassed. "We don't need any rent."

"Well, you may not need it. I don't know anything about your financial situation here, but we're going to pay you rent, so there. Now, when are you going to move in, Būchan?"

"I don't know really. As soon as I've found time to clear up the place, I suppose. Sometime before the end of the year?"

"So, why not pay rent from the New Year? That makes more

sense." Tatetarō is a great one for organizing things. We drink our *sake*, and Yamaguchi offers me his cup. Tatetarō exchanges with Hanako, and Inoshige offers his to Yamaguchi. I pass mine to Inoshige. We all have another drink.

"That's better." Tatetarō exhales his breath sharply in appreciation as he finishes his cup and passes it to me. I return Yamaguchi his cup. Inoshige exchanges with Hanako. We all drink again. A further exchange of cups takes place. This is the short road to drunken frivolity.

"Hey! I nearly forgot. We're supposed to be clapping hands on the matter. Where's the old lady?" Tatetarō asks, looking around, just in case Yamaguchi's mother had crept in silently behind his back.

"She's gone to bed," replies Hanako.

"Hadn't we better wake her up for this?"

"No, it doesn't matter. As long as Hanako is here to know what's going on. Right?"

We all climb out of the *kotatsu* and kneel on the floor. Hanako refills our cups.

"Who's going to do it, then?"

"You, Tatechan. You do it."

"No, you do it."

"Tatechan should do it. He's the go-between."

"Well, if you insist." Tatetarō looks around at us, his face suddenly solemn. "Right then. O-o-o-oh!" he booms out and we all clap our hands sharply together twice. "O-o-o-oh!" And twice more.

"Good, then." Tatetarō relaxes back into his normal voice, and we slip our feet back into the *kotatsu*. "Come on, Būchan. Drink up!"

An hour or so later, after each of us has gone through the facial contortions involved in singing a *shigin* poem, and Yamaguchi and I have sung "You Are My Sunshine" in duet, with me making up the words after the second line, we bid farewell and stagger out into the night. The cold air soon sobers us up.

"I hope you noticed what went on, Būchan," says Inoshige as he shuffles over to the edge of the front courtyard and unzips his fly. "When asking someone a favor, or acting as intermediary, you should make it clear that you're not acting for yourself, but speaking in the interests of a group of some kind. That's why I played down our personal friendship and emphasized how it was the North Oni *shigin* group who wanted you to live in the valley."

There is the sound of water, and Inoshige lets fly his *shomben dama*. Tatetarō and I soon keep him company.

"And that also means, of course, that Inoshige doesn't get too personally indebted to Takeshi," chimes in Tatetarō. "As for the rent, I'm sorry I set it so high. The trouble is, I know that Takeshi is a bit greedy when it comes to money. The more he can get, the happier he is. All that talk of not wanting any rent was just a charade. I was thinking of about ten thousand yen, but that was too round a figure. Twelve thousand would have been better, but that worked out to four hundred yen a day and that didn't seem right. One should never be able to calculate exactly favors that one owes other people. So I plumped for thirteen thousand yen. An ideal figure. A bit unlucky for you, though."

Ideal, unlucky or not, I have my house. A little bit more than ten feet square and seven feet high, perhaps, but it, too, looks out over Mount Toyama. Kyōko *will tune her koto to the echoes of the pines and, in our search for tranquility, may we rejoice in the absence of grief.*

9   When I first came to study in Kamayama, some people thought I was a tax inspector in disguise. Others suggested that I was a spy. While I could understand why a few innocent questions about income and expenditure could quickly give rise to the first accusation, I was at a loss to explain why the British government should be interested in sending one of its agents to a remote Japanese valley. Perhaps there were secrets here that I'd never dreamed could exist.

I had also heard about one man who was convinced that I was a Russian spy. That man, I have now discovered, is my next-door neighbor-to-be, Aso Masaki. Today I meet him for the first time when I come up on my motorbike to start work on the house. He is standing in the sunlit yard in front of his house when I arrive, so I go up and introduce myself.

"I'm pleased to have you as a neighbor," he says quickly. "It's been lonely here these past few years with just the one family, and it'll be nice having company."

"I'm sure my children will make a lot of noise and cause you trouble, but please forgive them."

"Of course, of course. How old are they?"

"First and third year at the primary school," I answer in the Japanese way of telling children's ages.

"And are they boys or girls?"

"Both boys."

"Congratulations," Masaki says approvingly. I am a real man. "Well, let's be good, friendly neighbors. If there's anything you want, please let me know."

I go off to the house and start clearing up the mess inside. One hundred and eight empty *sake* bottles later, I wearily make myself some space on the veranda floor and sit down for a packed lunch of rice balls wrapped in dried seaweed. The sun streams through the open doors; the pears droop firm and heavy from the trees in the orchard below; the bamboo waves gently to and fro in the crisp autumn breeze.

A slight sound makes me turn to find Masaki standing in the doorway behind me. He looks around disapprovingly. "What a mess!"

I tell him about all the rubbish that I have just collected.

"One hundred and eight bottles!" Masaki looks at me, slightly incredulous. Never trust a spy. "I knew people came up here sometimes in the afternoon or evenings for a quiet drink, but I'd never have guessed that they got through that much *sake*." He steps up into the main room. "You're going to have to do something about these cupboards, you know. And look at those walls," he exclaims, limping slightly through the dust into the upstairs part of the old house. "And the ceiling! Look at the window! And the floor! How are you going to live in a place like this? Look at the shōji. They've been gnawed away by rats."

I explain that Higuchi Daisuke, the carpenter from Amagase, is going to seal off that part of the house. We are going to live in the rooms downstairs and where I am now.

"It reminds me of Siberia," muses Masaki aloud. Then he goes on. "I was taken prisoner by the Russians, you know. Yes. It was

August 1945. We were marched out of Manchuria, a whole division of the Imperial Japanese Army, and taken off somewhere into the middle of Siberia. Between two and three thousand men with no water. When it rained, we all scooped up the rainwater with our hands from the horses' hoofprints in the caked mud. That was the only way we could drink. We'd thrown away all our equipment before we'd been captured."

Masaki comes toward where I am sitting. "I'd been wounded in the thigh here by machine-gun fire from an airplane and had to hobble the whole way. Those Russians didn't have any medicines at all, except for some kind of disinfectant they used for their horses. They put some of that on my thigh, but it only served to inflame the wound, not cure it. The thing became a pussy mess.

"When we reached some remote part of Siberia two weeks later, we found that we had to make our own prison camp. Have you heard anything like it, having to work to shut yourself in? We cut wood from the forests. I suppose that wasn't so bad because I was, after all, a woodcutter by trade. Then we had to dig great pits in the earth. We placed tree branches across them and lined the pits with wood. And those were our homes. We lived in those pits for the first four years."

Masaki is looking bitter now, as gently nodding his head he surveys the house in which we stand. I find myself thinking how ironical it is that Masaki should have survived this ordeal, only to lose a leg later in a logging accident. I try to cheer him up a bit.

"So this isn't so bad, by comparison, is it? This house is better than your primitive Jōmon-style dwellings."

Masaki ignores my comment and continues.

"It's not that I've got any grudge against the Russians as such. It's the military and the politicians that get me. You know, I was squad leader, which meant that I didn't have to do hard labor like the others under my command. Instead, I had to communicate with the guards. And that was tricky for someone like myself who can't speak even standard Japanese properly. But there were only a couple of soldiers guarding each squad—unlike another camp nearby where they had man-to-man guarding of the German prisoners. I used to try and chitchat with them. Using sign language to talk about girls and drink, so that the guards wouldn't do the rounds, and the men could take it fairly easy. And you know what?"

Masaki asks rhetorically. "When the time came for us to be transferred back to Japan, one or two of the guards actually asked me to
take them with us.

"Not that I thought we ever would get back home, mind you.
There was a rumor floating around that the Russians used to test all
prisoners at the dockside to see how much communism they had
drunk in during their stay in the camps. Those who managed to
convince their interviewers that they believed in equality, the red
flag, and all that, were taken aboard ship. The others were split into
two groups—the nearly-theres and the yet-to-be-educateds. The
yet-to-be-educateds were taken back into the mountains of Siberia
and were never heard of again. A lot of Japanese are still there, I
reckon.

"But we were lucky. When our division got to Nahodka, there
was a ship already docked, with nobody on board and the quayside
empty. The Russians had no choice but to load us all on board at
once, and so we all got home safely. Eight years!" Masaki almost
spits out these words, his mouth twisted with pent-up anger.
"Eight years of my life wasted on a nine-day war."

IO   "Marriage," muses Inoshige's mother, Den, "is like a water-
melon. You never can tell what it's going to be like until you've
tasted it."

II   We've been preparing to fire Inoshige's kiln. For the past
three days, the whole household has been gathered in and around
the workshop. Inoshige started by glazing the largest dishes and
jars outside in the drying yard—watched by Den, who sat quietly
on the veranda of the house in the wintry sunshine. Inoshige's sister-in-law Misae, wearing an apron and a peaked, checkered-cloth
bonnet to keep the sun off her face, worked at the back of the house,
tying together bundles of wood for the firing. Ayako wore the same
kind of apron, with a small towel draped across her hair and knotted
loosely at the back. Sitting at the wheel, she wax-resisted coffee
saucers, which I then dipped into a bucket of glaze.

But I could glaze only so many trays of saucers before being told
to switch to teacups and chopstick holders. Then Inoshige would

tell me to use a different bucket of glaze for more coffee saucers, slabware dishes, and flower vases, and yet another bucket for mugs, cups, and teapots. As time went by, I gradually understood that what at first sight appeared to be unstructured chaos had in fact a perfect logic. Pots were being prepared for firing according to a classification system that put glazes first, then size, then shape. The first pots I had done, which were in fact glazed translucent brown, were to be placed at the back of the kiln, where the firing temperature is low. The slipped wares with their transparent glaze fire best in the central and upper parts of the kiln chamber. The green teapots only come out well at the very front of the shelves well above the firemouth. Big pots must be placed at the top of each chamber. Small pots are the only ones likely not to be misshapen by the heat of the firing at the bottom of the chamber.

Now, as I carry tray after tray of pots across the yard to the climbing kiln, I begin to make sense of the complexity of this craft. Inoshige himself crouches in one of the chambers, carefully placing pots in rows along the shelves that he has arrayed on stilts along the back of the chamber. Nine shelves side by side along the arching wall that gleams glassily in the light of the single bulb, coated with glaze from former firings. Four tiers in all, the height of each tier being calculated according to the type of pot that will be placed there: four inches for teacups, six inches for saucers, eight inches for piles of plates. And on the very top, the largest plates and jars, vases and jugs. And then a second tier of shelves placed in front, and all of these packed with mugs, coffee cups, teapots and teacups, pitchers, sugar bowls, toothpick holders, chopstick rests, and all the other bits and pieces necessary for Japanese cuisine. It is the way that the Japanese cook and present their food that makes the potter's work so varied and profitable. Some 2,000 pots crammed into a four-chambered climbing kiln. The product of three months' hard work.

Inoshige backs into the topmost chamber, balancing three chopstick holders, one on top of the other. "Circus!" he exclaims in English, as he disappears through the narrow entrance, only to emerge half a minute later with one holder still in his hand. "It won't fit," he says. "But it's probably better not to try to make *too* much money." He grins. The kiln is fully loaded.

We brick up the chamber entrances and seal them with mud. It is seven in the evening and time to stop work. We go into the house, bathe and change into kimonos, with quilted jackets (*dotera*) on top to keep us warm. Ayako and Misae are in the kitchen preparing dinner. Inoshige's teenage children, Shigeki, Rumiko, and Mariko, are lying on the floor with their feet in the *kotatsu* watching television. Den, too, lies on the floor, stretched out sidewise with her head propped up on an old-style ceramic pillow that Inoshige had made for her some years before.

We slip our feet into the crowded *kotatsu*, and Ayako brings us *sake*.

"*Otsukaresama deshita*. Thank you for your tiredness," she says, pouring the *sake* into my cup.

"Not at all. It was great fun. Although there are times," I add ruefully, massaging my back, "when I wish I weren't so tall. Those kiln chambers aren't made for people my size."

Inoshige smiles and offers me his *sake* cup. Misae brings in some chunks of raw chicken, which we hungrily begin to eat, dipping the pieces in grated ginger mixed with soy sauce.

"Chicken used to be a great delicacy, you know. Not like now, when we eat it two or three times a week." Inoshige speaks with his mouth full and glances at the television comedy program that has made the children suddenly burst into laughter. "In the old days, we only served chicken on special occasions—like when the tax inspectors came up from town to see what we were up to. I remember once when they came, we decided to pluck a chicken before we killed it. Then we let it go, and the bird could hardly keep its balance. It began running around Daichan's yard and finally fell into the cesspit. We didn't have indoor toilets then. So we fished the bird out, gave it a quick but far from thorough rinse, and proceeded to serve it up to the tax inspectors, who were being entertained up at Haruzō's place, at the top of the hamlet. Then we carefully made sure we ate a different bird for ourselves. Ah! Those were the days."

Inoshige helps himself to more *sake*, and Ayako gives him a look that is half a frown of displeasure and half a smile of admiration.

"Really. The things you men get up to when you start drinking. You ought to spend more time around the house, talking to the children, instead of going off until all hours of the night and coming home so drunk you can't work the next morning."

"But that's the whole fun of drinking," rejoins Inoshige, who is clearly used to Ayako's little outbursts. "That feeling of empty forlornness, that *munashisa*, the morning after. That is what makes it all worthwhile." He smiles wryly. "Anyway, my father never talked to me and I'm all right. So I'm sure that Mariko and the others will survive and turn out okay."

Inoshige has already told me about his childhood. He is the ninth of ten children, but only one of two boys, born some 15 years after his older brother. As second son, Inoshige had been destined to leave Amagase and go out into the world to make his fortune, but his brother was killed in the last days of the war on one of the Pacific islands, leaving a widow and two small boys. Normally, Misae would have been returned to her family, but Inoshige's father decided that she should marry his one remaining son, who would then become head of the household. Not that he had let on about his plans at the time. Inoshige had still been at school and hardly old enough to appreciate what was going on in his father's mind.

And he didn't appreciate the idea much when he did grow up and was told about it. Misae was at least a dozen years older than he. It was then that Inoshige learned to make himself scarce, leaving the house as soon as he finished work and going off to drink with his friends in the valley. It wasn't that he had anything against Misae. She was a good sister-in-law. He just didn't want to marry her. That was all.

"Did I ever tell you about the time I had a fight with a gang of toughs?" Inoshige breaks in on my thoughts. "It was when they first built a road up to Amagase from the Todoroki bridge. The *oyabun* [construction boss] and his mob were all drinking together in Terukichi's noodle shop, just across the road. Terukichi himself and a few others in the community, including Haruzō, Daisuke, and I, were drinking in the main room of the house. Haruzō's daughter came to call her father home and, as she went through the shop to the back of the house, one of the laborers made some insulting remark—loud enough for us to hear. I was pretty far gone by then and decided to have it out with the *oyabun*. He'd been acting up for several weeks already, and we were all pretty pissed off at the way he was behaving.

"Well, that *oyabun* was spoiling for a fight. He ordered me to apologize for not drinking with him in the noodle shop. But I refused to bow my head to him, and I suddenly found myself surrounded by his gang, all with their knives out and pointing toward me. I tell you, I was scared. I had time to think that this was probably going to be the last night of my life, and that I'd better end it with dignity. So I grabbed hold of a beer bottle, smashed it on the tabletop, and stood facing the *oyabun*.

"Terukichi and the others had all slipped out of the main room by the window, and everybody in the community had come to peer through the glass at what was going on. Somebody tried to use the public phone to call the police. But they didn't seem to think that what was going on was any more than a drunken brawl, and anyway it was hardly likely that they'd get there in time. So we just stood there, me with my jagged-edged beer bottle facing the *oyabun*, and the others with their knives around me. But then, for some reason, I don't know why, the *oyabun* backed away. Very slowly, mind you, but he moved away and left the noodle shop without a fight taking place. His men just followed him. Then they got in their jeeps and drove away.

"My old man was standing outside with a large pair of pliers, ready to fight, if need be. And so were a lot of the others, armed with hammers and scythes and all sorts of tools. My father never said a word to me about my confrontation with the *oyabun*, either then or later on. He never even asked me if I was all right, but I could tell that he was really proud of me. For the first time ever, perhaps. And from that night on, he never pestered me again about marrying Misae. And the toughs never caused any more trouble in Amagase again. So I killed two birds with one stone. That is what *sake* has done for my life!"

12   Inoshige wakes me up at five-forty the next morning. It is still dark as I put on my work clothes and go out into the yard. One of the fighting cocks scurries away toward the back of the house, clucking nervously. Inoshige comes out of the shed across from the workshop with an armful of dry cedar brush. This he stuffs in the two firemouths of the climbing kiln, before carefully placing some thin strips of wood criss-cross on top. From a trestle table outside the workshop, he brings across a bottle of cold *sake* and places it on a shelf above the firemouths. He has a jar, too, into which he dips his fingers and scatters handfuls of salt over the kiln. Then he places three large pinchfuls of salt on the shelf in front of the *sake* bottle. Somewhere farther up the hill a cock crows.

Fumbling in the torchlight for a match, Inoshige strikes one and lights the cedar brush. The flames blaze away from us, sucked through the fire ducts into the black kiln chambers beyond. He throws in more strips of wood as I start splitting some of the logs piled up in the shed behind us. The mountain ridge above Amagase begins to be etched in early morning light.

There is the rattle of a door, and Terukichi comes out into the road where he yawns and stretches his arms. Still in his pajamas and quilted robe, he shuffles across to Inoshige's yard.

"So you're firing."

"Yes, we're firing."

"You're earlier than usual."

"I drank less *sake* than usual." Even at this time of the morning, Inoshige is ready with his repartee.

Terukichi grins shyly. A small man, with one arm withered from childhood, he is one of the strongest people I've met in the valley. A jack-of-all-trades, he can be found cutting down trees, working on the roads, even building Inoshige a small bisque kiln. And when his wife is really busy with the summer tourists who stop by on their way down from the sacred mountain, a famous pilgrimage center high above Amagase, Terukichi will help make the buckwheat noodles for his hungry customers.

"I wonder how the wind is today," Terukichi says, looking up at the sky.

"Seems all right at the moment." Inoshige is not committing himself.

There's more to this exchange than meets the eye. This much I know, for every word spoken in a country valley has a secondary meaning behind the word. It is this world of implication that I find so hard to fathom.

In this particular instance, the conversation between Inoshige and Terukichi has little to do with the weather. Terukichi lives directly across the road from Inoshige's kiln, and when the wind blows down the hillside from the northeast, the smoke from the kiln billows across the road toward Terukichi's house. There are times when people can hardly see their way in or out of the noodle shop, so dense is the black smoke from the firing. But Inoshige lets his neighbor have quite a few pots cheap so that he can sell them at a good profit to the tourists, and he always makes sure to deliver a box of tangerines at the end of the year when gifts are exchanged, as an apology for causing Terukichi's family such inconvenience. It isn't enough, of course. Nothing ever is enough in the give-and-take of valley life, and the matter of Inoshige's kiln can be brought up in any drunken argument when Terukichi may try to justify his own position or undermine Inoshige's.

It is to prevent things like this from happening too frequently that Inoshige was recently prompted to build a chimney at the top of his kiln.

"It's better, isn't it, now that the chimney is there?" Inoshige reminds Terukichi indirectly of the costs involved in being good neighbors. "The smoke seems to be drawn up higher. And so it should be. After all I paid more than half a million yen to get that chimney built."

Terukichi grunts.

"I suppose so," he admits. "But still the smoke can waft down again when the wind's really strong."

He shivers in the early morning cold and leaves us for the warmth of his house. As he crosses the road the sun beams down through a dent in the mountain ridge, and a ray of light catches his perfectly bald head.

"There are moments when Terusan is aptly named," whispers Inoshige mischievously. "*Teru teru bōzu*—the gleaming bald-headed monk who makes the rain stop, and whose image the children make from a handkerchief and hang from under the eaves of their homes on really wet days. But he's not bad, really. Terukichi's heart is in the right place and he means well enough."

By now the firemouths are really ablaze, and there is a thin wisp of smoke spiraling up from the chimney at the top of the kiln.

"Time to eat," Inoshige grunts, and puts a couple of large logs into the flames on each side of the kiln. "There. That should keep the fire going awhile."

We go back inside the house. Ayako is getting breakfast ready in the kitchen. The children we can hear thumping around upstairs, getting their things ready for school. The bus will be leaving at ten past seven from just below the Todoroki bridge.

Inoshige starts on his bean-paste soup, rice, and pickles. Ayako knows me well enough to put a jar of instant coffee down on the table, together with a thermos full of boiling water. Two slices of toast, and a butter knife with which to spread the strawberry jam. This is the nearest I can get to a continental breakfast.

Shigeki comes in with his satchel crammed with books. Seeing me eating toast, he calls out to his mother: "Hey, Mum! Bring me the same as Būchan. I'm fed up with rice." He slips his feet into the warm *kotatsu*.

Misae comes in from the backyard, where she has been collecting eggs. "Those cats!" she exclaims. "They've been after the chickens again."

This comment is aimed at nobody in particular, but succeeds in rousing Shigeki as he helps himself to a spoonful of coffee.

"It can't be the cats. They were sleeping with me all last night."

"Then it must be a weasel. They're in a right old flap, anyway, squawking away out there in the woodshed. Inoshige, you really ought to do something about it. Put up a fence or something to stop the weasels getting in."

"Yes, I must." Inoshige nods his head as he slurps his soup. "Ah! I'm sorry, Misaesan, but can you check the kiln for me before you sit down?"

As his sister-in-law's shuffling footsteps recede into the distance, Inoshige continues. "Women are a nuisance—always complaining about something. Not enough money; too much *sake*. The cats have been chasing the chickens; the chickens have been chasing the cats. You have to learn to agree with them and then proceed to distract them. They soon forget what it was they were saying." Winking, he calls out to Ayako, "Oy! More rice!"

The day goes slowly. There isn't much to do at first except doze in the sunlight and listen to the radio. Most of the wood we are using for the main mouth firing comes from the beams and pillars of old farmhouses that have been pulled down. Inoshige gets them for the price of the truck he has to hire to bring the wood to his pottery. Then Terukichi comes over for a day or two when he's got nothing else to do and cuts them up with Inoshige's chain saw. Later we begin splitting these logs with an axe. Inoshige's aim is unerring.

"Just like the old days," he sighs, bringing his axe down with a force that shears the pine wood. "Then we used to go up into the mountains to pick up wood. Sometimes somebody would be clearing a bit of forest land, and we'd get permission to root around there for the stumps of trees and any stray branches the foresters might have left lying about. We'd lug the wood all the way down here on our backs. Then Ayako and I would have to spend the best part of a week, splitting the wood and chopping it up into proper lengths. We'd each of us balance on one end of a branch and hack away, trying to split it down the middle with our axes, while the old man, my father, would sit over there where Den is now, smoking his pipe in the sunshine and watching us. We were only just married then, and the other men in the hamlet would pretend that they'd got some errand that brought them down to this end of Amagase, just so that they could see us at work. They wanted to know what sort of mettle Ayako was made of. And they'd work out how good we were at wielding our axes by the amount of wood that lay piled beside us at the end of each day. So, really, this is child's play." Inoshige cleanly splits yet another 12-inch-thick log.

"After we'd finished cutting up the wood, we had to dry it. On reflection, I think that that was the worst job of all, you know. We did the drying in the third chamber of the old kiln, the one before this. In those days, we didn't have anything like kiln shelves, just a sandy floor on which we placed our pots in a few piles. First of all, I had to block off all the fireholes with mud. Then I stacked the wood all the way up to the roof of the chamber. Next I had to cover the exposed ends of the wood with mud to prevent them from burning. And then I lit two small fires, one at each side of the chamber. The smoke from that green wood was awful. It had nowhere to go except out of the chamber entrance, and I had to stay inside all the time tending the fires, making sure that they didn't burn too bright or set the wood alight. I'd have a damp towel wrapped around my face to help me breathe, but things would soon get too much for me. I'd run out of the chamber spluttering and coughing my guts out. Two whole days of that, and I was really beat.

"And now what happens? We have a road put in to the valley all the way up to Amagase here. All I need do now is pick up the telephone, dial the number of a lumberyard, and get a whole truckload of wood delivered to my doorstep for a mere forty or fifty thousand yen. No more splitting wood with Ayako. No more choking myself to death inside the kiln. Instead, I can make a few more pots, drink a bit more *sake*, and spend more time talking to my friends. There's something to be said for progress after all."

Misae calls us for lunch, which has been laid out on one of the trestle tables in the workshop. Raw whale meat, fried chicken legs, seaweed (*hijiki*), bamboo shoots, pickles, and Misae's favorite boiled vegetables (*gameni*). Inoshige brings in the bottle from the kiln-mouth shelf and pours out the cold *sake*. This is a special meal because of the firing.

"To most people these days, *kuruma* means a Toyota car or Honda van, but we use the word to refer to the potter's kick wheel. And so the workshop is called a *kurumaza*, a place where you sit at the wheel making pots. And when men gather to drink they, too, form a circle called a *kuruma*. They say that harmony is a circle. Well, so is life. It's full of cycles. The agricultural cycle is an annual one. So are the community festivals that stem from agricultural activities. My pottery cycle is more or less trimonthly. Ayako prepares the clay. Misae dries out the wood. I sit at the wheel and make my pots for weeks on end. And then we all stop our separate tasks and help decorate and glaze the pots that I've made. We all load up the kiln. We fire it and rest for a couple of days. Then we unload the kiln together, and I get disappointed at the way the pots turn out. We pack up the good ones and send them away; the bad ones we chuck in the river there. One or two really good ones I put aside for a special occasion, like an exhibition. Then I loaf around for three or four more days, trying to summon up the energy to start all over again, and using my lack of enthusiasm as an excuse to catch up on correspondence and all the little things that I never normally have time to do. But, finally, I start work again." Inoshige drains his cup and hands it to his sister-in-law. "And all the time we grow older, don't we, Sister?"

Misae's sunburned face wrinkles as she flashes a gold-toothed smile. "We may grow older, but we never get any less busy."

"It could be worse, though."

"It sure could. Why! You only have to think back a few years to remember how bad things used to be. I'll never forget what it was like when I first came here. Your father had stopped making pots because there was a depression, and he couldn't sell them. He was working in that stone quarry up toward Ichinotsuru. I used to have to work with Granny in the fields." She jerks her head over her shoulder toward where Den is still sitting quietly enjoying the sunlight. "She may seem all right now, mumbling away and smiling sweetly at you, Būchan, but she was a real taskmaster, I can tell you. She used to strip bare to the waist in the fields, weeding the rice plants or digging the vegetable patch. And she made me do the same, even when I was pregnant. Many's the time I wanted to run away."

"And she would have, too, if only she'd known the way," chimes in Inoshige. "In the old days, you see, someone like Misae marrying into one of these mountain communities had to walk all the way up from Fujioka. The path was difficult and winding, running crisscross over the stream. The day of the wedding would be the first time a young girl ever met her husband. If she didn't like him, that was her hard luck."

"And the really terrifying thing was that, even if you did decide to run away, the path was so difficult, you'd never find your way back down the valley alone."

"How lucky I was," sighs Ayako, "having Misae here to help and protect me from Granny."

"And, you know," continues Misae, now well into this false nostalgia for the past, "when it came to food, we never had anything like this to eat. Just the rice that we grew. And the vegetables. And the occasional piece of wild boar that a hunter had shot. Or salted fish that we bought off a peddler who sometimes found his way up to Amagase. That was a real delicacy. Inoshige's father would get the best bit, of course. He was head of the household. And Den got the next-best piece. And then the children got their portions, boys before girls. And finally, all that was left over for me was the head. One great lump of salt. For years I was never allowed to eat anything except the head of a fish. The old days may have been better days. But they were hard days, all right."

Misae gets up to go and put more wood in the kiln, which is burning furiously. The wind is still being kind to us, blowing the black smoke away from the house up the hillside. Inoshige stretches and yawns. Ayako glances at her watch.

"Why! Look at the time," she exclaims. "The program's started, you know."

We pick up the bowls, cups, and dishes and take them into the house. Den has already shuffled from her chair on the veranda to take up her position on the living-room floor, with her feet in the *kotatsu*, watching television. Inoshige, too, puts his feet under the quilt covering and stretches out, his head propped on one arm. Ayako and Misae seat themselves against the far wall and abstractedly peel tangerines, eyes glued to the television set in front of them.

The program is a soap opera, with a wholly predictable plot involving a widowed mother whose only son goes off to fight in Manchuria and whose remaining daughter has been seduced by a smooth young man who is out to get her mother's entire savings by some devious trick, yet to be divulged. The daughter has fallen for him, failing to see through his sweet-tongued words. I find her stupidity quite exasperating. What is worse, the show has been going on now for the best part of an hour a day, five days a week, for the last six weeks and, by all accounts, has another month and a half to run. Past experience suggests that the somewhat effeminate young student, whom both mother and daughter this week despise, will eventually marry the girl, who may or may not be pregnant. As for the son called up to the war, he is almost certain to be killed in Manchuria—I suspect by the Russians. Before that, the smooth young man will turn out to be neurotic, but only after he has somehow managed to get hold of, and dissipate, the widow's pension and family fortune.

In this sort of program, Confucian values come to the fore. Honor men and despise women. A good wife and wise mother. Love, honor, and obey your parents. Crave not after money. Work hard and diligently. Value honesty, uprightness, and truth. A good, solid, almost Protestant ethic that the Japanese have managed to maintain throughout their modern development. Certainly, Misae and Ayako lap up these values. Even Inoshige makes a point of starting to watch the program each day after lunch, although he usually falls asleep in the middle. Ayako kicks him when he snores too loudly.

One of the cats climbs into Misae's lap and settles down, oblivious of the occasional strips of tangerine peel that fall down on its head. It's funny, I muse, how differently people here tend to work out their thoughts when they talk. Like Misae earlier when she was telling us about Den. Really, it was the sight of a good meal in the workshop that had started her train of thought. But she hadn't started with the story about dividing up the fish so that all she was left with was the head. Instead, she had begun with a story about Inoshige's father and his work, then Den and her work, and this brought her to the work that had produced the food they ate at table. I suspect that in England we'd probably have put things the other way around.

I've noticed this sort of thing before. Like a few weeks ago, when I talked to Haruzō about the valley road and the way that this might have affected household structure and kinship relations. Haruzō is Inoshige's father's second cousin and lives at the top of Amagase. There's no recognized kinship relation between the two men, but Inoshige advised me to have a talk with him. Haruzō is considered somewhat of an expert when it comes to having roads built. At one stage during our discussion, I asked him whether he thought a road would ever be put in up a certain valley nearby, which was at present inhabited by a single family.

"You see those woods there?" he began, pointing in precisely the opposite direction. "Well, I used to own all of them once. And then Inoshige came to ask me if I wouldn't give him a bit of land. And because he's my branch household from way back, I agreed and gave him some land. And then a few years later, Kajiwara Katsuhisa, from across the river in Inekari, asked me if I wouldn't agree to exchange some land with him. He had a piece next to mine up above Amagase, and my little bit adjoins a large area that he owns up toward the ridge there."

I was getting confused by this chronicle of landownership, and my attention wandered as Haruzō, always a stickler for detail, continued with who owned what, where, and why, and what had happened when the Town Council had decided to put in a road along the other side of the valley. He told me how much had been offered for the land, and who had bargained for more than the Town Council was prepared to pay. It was Gotō Chitose who had really held things up with his prevarications. "And it is Chitose who owns the land right at the entrance of the valley you are referring to," continued Haruzō, as I suddenly grasped what he had been trying to tell me. "When you've got to deal with somebody like Chitose, it makes it pretty hard for any road to get built."

Haruzō had not just given me a simple answer to my question.

Instead, I'd been treated to a full rundown on the kinds of people involved when it came to building roads in a country valley. My question had not produced the sort of (Western) answer I had anticipated: "Yes, because . . . " or "No, because . . . " Instead, Haruzō had told me a series of incidents, which had ended up with an "And that's why . . . " one could, or could not, build a road in the place I had indicated. Explanations here do not proceed in a series of occasionally tangential but generally straight lines. They operate in circles. Rationality, too, perhaps is an endless series of cycles in Japanese thought.

Soon I, too, drift into sleep. *A blue heron poised in nobility?*

Nine hours have passed since we lit the kiln. The flames are searing hot now, sucked with a roar by the updraft into the main body of the kiln. Inoshige throws in half a dozen logs on each side. Then, together with Misae, we get in a small truck and drive up to his woodshed above the hamlet. Misae has painstakingly tied with nylon tape bundles of six-foot lengths of cedar bark. This is the wood that is sent up from the lumberyards. Bundle after bundle we throw into the back of the truck, until it is so full that it will take no more. We drive back down the hillside and back the truck up the short, steep slope into Inoshige's drying yard. There we unload the wood, carrying it up to the top of the climbing kiln, and laying it on the stepped earth by the fourth chamber. It is safe from any rain here under the kiln's protective roof.

We go back up to the woodshed and load up the truck again. By the end of the third truckload, Inoshige figures that he probably has enough wood to last the firing. The workshop is now full of wood, and the area beside the second and third chambers is also stacked high with bundles of cedar strips. I pull one or two splinters out of my fingers. Even my work gloves couldn't prevent them from piercing the skin. Ayako goes to get tea.

A van pulls up outside Terukichi's house, and a clean-shaven man in his mid-fifties, hair just longer than an American "GI cut," gets out and bows slightly to us. It is Kazuo, the fishmonger who drives up the valley every day with fish fresh from the town. A quiet man, he lives in Kodake, close to the house that we looked at the other day. He is popular with many of the housewives because he brings them fresh fish to order when they ask and doesn't overcharge.

Misae immediately shuffles down to his van and peers inside the tarpaulin flaps that surround it, keeping the fish cool in their ice boxes. Within two or three minutes half a dozen women have joined her, all with their heads buried inside the van and only their blue-and-gray-checked trousers (*mompe*) visible to us in the drying yard.

"Like a row of assembly-line hens," mutters Inoshige, accepting tea and a pickled plum, and wiping his face with the towel that he has had wrapped around his head all day and has just rinsed under the outside tap.

"Terukichi used to have hens, you know. Several hundreds of them, all cooped up in a long shed in the rice field below his houses, clucking away, day in, day out. It wasn't the noise so much as the smell of them that got to me." He shudders at the memory. "When the wind was blowing from the southwest as it is today, and does most days, we had to put clothespins on our noses to keep the stink out. When I remember that, I forget to worry too much when the smoke from my kiln billows down across Terukichi's house. It's all part of what you like to call 'give-and-take,' I believe."

Misae comes up from the van with her purchases. The cats get up and stretch themselves, before stalking off—oh, so casually—toward the kitchen.

"That's the way the foxes were with the hens," continues Inoshige, looking after them. "Once or twice one would find its way into the hut, and then there would be one hell of a commotion. Then there were the wild dogs that live somewhere up near your new house, Būchan. Sometimes, one of them would get in, and Terukichi would come out with his gun in the middle of the night. He never dared let fly at them, in case he killed a chicken by mistake. So he'd just run around waving his arms in the air and shouting at the top of his voice. That only upset the chickens even more, and they wouldn't lay for days."

"What happened in the end, then?" I ask.

"Oh, we had a really bad winter. The snow was up to here." Inoshige motions with his hand to a point halfway up his thigh. "Terukichi couldn't get food up from the town for the hens. He got stuck once on the Todoroki bridge, and we all had to go down and help cart the stuff up for him. By the time spring came, he'd decided that there was more money to be made from the hikers who go up and down the sacred mountain over there. He was probably right."

Kazuo comes into the yard, and Ayako offers him tea.

"So you're firing, then."

"Yes, we're firing."

"I've got some cuttlefish for you," he says, pushing a plastic bag across the table. "It should taste good roasted on the embers."

"Now that is a good idea. I was just beginning to feel a bit hungry."

So Inoshige roots around in his shed for a piece of corrugated iron on which to grill the cuttlefish, while I go off in search of potatoes. I manage to find half a dozen or so very old ones in a bag in the earth-floored storeroom below the kitchen. With a long iron rod, I then shake some of the embers so that they fall through the grille and form a bed of red hot coals below each of the firemouths. On one side we cook the cuttlefish and on the other the potatoes. It is very, very hot, and we have to turn our faces away from the heat when we approach the firemouths.

"This is when your eyelashes start burning off," warns Inoshige, "so be careful. And roll your sleeves down or all the hairs on your arms will be singed off. We don't want that to happen, because then we won't be able to call you *ketō*, the red-haired barbarian, behind your back anymore."

We both laugh at his use of this old-fashioned word to describe foreigners in Japan. We throw in more wood. Inoshige calls to Misae to bring out some cold beer. The sun has gone from the drying yard now, and it is suddenly chilly away from the roaring flames. We squat down with our backs to the kiln and chat idly. Kazuo is the bearer of news from all the way down the valley, for in every community in which he stops he has a chance to listen to the housewives gossiping as they purchase their fish. He knows who has died; whose marriage is being arranged. He has heard who has spent how much on building a new house and what the neighbors think about it. As we sip the cold, refreshing beer and pick off pieces of cuttlefish from the corrugated iron sheet that we've dragged out of the embers, Inoshige listens attentively. Mostly he just nods his head and makes noncommittal comments; once or twice he casually asks Kazuo some questions to elicit more information. This Kazuo freely gives. The two of them live far enough apart and their interests are sufficiently diverse for them not to have to hold back at all or prevaricate in the way that they might do with immediate neighbors. They are both men of the same valley, though, and it is this that ultimately binds them together.

We throw in more wood—log after log hurled into the back of the roaring fire. We have to stand two or three feet back and aim the logs through the narrow firemouths, firing them like arrows right to the back of the yellow-white flames. Quite often my aim is bad, and a log comes tumbling back off the face of the kiln, or else lodges awkwardly in the very front of the firemouth. I use a long piece of wood to push the logs deeper into the kiln. It catches fire at once, then smolders in the dust as I put it down and throw in more logs to fuel the voracious appetite of the roaring kiln.

Suddenly I remember the potatoes and pull them out of the embers, one by one. They are as black as coal. I use my long piece of wood to bat them across to where Kazuo is still squatting, sipping his beer, his face glowing a pinkish-red in the firelight.

"What on earth's that?" he asks, pointing warily at one of the steaming black potatoes. "It looks as if it's about to explode."

I put on a second pair of gloves, and try to peel one of the "bombs" with a knife. Cutting it in two, I add a blob of butter and salt, before placing the two halves on the corrugated sheet.

"Try some," I encourage him with my best smile.

Kazuo, too polite to refuse, does as he is told. He munches the potato warily once or twice. Then his eyes widen slightly in surprise. "Hey, Inoshigesan! This is good. You ought to try a bit, too."

Inoshige puts the second piece of potato in his mouth. "Well, well," he says with his mouth half full. "You foreigners occasionally have a good idea, after all. Not bad. Not bad at all."

I peel the remaining potatoes, and we open another bottle of beer. It is almost half past five.

"Another half hour and we'll be finished," says Inoshige, seeing me glance at the clock on the workshop wall. "Then comes the hard bit. Four chambers at three hours apiece. If all goes well, we should be through by dawn tomorrow."

We throw in more and more wood. Kazuo leaves us to drive back down the valley. It is dark now, and we can see the headlights of his van picking out some tall tree trunks here, the gleam of a damp rock

there, and lower down—briefly—the roof of the small shrine that
stands by the road to Ōkubo. There is a sudden gust of wind, and
the smoke from the kiln comes wafting around us, sooty and black.
*The day grown dark, our visitor gone home. All that remains in
this remote hamlet is the howl of the wind from the mountain's peak.*

So the firing comes to an end. At ten minutes past six, with the
night turning back to day, Inoshige takes one last long look
through the single brick stoke hole of the top chamber of his climbing kiln. Shielding his red eyes with a sooty hand, he peers into the
white-hot fire, checking whether the glazes on all the pots across
the kiln are glistening in the heat and truly melted. He looks down
and along the shelves. Then, angling his head down in the dust
where he is kneeling, he looks up and across.

"That'll do," he says, throwing in one last handful of cedar wood
and a few leftover scraps of bark, before quickly blocking up the
stoke hole with a brick. We add a bit of water to the pile of mud in
the yard, turn it over with a mattock, and use it to seal up the kiln
chamber's arched brick entrance. The firing is over.

Inoshige sends me into the house to have my bath first, while he
clears up around the kiln. My whole body smells of wood and
smoke and grime. I splash around in the cold bathroom, washing
myself clean, and then finally sink into the steaming hot bath, my
body trembling with fatigue. Memories of the past twelve hours
flash through my head. The night birds calling in the woods above
us. The smoke blowing back down the kiln's slope, smothering us
in its black mantle (Oh, that I, like a Heian lady, could have turned
it inside out to dream of my loved one). The radio that we kept on
all night to help keep us awake, and the sudden clear voice of an
announcer talking to us in Spanish from Peru. The nylon tape
around each bundle of wood that I carefully untied and retied
around the four fingers of my right hand, knotted, and threw onto
the trestle table by the workshop floor. The endless drinks that we
consumed through the night, and the occasional walk down to the
stream below the house to pee under the starlit sky. Our taking
turns to feed the kiln, leaving the other to lie back and doze on a pile
of wood. The first drops of rain before dawn, and the gully in the
dust that I dug to prevent the water seeping down among the piles
of wood—

"Būchan! Is the water warm enough?" Ayako's voice wakes me from my reverie.

"Ah, yes. Thank you," I call, stirring myself in the water. Inoshige must be waiting. I get out and dry myself and put on fresh, clean-smelling clothes. Ayako is in the kitchen making breakfast, Misae is out in the yard feeding the hens, the children are thumping around upstairs getting ready for school. This is one cycle that Inoshige and I were not a part of today.

We have breakfast, with *sake* and beer, and finally go to bed, longing for sleep.

13 For a month now I've been coming up to the house almost every day to clean it up. I've had most of the rubbish taken away; the rest I've burned, since there is no regular garbage collection here in the valley. I've clambered up a rickety ladder onto the roof and straightened a few tiles so that there are no more leaks in the veranda cupboard. Daisuke, the carpenter, came one morning with two of his apprentices, and in the short space of half a day fixed the bathroom door, made a cupboard for our bedding, put in a new window, and sealed off the old part of the house upstairs. I was left to put in the plumbing for the bathroom and kitchen sink, and to empty out the cesspit into wooden buckets, which I borrowed from my new landlord, Takeshi, and balanced precariously on a wooden pole across my shoulders as I carried the "night soil" down to the bottom of the orchard below the house.

The water supply to the house was hardly more than a trickle from the tap and I had to ask Masaki next door where it came from.

"There's a pipe running underground along the bottom of the wall below my house and into the woods," he told me. "If you walk along the path, you should be able to see it occasionally where it isn't covered with pine needles and cedar brush. There's a tank in the woods, a couple of hundred yards up. The water comes out of a hole in the hillside just next to it. But it gets clogged up with sand whenever it rains. That's the disadvantage of mountain water. The good thing about it is that it tastes really good. When you're thirsty, there's nothing better to drink. The pity of it is that it isn't as good as it used to be, because Buntarō and Tōsuke have started using insecticides on their pear trees. We're going to have to do something about that soon, or we'll all be poisoned."

I wandered off into the woods as directed. Masaki was right. I caught a glimpse of a length of red hosepipe running along just below the path. Following it up the gentle slope, I eventually came across a small concrete tank covered with plastic fertilizer bags, themselves held down with stones. I slid the lid off the tank and found it almost empty. There was no water coming through the feeder pipe, and I shook it a bit. Nothing happened, so I slid the lid back onto the tank and covered it with the fertilizer bags as before. Then I followed the pipe where it ran along a ditch at the edge of a disused rice field and into a narrow hole that was blocked by two very large flat rocks. These I heaved aside, before getting down on my hands and knees and feeling inside. I could make out a small concrete ridge, behind which was a very small pool of water. The pipe from the tank had been fixed into the concrete and a filter had been attached to its end. It was covered with sand, just as Masaki had warned, so I scooped out handfuls of it and could soon hear the water pouring gently from the pipe into the water tank a few feet away. I heaved the rocks back to cover the mouth of this hole in the hillside and went back to the house, where I turned on the taps. After a minute or two of spluttering air, water began to run into the basin. It was muddy at first, but soon cleared, and I took a sip. Without doubt, it was the best water I had ever drunk.

Daisuke had left me some varnish so I could paint the veranda floor. What had at first seemed like tired and dirty wood was suddenly transformed in the late afternoon sunlight into a gleaming auburn brown. Since I still had a little varnish left, I used it to paint a small wooden shrine that I had discovered among the empty *sake* bottles. There was a shelf for the household gods (*kamidana*) in the small room downstairs, and I placed the three figurines that I had found there in the shrine. Clapping my hands twice, I asked them to look after the house and all who lived in it. Then I placed a small amount of rice from the remains of my lunch on a broken saucer and placed it on the god shelf with a *sake* cup full of water.

Misae came over a few days later and spent the afternoon showing me how to paper the shōji screens. Like Daisuke and Inoshige when they first saw the house, she thought the place was *sabishii*, lonely. By the end of the afternoon, however, she began saying how lovely and quiet it was, and how much she enjoyed the sunshine and the view.

"It's so peaceful," she exclaimed, sitting down to rest on the sunlit veranda. "And what a view you have, too. Not like our place where we face straight out onto Terukichi's noodle shop. And you have the sun for so long here. Why, this must be the sunniest place in the valley. Close to five o'clock on a December afternoon and the sun still hasn't sunk behind the ridge of hills over there above Takao. You chose a good place, Būchan. I hope your Kyōko will like it."

And that is what I find slightly worrying. Will Kyōko like the house? More important, will she like the valley and its people? It's all right for me. I have come here to study just this sort of out-of-the-way community. But to ask a downtown Tokyo girl to come and live here might just be a bit unfair. Especially since I know that she used to stay near here during and after the war, when her parents moved out of Tokyo to avoid the air raids. The stories Kyōko's mother tells about country people are far from flattering: the way she used to have to hand over expensive kimonos in exchange, for example, for a few pounds of rice; or how her daughter was teased and bullied so much by the other children that she refused to go to school. Kyōko doesn't have many happy memories of this island, where anybody not born and brought up in the immediate neighborhood is always treated as an outsider.

14   Finally, we move into our house in Ōkubo. We rent a van and drive down the highway to Osaka, where we get on the ferry that takes us through the night to this southern island of Japan. Another hour's drive, and we arrive at Fujioka. Like a tourist-bus guide, I start pointing out the local sights.

"That enormous bowling pin there was put up by the valley Youth Association," I point to the extraordinary bottle-shaped form that towers above the roadside. Painted in red from top to bottom of the pin on its uphill side is the usual farewell made to parting friends or relatives: ITTE IRASSHAI, "go and come back." For those entering the valley, however, is written the somewhat

sterner warning: THE ONI ROAD DOES NOT ADMIT DRUNKEN
DRIVERS.

Cold sober at this time of the morning, we drive up past the
bamboo groves. There is a workshop some way below the South
Oni school, and bamboo has been laid out to dry in the field nearby,
stacked neatly in squares or made to stand end to end like miniature
wigwams. "They make chopsticks here for the tourists who come
to town. And back scratchers, too. Some people make really sturdy
woven bamboo trays."

We are approaching Yamaguchi Takeshi's house, so I stop the van
and we all walk up to pay our respects to our new landlord. Hanako
comes out and bows as I introduce Kyōko and the children. She
calls out to her mother-in-law, who comes to the door, wiping her
hands on her apron. We pay our respects, thank them for being so
kind as to lend us their house, and apologize for the inconvenience
that we have been, are, and will be, causing.

"Not at all, not at all," Takeshi's mother smiles. "We're delighted
to be able to help. Aren't we, Hanako?"

"Of course," says the younger woman and asks us when we arrived. When she hears that we have just got off the ferry and are on
our way to unload the van, she immediately insists on coming up to
the house with us to help. It seems that Takeshi is already working
in the orchards around the house.

We get back in the van, while Hanako goes to get her car. As we
drive on up the hillside, I point out the Valley Coordination Office,
the house I decided not to live in, the Pear Sorting Station, and the
Agricultural Cooperative. We pass our local barber's shop and turn
up the narrow road for Ōkubo. The children, unused to so much
countryside, are very excited as we glide down the last slope of the
track toward the house.

"What a crummy place!" they exclaim in disappointment when I
show them where we are to live. It's a hard life being a father.

As we pull up in the parking space below the two houses, Aso
Masaki comes out to see who it is.

"*Irasshai!*" he calls, welcoming us.

More introductions, which have to be repeated a few seconds
later when Takeshi appears in his army-like gray uniform of soft
cap, jacket, and trousers tucked into his short rubber boots. He is

carrying a yellow plastic box filled with pears and gives some to the children.

"Oni pears are famous around here, you know," he says proudly. "It's still early in the season yet, and these aren't so good. But if you wait a month or two, you'll be able to eat some really delicious crisp fruit."

As we begin to untie the cords keeping our furniture and belongings in place on the back of the van, there is the sound of a car. It is Inoshige, accompanied by Ayako and Misae, together with a big burly man whom I have never met before.

"Hanako phoned to say you'd arrived," Inoshige explains as he gets out of the car. He immediately greets first Masaki, the older man, and then Yamaguchi, all three of them doffing their caps and bowing to one another.

"Būchan, I don't think you've met Katchan before." Inoshige motions toward the big man he has brought with him. "This is Kajiwara Katsuhisa. He lives just down the road from you. At the big house on the corner by the temple. You're in the same hamlet now, so if you're stuck for something, ask Katsuhisa here or Asosan for help. That's what neighbors are for."

"That's true." Katsuhisa takes a long toothpick from his mouth and uses it to scratch the stubble on his chin. "Glad to meet you." He bows slightly with a shy smile.

"He's a bit under the weather because we drank too much last night," Inoshige explains. "Which is why he hasn't gone to work today. Katchan's a schoolteacher, you know."

"Not much of one, though. I'm always cutting classes. More so than my students."

We start to unload the van, and the children wander off into the orchards, glad to be able to stretch their legs after the long journey and eager to explore.

Half an hour later, we have managed to put everything more or less in place. Katsuhisa and Inoshige between them have fixed the kitchen sink. Misae and Ayako have put up some old curtains that they say they don't need anymore. They start peeling tangerines, which they have brought with them, and Takeshi goes off to his store near the house to get some more pears. These he peels deftly with his jackknife. We all sit ourselves down on the veranda and on the floor of the upstairs room, the women together in one group, the men in another. Without noticing it, Kyōko and I have slipped into our socially expected male and female roles. From now on we will almost always be separated in public.

We hear the children running breathlessly up the path toward the house. Kicking their shoes off at the entrance, they jump up into the room.

"Look what we've found," they chorus in unison, letting go of the bottoms of their sweaters and allowing dozens of mushrooms to cascade to the floor. "Isn't this place marvelous? We've seen fish in the stream. There are strawberries growing wild along the path. And look at all these mushrooms that we found growing on some silly rotten-looking trees."

There is a slight silence, before everyone suddenly bursts out with laughter. The mushrooms referred to by the children are in fact very carefully cultivated by some of the local farmers, who inject bacteria into oak-tree (*kunugi*) branches and grow mushrooms that in a city like Tokyo can cost several thousand yen *each*. It is definitely a hard life being a father.

"Don't worry. Those mushrooms belong to Jirō, who lives at the bottom of the hill," Katsuhisa soothes me. "He's a good sort, and anyway he's got so many of the things that he'll never notice if a few are missing. At least, you won't have to buy anything for your supper this evening."

15   And, slowly, we settle in. The next day the weather turns bitterly cold, and there are flurries of snow. We have no telephone and I don't fancy trying to go down to Fujioka to get some kerosene for our single stove, so we walk up through the woods together. I show the children where our water comes from, and then we go on up through the brown stubble of the rice fields to the huddle of houses that make up the bulk of Ōkubo. I've already met most of the people living here. Kajiwara Buntarō owns what is called "the main house" right on the top of the hill. Like Yamaguchi, he spends most of his time growing pears. So does his cousin, Tōsuke, who lives in the house next door across the orchard. Both these men are members of the *shigin* singing group. Then there is Kajiwara Munetoshi, a traveling salesman whose house also branched from Buntarō's at some time in the past. Below him, looking out over the valley towards the school, is a house owned by yet another man named Kajiwara: this time an elderly man called Shichirō, whose son has gone away to work in Osaka and whose elder daughter, Yasuko, is married to Tōsuke and has borne him two sons.

"We're a close-knit community, here in Ōkubo," explains Buntarō as he willingly pours out some kerosene for me into a large square can. "My family owns the main house. It's been here now for almost two hundred years, you know. I've been told that by some local historian who came around here once a few years ago and began marveling at how old it was. There's something about the way the roof has been constructed that enables him to date the house. He drew plans of it. Later on a television company came and filmed it."

This doesn't mean much. Japanese television companies often come out into the country to film "traditional" scenes to use as backdrops for the weather reports. I know this from one I've seen of Inoshige making pots. Bent over the wheel, his balding head had gleamed unflatteringly in the camera lights. The forecast was superimposed—*hare, toki doki kumori* ("fine, with occasional clouds"), which one wag during *shigin* later that week had transformed to *hage, toki doki kemori* ("bald, with occasional hair").

"Katsuhisa's was the first branch house to be formed. About four or five generations ago. But he lives down at the bottom of the hill by the temple, and that's too far away for us to keep up the customary main-house / branch-house relations. Anyway, he's far wealthier than I am, and that's not the way things should be between main house and branch house. His great grandfather worked in local government, you know."

I knew enough to realize that people distrusted minor officials in the local government bureaucracy. It was always being implied that shady, underhanded deals went on there. That was the only way people like Katsuhisa's great grandfather could have got rich.

"Shichirō's my uncle. He's my father's younger brother and was adopted into the house down the hill—the one we call Shimo—because they didn't have a son to succeed as head of the family. His elder daughter, Yasuko, is married to Tōsuke, whose father was my mother's elder brother. They live in Shintaku, the 'new house,' over there. My parents are cousins, too. It used to be quite common for cousins to get married here, you know."

"What about Munetoshi?" I ask, marveling at the way people intermarry here in the valley. Form a branch house and receive a daughter in return the following generation; give a daughter in marriage one generation, and you can expect to adopt a son into your own household the next, if you haven't got a son of your own. The give-and-take of kinship relations.

"Funnily enough, we've never married into Mukei, the 'house opposite.' I don't know why. Probably got something to do with their never having sons and daughters the right age to marry ours. Munechan's wife, Sumiko, comes from a different part of the country altogether."

"And the others?" I prompt.

"The others. Well, Kumao used to live in Aso Masaki's Naka, 'middle,' before he moved down to Atarasha, the 'new house,' beside the barber's shop. Haruo lives in Uazē, the thatched-roof house in the orchard above us, and at the very top, in Uendan, 'top ledge,' lives another Aso. No relation to Masaki, although I suppose they might have been once upon a time. Only the old lady lives there now. Her son works down in the town and doesn't come back much. Like Shichirō's only boy, who lives in Osaka. There's not enough work around here for all the young people. Tōsuke and I, we were lucky, but Munetoshi has to drive off for as much as two weeks at a time as he travels around selling his company's medicines. Poor Sumiko has a hard time, what with her children being so small and her mother-in-law not well."

Buntarō bends down to screw up the lid of the can of kerosene. "And that is the entire hamlet of Ōkubo. Oh! I forgot to mention Gotō Jirō, the mushroom-grower. Do you know him? A bald-headed man with rather small eyes. He lives at the very bottom of the hill in the middle of Inekari, but is in fact a member of our community. You'll probably meet him at the Kōshinsama celebration, which is going to be held fairly soon. That's the god whose stone effigy you can find above the hamlet. The person whose turn it is to entertain always takes the children up there in the afternoon. He puts a bottle of cold *sake* in front of the god and distributes dumplings [*dango*] to the children. Now that Atchan and Maya-chan are here," he jerks his head toward where my children are looking in wonder at a wild boar caged in Buntarō's backyard, "they can go along, too. Every sixtieth day. Kanoesaru it's called on the lunar calendar. I'll let you know when that is."

16   The children have started going to the primary school situated along the road leading up to Noda and Ichinotsuru. Every morning they go off, with satchels on their backs, wearing green track suits and gym shoes. The other children from Ōkubo wait for them at the end of the track by the Inari (fox-deity) shrine in the orchard. There is Tōsuke's boy, Naruhisa, and Buntarō's elder son, Sugihiko, together with Munetoshi's eldest daughter, Akemi. The five of them walk down the road to Katsuhisa's house, Mon, where they are joined by his two girls, Naomi and Akiko. In single file, they walk on down past the shrine to the main road and the houses of Inekari, where they pick up Kuroda Tatsu from the *sake* shop and Inekari Norihisa from the general shop next door.

It is only a 15-minute walk to the school for these children, but for those who come down from Kamayama, Ichinotsuru, and Noda, the walk is much longer. The children from Ichinotsuru find themselves walking at least three and a half miles a day during the term time, and I often come across them on my way back from Kamayama, sitting or kneeling in the middle of the road, poring over a book together. The headmaster of the school, a jovial man who occasionally drops by Inoshige's workshop on his way home, is firmly convinced that it is good for the children to walk to school.

"That's the way things used to be, after all," he says, sipping a cup of green tea and standing with his back to the workshop stove as he watches Inoshige work miracles with a lump of clay. "In the old days there weren't any cars, so people had to walk. Children have life too easy now, so I think that it's right they should walk to school and back. Whatever the weather. It toughens them up."

"You're right, *sensei*," Inoshige agrees. "I remember going to school as a kid. It wasn't that far for us, of course, compared with those coming down from Ichinotsuru. But there were no roads then, and we used to take a short cut across the hill behind this house. Katō Michiya and I were the only two boys going to school at one stage. He was a real little rascal—catching snakes and throwing them at the girls. They used to squeal with fright. Like pigs.

Haruzō's sister fainted once, and we had to carry her piggyback down to the school. When Haruzō heard, he gave poor Mitchan a real drubbing."

Inoshige wipes the clay from his fingers on the edge of an iron bowl of water beside him. Then he begins rummaging among his tools for a special throwing rib. "In winter once it snowed so hard the only way we could get across the drifts on the Otomai pass was by tunneling our way through. That was really exciting." He finally finds the tool he has been looking for and turns his attention to the clay on the wheel. "We didn't have any shoes, then. I remember having to sit down for a whole day occasionally and my father would teach me how to weave my own straw sandals. They'd disintegrate every time it rained, and then I'd have to make some more."

"Yes. That's the way children should be brought up. Your Alyosha and Maya are lucky, Būchan, getting the chance to experience this sort of education just once in their lives. Good, practical knowledge and not so much of that airy-fairy stuff they teach you in books. Picking tea leaves in the spring, so that they can make enough tea for school visitors during the year; helping transplant the rice in June and cutting it in the late autumn. It'll be an experience I hope they will always treasure. How do you do that, Inoshigesan?" Fujita, the headmaster, asks admiringly, as the potter deftly cuts a tea bowl from the top of a lump of clay, places it on a wooden bat beside him, and immediately makes another bowl almost identical in size and shape.

"Practice," answers Inoshige shortly. "How are the boys getting on, anyway?" he asks me.

"Marvelously. They've never been so happy and content in all their lives. We hardly ever see them at home now because they're out playing with their friends."

"Yes, it's a good time of year now that the rice has been harvested and the fields are dry enough to run around in. Plenty of baseball and games of hide-and-seek in the straw. I saw Gotō Jirō's old woman chasing away a whole bunch of kids who were frolicking in her haystacks."

"It's lucky so many of the boys in Atchan's age group should be living in Yashiki village," the headmaster says, picking up the thread of the conversation. "There are only fifty-six children altogether in the school, and Atchan's class is larger than average with thirteen children in it. All six of the boys come from Inekari, Ōkubo, and Takao near the school. I feel a bit sorry for Mayachan, though. There are only six children in his class, and he is the only boy. I guess if he stays long enough in the valley, he'll begin to appreciate his classmates." Fujita chuckles and shakes his head in disbelief as he watches the potter throw yet another identical form.

"How *do* you do that, Inoshigesan?"

17   To my surprise, I've discovered that Aso Masaki has quite a large family. While I was clearing up the house, Masaki was the only person I met, although the way he bawled out in the house sometimes made me suspect that someone else was there, too. Not that I ever saw who it was.

"That'll be Mihoko," Buntarō explained as we sat together over a few drinks after a *shigin* session. "Old Aso is always shouting at his wife to do this, do that, and telling her what a bloody fool she is. And when she does what he tells her, he curses her for being so stupid. But she's not at all. Her only trouble is that she's too shy and gentle to stand up to her husband."

We used to see her once or twice after we moved in, a thin, wiry woman with her hair in a bun, who would walk quietly down to the few fields that Aso owned below Takeshi's orchard, where she grew vegetables. But when we greeted her, she never replied, and we wondered if she was perhaps deaf.

"Not deaf at all," insisted Buntarō. "As I told you, she's really shy and withdrawn. Aso has beaten her into silence."

Mihoko is not the only person living in the Aso house. There are three children there, too. Masaki's eldest son works as an electrician in Osaka, and his youngest boy has recently been employed by a car manufacturer in Hiroshima. Masaki is very proud of the fact that he has also managed to find a job in a lumberyard down in the town for his second son, Akihito, who will take over the headship of the household in due course. Still in his early twenties, Akihito seems to have more of his mother's than his father's temperament. On weekends, or sometimes in the afternoon if he gets home early, he starts talking to my children and shows them how to spin wooden tops, which they bought down at Inekari's general store (too grand a name for the room at the front of the house, piled high with anything from tōfu to cigarettes). Akihito patiently teaches them how to wrap the spinning cord around the metal spindle that he has hammered into the wooden top for them; how to grip the cord so that it doesn't slip; and then how to hurl the top with all the force of one arm downward onto the hard earth in the yard outside his house, allowing the cord to unravel and spin the top at great speed. Soon the three of them are busy trying to see who can keep his top going the longest.

This is the season for tops. I meet Katsuhisa down in the *sake* shop this evening, and he insists on taking me to the small shrine by the fork in the road to Ōkubo. We climb the flagstone steps set deeply in the hillside, his flashlight picking out the sculptured figure of a dog guarding the entrance to the community shrine.

"Look here!" He pauses and shines his flashlight directly into the dog's mouth. "Here's a puzzle for your university brain to work out. How did the man who made this dog get that large stone ball into its mouth?"

I look and am puzzled. Sure enough, between the clenched teeth of the stone dog I can see a large ball. I prod it gently and it moves.

We walk across the open space at the top of the steps to the building itself. Katsuhisa directs the beam of his flashlight onto the wooden floor.

"You see," he says. "The whole floor is covered in pockmarks where the children have thrown their tops. For years they have been coming here to play on cold winter days when there is nothing else to do. I used to come myself, you know, with Buntarō and Tōsuke. Great battles we used to have, too, trying to knock each other's tops off course."

Masaki also has twin grown-up daughters living in the house. We never see very much of them, for they go down to the town with Akihito in the early morning and come back with him in the evening. The rest of the time they are kept closeted up in the house.

"Masaki is probably afraid that somebody will try to do a bit of night crawling in his house," said Daisuke, the carpenter. "Not that you could really get close to the house without those dogs barking their heads off. Hitomi and Futami, the two girls are called—first and second beauties. I haven't seen them for some years now, but they weren't much to talk about when they were younger. I wonder what they're like now," Daisuke paused to muse. "Terukichi tells me that Aso is looking around for a husband for one of them."

"Beauty!" chuckled a garage attendant down at Fujioka while he filled up the tank of my motorbike. "You know the definition of a 'beauty' around here, don't you? Swarthy skin and squashed nose. That's what people mean by beauty around here."

18   There are three wild dogs living around our house. At first I thought they belonged to Masaki, but the way he spent so much time cursing and throwing stones at them, I soon began to wonder. One day Akihito explained that they were wild, but that the black one answered to the name Kurochan, "Blackie." She would eat from your hand once she got to know you. Now she was pregnant and spent most of the time lying under the house. As for the other two, you could never get near them. Even when they appeared to be fast asleep, they would always leap up nervously and dart away the moment the children approached them. They've named them, though—Otōsan, "Daddy," and Onīsan, "Elder Brother," because they figure that one sired the other by way of Kurochan. Akihito says that in fact Elder Brother is the father of the other two, but the names have stuck now in the curious way that names do, and the children put out scraps of food for the dogs every morning, patiently hoping that one day they will become less timid.

Right at the end of the year, Kurochan gives birth to a litter of puppies in the cold, narrow space under one wing of Aso's house. Only one of them survives the frosty night and Akihito names it Rokuchan, "Six," a neat inversion of the syllabary for *kuro*. The children are delighted to have a dog to play with. Masaki goes around cursing and threatens to have all four of the dogs put down. Almost every time I see him, he mutters something about phoning up the town hall and getting the environmental health people to come and take them away.

Even though two of the dogs are so wild—I've come across them way up above Kamayama before now—the pack never leaves us entirely alone. When the dogs go off on their forays, they always make sure that at least one of them stays to guard the house. It's almost as if they've adopted us.

19   And so we slip into the rhythm of life in the valley. In these last days before the New Year, we go over to Inoshige's and learn to make rice-cakes (*mochi*), taking it in turns to pound with wooden mallets the steaming rice that Misae quickly turns in the wooden mortar between our blows. Living dangerously, she helps us create and maintain a steady rhythm, uttering little cries of encouragement as the rice is gradually transformed into one smooth, pudding-like lump. Kyōko, Ayako, and the children pinch off pieces of this dough, which they then shape into round cakes and cover with flour. Between us we prepare two *tō*, just over 75 pounds, of rice. By the time the New Year festivities are over, none of us wants to eat rice-cakes ever again—until next year, at least.

The Kōshinsama community gathering takes place early in the new year. Buntarō, true to his word, sends his wife, Hideko, down to inform us that we should meet at Kumao's house at seven thirty one evening. He needn't have taken so much trouble, though. There is a loudspeaker set up on the hillside at the edge of Tōsuke's orchard, and this is used to inform everyone in Ōkubo of community occasions. At about six forty-five this morning we were awakened by the ding-dong-ding-ding of musical chimes, followed by somewhat rude-sounding noises as Masaki, whose turn it has been this year to be hamlet chief, blew down the microphone to check whether it was working.

"Good morning, everybody! Since it is Kōshinsama today, will everybody please gather at Kuroda Kumao's place this evening at half past seven. I will repeat . . ."

The gathering itself is little more than an opportunity for people in the community to get together and have a chat over a few bottles of *sake*. There is a scroll hanging on the wall of the guest room in Kumao's house and, on entering the room, we each of us kneel before it, place 100 yen on the tatami mat, and bow our heads briefly in respect to the god. Then we sit ourselves down at the low tables set out in the guest room and start eating the food prepared for us by Kumao's wife, Fumiko. Toward the end—and it is clear that this is not an occasion when people stay until all hours of the night drinking—Fumiko comes with a lacquer box full of rice dumplings. These she plucks out one by one with a pair of chopsticks and places in the cupped hands of each of the guests.

It is a good opportunity to meet everyone in Ōkubo, and I have brought with me a bottle of *sake* for people to drink on a suitable occasion. I make a short speech thanking everyone for allowing us to live in the community and expressing my hope that we will be good neighbors and not cause people too much inconvenience. This seems to go down very well, and Gotō Jirō, the bald-headed *shiitake* mushroom–grower who lives down in Inekari, immediately hands me his *sake* cup.

"It sounds a bit rude calling you by a name that means piglet, Būchan, and I hope you don't mind my calling you that." He laughs, and his eyes seem to narrow so much that they all but disappear into the folds of skin under his heavy eyebrows. "But I've been to your country, you know. Oh yes, I have. A long time ago, before the war. I suppose you weren't born then? No. Well, anyway, I was a sailor on board one of our biggest battleships, and we put in an appearance for the coronation of one of your kings. We docked at a place called, what was it now? Ah yes. Chat-ham?" He seems surprised at himself for remembering the name. "Yes, Chat-ham. It was a long way to go for a coronation, but in those days we did what we were told by the great British Empire." He laughs again. "Anyway, you've chosen a good place to live. That's all I wanted to say. And we're glad to have you here. Ōkubo's a happy community. We don't quarrel with each other, the way they do in some other hamlets around here."

The others all nod their heads in agreement. "You're right, Jirō-san," says Katsuhisa. "Ōkubo's a much better place than somewhere like Kamayama where you're studying. Some of the things that go on there! You wouldn't believe it. Like that tree that juts out in the middle of the road halfway up the hill."

"You mean the one between Fujinori's and Etsuo's potteries?" I ask, eager to learn a bit of gossip that might prove useful to my understanding of the community there.

"That's the one. There's a long, long story about that tree, and you'd better ask somebody in Kamayama about it. But the way I heard it was like this. Way back in the past, those two houses had some row, apparently over land. Fujinori's great grandfather, I think it was, thought that he'd been cheated, so in revenge he decided to plant a tree in such a position that when it grew properly, it would cast its shadow right across Etsuo's courtyard in front of his house. In other words, the idea was that Etsuo's family wouldn't be able to dry their pots properly because of the tree."

"Well, well. Who would believe it?" Kumao shakes his head in wonder as Katsuhisa continues.

"It made no difference to Fujinori's great grandfather that he would never live to see the day when all this happened; but he was happy enough in the thought that one day Etsuo's family would suffer." Katsuhisa gives one of his chubby smiles. For a big man he has such a gentle face. "And suffered they have, of course. The tree is fully grown now, and its shadow nicely blocks the sunshine from Etsuo's yard. It takes the poor man at least a day longer than anyone else in the community to dry his pots.

"But that isn't the end of the story. Two or three years ago the Town Council decided to widen the road to make more room for the tourist buses to go up and down Kamayama. Remember? Well, the planning authorities managed to arrange everything—except for that tree, which Fujinori absolutely refused to allow them to cut down. The planning people got Haruzō to intervene on their behalf—you know he's a great one for keeping in with them, because he relies on the Town Council to give him his contracts. But even old Haruzō wasn't able to make Fujinori change his mind. I was delighted, of course. After all, I teach forestry at the local high school, and the last thing I want to see is a big tree being cut down for the sake of a tourist bus or two. All the same, I feel a bit sorry for Etsuo. Anyway, now you have a nice wide road all the way through Kamayama, except for that one place in the middle where it narrows to half its width because of the tree." Everybody laughs. "That's what we mean when we say that Ōkubo is a happy community. We don't have that sort of vicious, long-standing family feud here."

"Yes," agrees Munetoshi, a dapper young man whose gold-rimmed glasses give him an earnest appearance. "There aren't many hamlets in this valley that will arrange to take a few days off from work so that everyone can go off on an outing all together."

"Like when we went on our *sangū* pilgrimage several years ago." Tōsuke grins, his dark-skinned face slightly reddened from the effects of *sake*.

"Which pilgrimage was that now?" asks Kumao, who somehow reminds me of a Greek fisherman I once knew on Seriphos.

"You know, the one where we started off in Izumo," Buntarō reminds him.

"Ah, yes. And then we went to Kyoto."

"No. We went to Amanohashidate first."

"Did we? I can hardly remember. I was drunk most of the time."

Munetoshi is determined to let me know the details of the journey. "We visited the Higashi Hongan temple in Kyoto, along with Kiyomizu temple and the Gojū-no-tō pagoda, and one or two other places whose names I've forgotten. After that we went to Ise. Or did we go to Tokyo first and Ise on the way back?"

"Can't remember," says Katsuhisa. "All I know is that by the time we got to Nikkō, we were rushing into one shrine, chucking a coin in the donations box, rattling the bell-rope to say hello to whichever deity it was, and rushing off again."

"Yes, that's right," Jirō takes up the story. "When I started at Izumo, I was donating one hundred yen a time. When we got to Nikkō, I had cut my contributions down to ten yen. And in Matsushima and Sendai in the north of Japan I couldn't afford more than one yen a shrine. No wonder they're so poor up there."

"Twelve days that trip took," Munetoshi reminds us. "That was a really good long holiday. We ought to do something like that again."

"You're right, Munechan. It was good fun. Do you remember how black our faces were when we got off that train in Sendai? Those old steam engines may sound nice and romantic, but they were really dirty, weren't they?"

It is occasions like these that allow people to reassert their sense of togetherness. Nostalgia for the past keeps alive, sometimes creates even, a sense of community history and reinforces community ideals.

20   On my way home from Kamayama, I stop by Inoshige's workshop. The building is in darkness, which is unusual, and so I slide open the front door and call out to ask if anyone is at home. A weak voice answers, and the shōji of the *kotatsu* room is slid open a little by Den, who is lying there in the darkness.

"Hello, Granny. Shall I switch the light on? Where is everyone?"

"Ah, thank you," she says, trying to prop herself up in a sitting position as I step up and pull the cord below the light above the *kotatsu*. "They're all gone, you know. There was a phone call a few days ago from one of my grandchildren asking Inoshige to check up on his sister. Nobody could get in touch with her, and we live nearest to her—even though it is an hour's drive away. He went over straight after Kōshinsama, only to find her dead. I can't believe it. Dead. And for five days, too. The doctor said she'd bled heavily from the mouth and nose."

I don't know what to do or how to comfort the old woman except to say how sorry I am.

"Sixty-three, Hisae was. You never met her, did you? Sixty-three and I'm eighty-three. And she's dead and I'm still alive. I never thought I'd see any of my children leave this world before I did. I think that's the worst thing that can happen to any parent."

I stay awhile to keep her company. The rest of the family has gone to the funeral, but Den is too weak to make the trip. Her legs wouldn't stand it. Fortunately, Ayako and Misae come back with the children soon after and I am able to leave.

As I ride up the hill on my bike, I meet Akihito coming down in the car. We stop and exchange greetings.

"Off to enjoy yourself, then?"

"Yes," he smiles. "A bit of fun with my mates."

Much, much later, in the middle of the night, there is the sound of an ambulance's siren wailing as it comes up the valley. Only slightly conscious of this strange sound in my dreams, I turn over restlessly. Later, I seem to hear the siren again, but I don't wake properly until the morning.

There is a lot of activity outside the house. It seems as if Aso Masaki's car has just been driven *down* the road to the car-parking area. I can hear voices and, quickly splashing cold water over my face to wake myself up, I slide open our front door.

One of Masaki's twin daughters, Hitomi, is standing there looking shell-shocked. "I'm sorry to bother you, but I'm afraid we shall be causing you a lot of trouble during the next few days," she begins, bringing out the standard series of formal expressions required when asking a person's favor. "But please be so good as to bear with us."

"Of course," I reply, returning her bow. "What is the trouble?"

"It's my brother," she says and, suddenly unable to restrain herself any longer, she blurts out, "He's not well at all. He's not at all well." Then she bursts into tears and runs toward her house.

Masaki comes limping up the path.

"I'm sorry to hear about Akihito. Has something happened?"

"The silly fool's gone and fallen from a precipice into the river above Amagase. You probably heard the ambulance last night." Masaki somehow manages a bitter smile. "Broken a leg and massive internal and head injuries. He's not going to make it."

I try to say something that will help. On occasions like this, though, words are so useless. "I'm sure he'll get better."

"He's as good as dead," Masaki says shortly. "He's unconscious and in an oxygen tent. The doctors gave up hope hours ago. It's just a matter of time. We're preparing for the funeral. Please accept my apologies for any disturbance we may cause."

Stunned as much by Masaki's ability to distance himself from the accident as by the accident itself, I go back into the house and tell Kyōko what has happened. The children are still asleep, and we decide to say nothing to them when they get up.

But they soon hear about the accident at school that day. I find it hard to believe that gossip can travel so fast. When I go down to Inoshige's to express my condolences over his sister's death, he already knows what has happened to Akihito.

"The ambulance came wailing its way right past the house at two in the morning," he says shortly, his eyes tired and red from lack of sleep. "How could I avoid hearing what happened and who was involved? They were out drinking—Akihito and three of his friends from lower down the valley—and it appears they decided to light a fire to keep themselves warm. It was cold anyway last night, and it must have been freezing above the river gorge. Goodness knows what they were doing there. Anyway, they started gathering wood, and Akihito reached for the branch of a dead tree on the edge of a precipice, above where the river comes down in a series of waterfalls. They say his foot slipped and he fell. He tried to grab hold of the tree, but the wood was rotten and didn't hold him. It took the ambulance men at least an hour to get him out of the gorge."

Later on in the day, Masaki's two brothers arrive from distant parts of the island to help with funeral arrangements. They clear away all the wood that Masaki has stacked along one side of the house and sweep the courtyard clean. They pull out the weeds growing in cracks in the stone wall and manage to tie up Kurochan and her puppy at the back of the house somewhere. They help the women clean the inside of the house from top to bottom. And when that is all done, they sit down and wait.

21 For two weeks the Aso household waited for Akihito to die. The residents of the hamlet of Ōkubo waited with them, ready to drop everything once they knew that the funeral had to be arranged. But Akihito was young, and his body wouldn't give up. According to the doctors—or rather according to rumors of what the doctors had said (Shichirō's daughter-in-law's younger sister was a nurse at the hospital where Akihito had been taken)—the boy was brain dead soon after the accident. In a coma, he was nothing more than a breathing vegetable whose pulse just would not stop.

Masaki's brothers went back to their separate homes at the other end of the island. I went about my studies. But I knew that the moment Akihito did die we would, as next-door neighbors, be called upon to help. This matter had already been discussed when I met Katsuhisa and Buntarō down near the drinking "fountain"—a trough by the roadside where tired foresters and farmers could slake their thirst with refreshingly cold water piped in from the mountains.

"Normally, you would be expected to offer your house for the funeral feast," Katsuhisa started, before adding quickly, "but it isn't really normal having you as next-door neighbor to Masaki. After all, you're only temporary residents. Anyway Kyōko isn't used to our ways and wouldn't know what to do."

I pointed out that as long as someone else took charge of matters, we were quite prepared to open our house to the funeral guests.

"Let's wait until the time comes before making up our minds," said Buntarō. "It would probably be better to use your house as a resting room. Then people who don't want to go all the way to Haruo's or Shichirō's or Kumao's or wherever can rest in your guest room."

So we, too, clean up the upstairs rooms and wait for the fateful day. Masaki, Mihoko, and their two daughters take turns staying at the hospital, only coming back to the house to get some sleep. The others, who for a time included Masaki's youngest son come back from Hiroshima, keep up their vigil by Akihito's bedside.

And then one afternoon there is the sound of their car, and we watch as all four of them get out, looking purposeful and solemn. "I'm afraid Akihito died. At approximately two o'clock this afternoon." Masaki announces the news to us through the open door.

We both bow and express our sorrow. Masaki limps back to the house, head bowed. The dogs, eyeing him nervously, get up from where they are lying in the yard and move away. This time Masaki ignores them.

I go off to tell Buntarō the news. He, Tōsuke, and Munetoshi are all standing outside the main house, dressed in their town clothes. Masaki has already phoned them the news, and they are about to go off and inform other members of the valley community. Munetoshi is being detailed to go down to the main Agricultural Cooperative in town and arrange for the people there to do the funeral service.

"They do a really good job," Tōsuke explains. "And so cheap, too. There's nowhere else around here that will do you so proud for seventy thousand yen."

A rusty old Toyota truck comes grinding its way up the hill. Katsuhisa is sitting behind the wheel in his suit, having just come back from school to help deal with the funeral arrangements. He has managed to find time to whittle himself a toothpick, which, as usual, he has stuck into one corner of his mouth.

"Canadian pine," he says proudly, showing it to me. "You'd know immediately by the smell of the wood. Not that I'm suggesting you have a sniff right now. I had garlic for lunch. But I'll show you some more of the wood next time you drop by my house. Now what's to be done?" he asks, turning to the others.

"Has Kumao been told?"

"I think so. Misako said she'd phoned him at work. He should be on his way back. What about Haruo?"

"He's on his way home, too. And Shichirō's gone to fetch Jirō down from the hills above Takao."

"Katchan, could you let the old priest at the temple know. And I'd better go and talk things over with Masaki once Kumao gets back," says Buntarō.

"In that case, I'll go with you, Munechan," Tōsuke says.

"So we'll meet at your place, Būchan. At half past five. That's when the community as a whole will pay its respects. Two members from each household."

Two hours later, people start to gather outside our house—one man and one woman from each of the other nine households that make up the community of Ōkubo. The women are all carrying floppy quilted patchwork bags, which are filled with about two pounds of rice. This is each household's contribution toward the funeral feast.

Once everybody is present, Kumao leads us towards Masaki's house. We cross the yard and go into the hall.

"*Gomen kudasai*. Please excuse us," we call and, leaving our thonged sandals in the entrance, we step up into the main room. Ignoring Masaki and his family, who are sitting quietly at the end of the room, we go straight up to the ancestral shrine and kneel before it. Kumao, Shichirō, and Jirō line up in front because they are the eldest. The rest of us take up our appropriate positions, more or less fixed by age, behind them. The women, I now notice, have stayed in the hall. Each of us throws a coin toward the shrine and places his hands together, bowing his head in silent respect. Akihito's corpse, covered in a white sheet and with a white handkerchief over his face, lies right beside me, facing north. This is the direction in which the dead are laid to rest, and for this reason people normally take care to lay out their bedding in some other direction when they go to sleep at night.

After half a minute or so, we get up from our knees and walk together down the long room toward the Aso family. The women step up into the room and pass behind us as they go to pay their respects at the ancestral shrine. We kneel down across from where Masaki is positioned, slightly ahead of his wife and two daughters. Kumao bows first, and we all follow.

"Good evening," he says, and we chorus his greeting.

"Good evening," Masaki and his family return our greeting.

"We'd like to express our condolences at this time," Kumao begins, and we all follow, although nobody really enunciates his words very clearly, and it is difficult to hear what exactly is being said. It is the form that seems to matter, not the content.

"Thank you very much," Masaki replies and bows again.

We shift sideways a few feet to make room for the women to kneel down beside us. They, too, repeat the same set phrases. When the greetings are finished, there is a short silence, before Kumao asks hesitantly when Akihito died.

"Did he ever regain consciousness?" asks Shichirō sympathetically.

"No, he didn't."

Another pause. Kumao asks when Masaki would like the funeral to take place.

"The day after tomorrow would be better. We haven't been able to get hold of my eldest son yet, and he may not be able to get home from Osaka till tomorrow evening. It'll also give other members of my family more time to get here."

"Fine. On Friday morning then. At about noon?"

People nod their heads.

"Now where shall we hold the funeral feast? Normally, of course, we would ask Būchan to oblige. But he's new here and his place is a bit cramped. Shichirōsan, do you think . . . ?" Kumao asks.

"Of course," Shichirō answers immediately. "Please feel free to use my house."

"You're welcome to use my place, if you'd like to."

"No, Būchan. It would be too difficult, especially with your kitchen being downstairs and your guest room upstairs. If it's all right with Shichirōsan, let's hold the feast there."

There are murmurs of assent.

"Right! That's settled, then." Kumao bows, and we take our leave. Outside it is dark. The dogs bark at us as we open the door of the hall.

"Those dogs!" I hear Masaki mutter. "I'd better shoot them before the funeral."

Preparations start early. Tōsuke and Buntarō arrive in a van just after seven in the morning and unload a trestle table and two folding chairs, which they carry up to the entrance of Aso's yard. They set them up facing out across the valley and attach a long strip of paper with the word "reception" handwritten across it. Another, similar strip marked "resting room" they give to me to place on our upstairs front door. Masaki has already lent us a smart black imitation-leather sofa for people to sit on.

Everyone else is over at Shichirō's house—one woman from each household working in the earth-floored kitchen, while the men gather around a fire at the back.

"We wondered if you'd put in an appearance, Būchan," Katsuhisa says, waving his toothpick at me in greeting. "You're just in time to learn how to cook rice."

Jirō comes out of the back of the house with a large cauldron, which he places over a fire tended by Kumao and Munetoshi. Haruo stands close by, warming his hands. It is a cold and frosty morning. Katsuhisa and Shichirō continue washing the rice in the mountain water that runs into the fishpond at the side of the house. A burly youth, whom Katsuhisa introduces as "the other Aso up the hill," is splitting wood for the fire.

"Our job is to cook rice. In the old days when there was a funeral, the young men had the job of digging the grave, and the old men made a coffin for the corpse. The in-betweens used to go down to the temple and bring back special trays and dishes for the feast, and parasols, which they'd set up for the funeral service. Nowadays, the Agricultural Coop does everything for us, so we've found ourselves with a bit of time on our hands. It seems only fair to give the women a hand, and we've taken over the job of cooking the rice."

"And a much better job than the women we do of it, too," puts in Munetoshi seriously, as he watches the rice simmering in the cauldron over the fire. Ash flies up, and he has to turn his head away sharply to avoid getting any specks in his eye.

Shichirō comes back from the wood at the end of his vegetable patch with a handful of bamboo stems. These he cuts to a length and sharpens at one end. Haruo, who occasionally does carpentry for a living, is busy sawing off blocks of wood, which he then hammers into L-shaped candle perches. Kumao joins him, and together they fashion lantern bases by tacking together a square frame of wood and then drilling a small hole at each corner. Shichirō meanwhile has been splitting one of the bamboo strips into yet thinner strips.

"It's lovely, isn't it?" says Katsuhisa, caressing a piece of bamboo. "The perfect wood. You can split it and split it again endlessly. You can soak it in water and bend it into almost any shape you please."

Shichirō bends a bamboo strip into an inverted U-shape, placing each end in two holes diagonally. Then he does the same with a second strip, to form a crude cage. Jirō comes out of the house with some red and white streamers and paper, which Katsuhisa cuts to shape and glues to the frame of the paper lanterns.

By this time the first pan of rice is ready, and the men ladle it out into shallow wicker baskets before taking them into the kitchen. Munetoshi, who appears to have put himself in charge of the rice cooking, proceeds to sprinkle salt over the rest of the rice stuck to the side of the iron cauldron.

"This is the best bit," says Jirō as he helps scrape the crusty brown rice from the inner surface of the cauldron. "And it tastes even better when it is washed down with some form of liquid." He grins as he watches Shichirō hauling a crate of beer out of the fishpond. They open two or three bottles, and the beer froths over the lip of brown glass.

Munetoshi refills the cauldron with rice and water. Haruo adds more wood to the fire. Kumao comes out of the kitchen with a hunk of whale meat and cuts it up with his forester's knife, after giving it a brief rinse in the pond. The poor fish must be wondering what on earth is going on.

"Strictly speaking, this is against the rules," says Katsuhisa. "Beer drinking, I can assure you, is not an official part of the funeral preparations."

"It may not be official, but it's an important part of what goes on. Isn't that right, Jirōsan?"

Jirō's eyes begin to melt away into creases of skin as he laughs. "And it has a history, too. In the old days we had to dig graves ourselves. We used to bury people in a sitting posture, with hands clasped around the knees. Not flat out on their backs like they do nowadays in some places. So the coffin was more box-like than it is now. And that meant that the grave had to be deep." He poured himself a second glass of beer.

"That's right, Jirō. I suppose it was your brother, Kōsuke, who was the last person to be buried and not cremated."

"Yes, I guess so. He was apprenticed as a carpenter in the city in the north of the island, you know. Somehow, he got mixed up with some gangsters and started borrowing money from the old man to pay off his debts. Not that he ever told us why he needed so much. And then one night he came home and hanged himself from the roof of the store where I dry my mushrooms. You know, the one just below Katsuhisa's place. We buried him because you don't cremate people who've committed suicide."

"It was hard work digging a grave as deep as you were tall, I can tell you," Kumao continues. "In summer, especially, it would get really hot."

"And occasionally you would dig too far to one side and the bones from some other grave would fall in on your feet."

"That's right, Shichirōsan. I remember one occasion. I was the youngest around then, and all the others left me alone to dig Buntarō's granddad's grave. Down I went. Six, eight, ten feet into the ground, until all I could see was the sky above my head. And then, suddenly, the earth fell away at my feet, and a skull came tumbling into the grave. Boy, did I scream!"

Everyone laughs, and Katsuhisa pours out more beer, before helping himself to some whale meat, which he plucks from the plate with his toothpick.

"What a stink there was," continues Kumao. "It wasn't the face so much that disgusted me as the way the hair still clung to the skull. It was awful."

"I wonder who it was."

"One of the children, I think."

"Ah, yes. They used to die young in those days. Quite often from drowning. Like my sister who fell in the river and couldn't swim," says Shichirō.

"My younger brother nearly went that way," recalls Haruo. "My mother was up in the hills collecting fern tops when the old man bellowed up from the valley below: 'He's dead!' She fairly flew down that hillside, to find everyone gathered around my brother's lifeless body. Fortunately for us, there was a relative staying with us who knew how to give artificial respiration. That's what saved my brother's life."

"Yes. I remember that, Harusan. You were really lucky, weren't you?"

Munetoshi decides that the second batch of rice is ready and scoops it out of the cauldron into the shallow wicker baskets once more. Again we sprinkle the pan with salt, and again we scrape the crisp rice off the sides of the pan. More hors d'oeuvres to go with our beer. Everyone is looking flushed and cheerful as we stand, huddling together for warmth, around the fire. Tōsuke has joined us.

"My mother likes to tell the story of when her mother died," he says, doing his best to catch up with us by downing a glass of beer at a single gulp. "After the cremation, they took the ashes home and went to bed. But my mother was sure she could smell something burning, so she woke everyone up. One of her brothers was sent up to examine the roof, just in case an ember from the kitchen stove had set light to the thatch. Somebody else checked the place where they heated the bath. But nobody could find the fire, even though everyone was by now convinced that he could smell something burning." Tōsuke finishes a second glass of beer.

"Eventually, one of her relatives suggested that the body was still burning in the casket. And do you know what? They actually decided to take the casket down from the ancestral shrine and—very hesitantly, mind you—open it. They were scared stiff. But all was quiet within. Not a hint of a fire among the ashes. So they put the old woman back to rest with the ancestors, and it was then that my mother discovered that one of her cousins had wrapped his trousers around a hibachi to keep them warm for when he got up in the morning. Instead, they had caught fire and were gently smoldering."

This story is much appreciated, and everyone has a good laugh before repeating parts of the story again to one another.

"Opening the casket to see if the ashes were still smoldering. That's a nice idea."

"And it was only somebody's trousers burning. I wonder which part was burned."

"The bit around his balls probably."

Everybody laughs again. A story like this helps put distance between them and the death of Masaki's son, Akihito. At the same time, it gives them an opportunity to reinforce a sense of community by recalling a more or less shared past experience.

"There don't seem to be that many people coming for the funeral feast," Tōsuke says, "so perhaps some of us had better go in now, while there are still empty places."

It is agreed that the elder men should go, and Kumao, Jirō, and Shichirō leave us. Talk turns to athletics, softball, and future babies.

In due course Kumao and the others come out of the house, and we are asked to go in. Seating ourselves in order of age, we are joined by many of the women, who sit below us in the main room. Kumao and Jirō, somewhat the worse for their beer, decide to serve rice and soup to everyone. There is much merriment at the way they mimic a young girl's mincing steps as they move across the tatami, pigeon-toed, with bowls of soup and rice raised high in their hands. Jirō then serves the women *sake*.

I ask Katsuhisa about the existence of a reverse ritual.

"No. This isn't fixed by custom or anything. It's a pure coincidence, really, that men have taken to cooking rice at funerals. After all, they have to do something. And it is only because we now have good roads that we no longer have to do the unpleasant jobs of grave-digging and burial. So it seems fairly sensible that we men help out the women in preparing the feast. Cooking rice would seem to be the simplest answer and a job for which we men are suited. After all, you can hardly imagine someone like Jirō here slicing bamboo shoots into thin slivers or Kumao arranging raw fish in pretty circular patterns on a large dish. Not that we eat fish, of course, when somebody dies. But you know what I mean." Katsuhisa, too, is finding the combination of *sake* and beer somewhat overpowering. "Anyway, as I was saying, it's better that we men stay outside and develop an appetite because all the food here has to be eaten. Yes, everything. It would be extremely impolite to young Akihito if we left anything behind."

"You're right there, Katchan," says Buntarō from my other side, pouring him some more *sake*. "But you may be right about things being done the other way around when there's a death, Būchan. Tonight it'll be Masaki's turn to entertain us and thank us for making the funeral arrangements. And usually the head of the household of the dead person makes sure to serve *sake* to all his guests— especially the women. You'll be able to see for yourself later on."

We drink a little more *sake*, and then Buntarō says, apropos of nothing in particular, "you know, it was Akihito's birthday, the day he died."

"It doesn't surprise me," replies Katsuhisa. "It's not unusual for people to die on their birthdays. Like old Inekari Gorō's father, who died a few months back on his seventy-sixth birthday. You know, my father and my grandfather both died when they were twenty-seven years old," he continues, shifting the subject slightly. "When I was twenty-seven, therefore, I took special care not to do anything silly or dangerous. But once I had got through that year safely, I suddenly remembered that I had been three when my father died. So when Naomi was three, I took no risks. Having got that

year over with all right, I was free to breathe easily for twelve
months or so. But then Akiko turned three. And the very next year
it was Norihisa's turn. Now all my children have got through their
fourth year and I can relax—until they get to twenty-seven, that is.
Life's a bit better now, all right."

The funeral service is to be held at midday. After the meal, we
walk around the hill to Masaki's house, and the cold air soon sobers
us up. Quite a number of people have gathered, all in their dark
suits and black dresses, and Tōsuke and Kumao accept funeral gifts
of rice and money wrapped in black-and-gold-trimmed envelopes.
These they note down, writing the name of each visitor in a special
book, together with the size of his or her gift. Later on, Masaki will
have to return these gifts in part to each of the mourners, unless he
decides to donate all the money to a local school or other worthy
cause, in which case he does not have to return anything.

The sliding window-doors of the guest room in Masaki's house
have been removed, so that we can look right into the depths of the
building. The ancestral shrine has been illuminated and decorated
with special lamps, and a photograph of the dead boy set up in the
center of the shrine amidst vases of flowers. Sticks of incense have
been lit before the shrine, and large wreaths of flowers are standing
up against the wall of the house outside.

As members of the community of the deceased, we occupy a
special position in the ceremony. Standing close to the house with
our candle stands and paper lanterns, we are the only people not
dressed in mourning clothes. Instead of dark suits and ties, we wear
our normal working clothes—dresses and white aprons for the
women, khaki trousers and warm, fur-lined jackets for the men. We
at least are snug and warm, while everyone else shivers in the cold.

There are two priests. One sits on a wide, throne-like seat with
red-and-gold-lacquered armrests. This has been set in the center of
the room in front of Akihito's photograph. The other, the priest
from the local temple, sits beside his associate. In his left hand he
holds both his beads and a bronze bowl, which he periodically taps
with a wooden clapper as he drones in accompaniment to his fellow
priest's chanting. Both wear white undergarments and orange
surplices, with gold-embroidered heavy vestments slung over one
shoulder and closed fans tucked handle-first into the open neck of
their robes. The chief priest recites the funeral chant from a book,

but occasionally gets spasms of coughing and has to stop, much to a couple of people's consternation.

"He sounds as if he's the one about to leave this world, does that priest," comes a drunken voice from the back of the crowd.

One person turns in slight annoyance, but nobody else in the congregation pays any attention. The priest starts intoning his prayers once more, and soon Haruo and Munetoshi light two bundles of camphor, which they hold up in the air and point, along with the candles and paper lanterns, toward the ancestral shrine.

The priest nods at a smartly dressed young man who stands with his back to the deceased's photograph and faces the congregation. He has been hired by the Agricultural Cooperative to act as master of ceremonies and speaks in a suitably funereal voice, informing us that relatives will now be called upon to take their final leave of the deceased. Masaki's name is called first, and Akihito's father raises himself from his knees, quickly clicks his artificial limb into position, and walks across to the ancestral shrine. Raising a pinch of incense between the thumb and forefinger of one hand toward the dead boy's photograph, he sprinkles it over the mound of burning incense to his right, letting it go in three movements. He then clasps his hands together, closes his eyes briefly, and lowers his head.

"No right to die, the way he did." The man's voice comes clearly across the heads of those standing outside, but it is ignored. The master of ceremonies calls on Masaki's wife and children to pay their respects to Akihito.

"He was too young."

The name of Masaki's older brother is called, and he gets up to make his way with his family to the ancestral shrine.

"Never even had a woman." The voice at the back continues. "Died a virgin."

Masaki's younger brother's name is called.

"And it's not as if there aren't any good women around here, after all."

The master of ceremonies calls out the names of relatives on Mihoko's side of the family. Kumao looks at Buntarō, and the two men slip quietly away.

"You're not so bad yourself." The drunken voice continues, and there is a sudden squawk from a woman standing nearby.

"That's a nice pair of legs you've got."

Buntarō and Kumao catch the drunk and usher him away up the path toward our house. His voice can still be heard grumbling amid the monotonous chanting of the priests and the rhythmical clanging of the bell, but it is no longer so penetratingly clear.

More and more names are being called—Gotō Chitose, Wada Tatetarō, Sakakura Haruzō, Sakakura Inoshige, Inekari Gorō, Noda Moriyuki. As each person reaches the front of the room, he bows slightly toward the priests; some bow again toward the bereaved on their way back from the ancestral shrine. The main priest interrupts his chanting to tell people to hurry up by using the second incense-burner provided. Nobody seems to pay any attention. The master of ceremonies had first of all waited for each person to raise the incense toward the photograph of Akihito before calling on the next member of the congregation. But as kinship relations grow more tenuous, he steps up his pace. People who are called up from the back of the room prefer to walk along the veranda, rather than make their way up through the throng of mourners in the center of the room. As they bow in the direction of the priests, they find themselves also bowing in the direction of Masaki's family, huddled in a small group by the wall. The family members start bowing back, whereupon people returning from the ancestral shrine are caught in a cross fire of bows and immediately start bowing to those queuing behind them, as well as to the Aso family. For a minute or two, people are bobbing backward and forward like those toy dunking birds.

Eventually the "representatives" are called up—the head of the Valley Coordination Office, the chief of Yashiki village, the chairman of the Valley Youth Association, the headmaster of the North Oni Primary School, and the boss of the lumberyard where Akihito was employed. These men are rather more elaborate in their bows to Akihito's family. Finally, the master of ceremonies reads out simple telegrams from the head of the Agricultural Cooperative, the city mayor, and the chairman of the Forestry Commission, followed by the names and titles of half a dozen people who have sent condolences.

Masaki is asked to address the assembly of mourners. Obviously upset, he stands at attention, holding the microphone firmly in one hand, but finds it hard to say anything apart from a few standard formal expressions.

"Thank you all very much for taking the time and trouble to gather here today . . . It is a very difficult and sad occasion, and we are much indebted to you . . . The weather has been kind to us . . . thank you for being here at such a busy time." He stops, clearly at a loss to find anything else to say. Then, abruptly, he hands back the microphone to the master of ceremonies, who apologizes for the inconvenience and the brevity of the service, and asks us all to pay our last respects to the deceased.

Katsuhisa gives me a nudge and guides me gently forward toward the edge of the yard. There is a great pile of flat boxes, carefully wrapped and neatly stacked on the reception table. These contain the almost mandatory gift of handkerchiefs, together with purificatory salt, which is thrown over anyone arriving home from a funeral. These we hand to every guest as he or she departs.

Finally, everyone is gone, and we stand in the yard at the back of my house. Suddenly there is the sound of loud snoring.

"It's Katō Tamaki," explains Buntarō. "The one who farms chickens down in Inekari. You know, the old man who lives by the road up to Ōkubo."

"Tight as a tick, wasn't he! It's always the same, whenever there's a funeral."

"It's not right, though. Shouting out like that. It brings shame on the community."

"You're right there, Munetoshi. It's lucky for us he lives in Inekari and not in Ōkubo."

"Even so. People lower down the valley will get to hear of it. He'll give us people of Yashiki village a bad name."

The snores get louder.

"Hey, Tamakisan! Belt up!" Tōsuke shouts, but his voice fails to wake the sleeping drunk. "We'd better take him home, or else Būchan will never get any peace at all."

"I'll take him then," volunteers Jirō. "After all, we live almost next door to each other."

So Jirō, accompanied by Kumao, goes to shake Tamaki awake.

"Jirō! It's you!" comes a sleepy voice. "Have you got some *sake*? That wretched foreigner who lives here wouldn't give me a thing. Hey!" he shouts loudly. "Bring us some *sake* here. We're thirsty."

Eventually Jirō persuades Tamaki to leave and, with the promise of a drink down at the *sake* shop, he and Kumao haul him off down the road. The others follow at a respectable distance, their voices receding as they round the bend past the bamboo grove.

Finally, everyone is gone. Akihito is no more. *Though I knew it to be a road that one day finally we all must take, I never dreamt that he would have to tread it so soon.*

22   Kyōko has been asked to teach some of the wives cooking. Ayako has heard how she makes bread at home and, having just bought a small electric oven, wants to learn how to do it herself. But as with most things in this valley, Ayako knows better than to learn things alone from Kyōko, and so she has arranged for a number of wives from Ōkubo, Inekari, and Amagase to gather once a week for lessons. Katsuhisa's wife, Misako, has offered her kitchen, since it is large enough to accommodate the class.

And, of course, as they stand around learning how to knead dough, make a potato salad, or brew a vegetable broth, the women soon start chatting about things that I, as a man, rarely get a chance to hear.

One theme that continually crops up, so much so that it could almost be called an obsession, is a woman's relations with her mother-in-law. This is itself tied up with the way in which women are expected to work all their lives. Misako sometimes accompanies Katsuhisa and his mother, Yuki, to work in the fields. The married couple almost always walk behind the older woman, chatting together about this and that. And when they start laughing about something, Yuki will turn around sharply and tell them to be quiet. "Daytime's not the occasion for laughing," she growls. "Laugh when you're in bed together at night."

Comments like this I find hard to believe, because Yuki always takes pains to be so correct and pleasant in my company. A still comparatively young widow, she wears expensive kimonos around the large house in which she lives with Katsuhisa and his family. She takes care with her makeup and does her best to make people feel that her family really is a cut above the families of the farmers around about. As for Misako, she is infuriated by comments such as these and tears up the earth with her mattock before going back to the house and cooling off in the toolshed.

Even now, most of the valley people believe that a woman's purpose in life is to work and nothing else. Old Den will call out for Ayako or Misae whenever she fails to find either of them in Inoshige's workshop or out in the yard. Sometimes she will climb all the way up to Misae's room on the second floor to see what she is up to. But then she can't get down the stairs by herself and has to be more or less carried down. If ever she has occasion to leave the house, on a visit to relatives, for example, Den always reminds Misae to fold up the washing, check the clay, feed the chickens, do this, do that, clearly convinced that the younger women are going to take advantage of old Granny's absence to lie around the house all day. Certainly, they do relax when Den is away, but it's hardly surprising when they know that the old lady is always snooping about—checking the large clay crusher, for example, which is driven by the mountain stream below Inoshige's house, and making sure that Misae is doing her job properly, turning over the clay piled under the seesawing pine-log crusher. Once, she went out in the evening and was hit in the dark by the falling crusher. It was some time before anybody noticed her absence, but eventually Inoshige found her, lying curled across the powdered clay with the crusher thumping down rhythmically between her head and her knees. How she didn't get knocked unconscious, or even killed, nobody knows.

Reiko, the wife of Daisuke the carpenter—a cheerful, plump-cheeked woman with a high-pitched voice and frizzy hair—thought it was just as bad having a sister for a mother-in-law. Precisely because she and Daisuke's (adopted) mother are sisters, they fight hammer and tongs, to the point where, in the past, Reiko used to run away from home after one of their rows. She would arrange for one of the other young wives to take her belongings quietly out of the house and wait for her down at the Todoroki bridge, where she would get on a bus and leave for her parents' home. She was only nineteen years old then, and her sister in her early thirties. But no sooner would Reiko escape back home than her sister would arrive quite nonchalantly, behaving as if nothing had happened, ready to take the girl back to Amagase. Her brother would drag her, still crying, into a taxi and send both women back up the mountainside.

Women work very hard here in the valley. I've seen them picking pears in the orchard before seven in the morning, and some wives are out in the rice fields well before that. What is difficult to accept is that housework is not considered to be work as such. This is why in some houses like Katsuhisa's, where the mother-in-law is a real taskmaster, Misako finds herself doing the washing either late at night, after everyone else has gone to bed, or at five in the morning, before anyone else is up. On top of this, women are expected to get up at any time of the night to entertain their husbands' drunken friends. Under the circumstances, it is hardly surprising to hear that the wives in this valley envy the women who are married to city men. Their husbands are away at work all day, leaving them to look after the house and the children. Here children belong to the old people. And few city men invite their friends home for a night of hard drinking.

Still, there is one type of work that women are not allowed to do when their husbands go off to the fields or the forests. They can't do any kind of cooking that involves putting food directly over a fire—sautéing or frying—since this is said to annoy the fire god. Accidents have been known to happen to men whose wives disobey this rule. There was a forester in Takao, for example, whose bull-dozer overturned and crushed him to death a few years back—all because his wife was steaming rice-cakes at the time. And it was suggested that something like this must have happened when Aso Masaki had his leg crushed by a falling tree. Tōsuke's wife, Yasuko, and Buntarō's Hideko are very careful not to cook anything while their husbands are out working in the forests.

The saying goes that the daughter belongs to the village and the son to his young wife. Yasuko shocked everyone by saying that if things didn't go well between her and her daughter-in-law, both son and wife could leave. It was not the sentiment itself that was surprising so much as the fact that Yasuko's son is only eleven years old and not likely to get married for at least a decade.

23   It is a custom in the valley for people to celebrate and share their good fortune by holding *sake* parties for their neighbors, friends, and relatives. One such occasion is the completion of a house, or extension thereof. Another is the purchase of a new car. The other day Haruzō held a celebration when he bought himself a brown sedan—the posh kind with white-covered headrests and lace curtains to make him seem more like the president of a corporation than the boss of a small road-building firm that boasts two trucks and a bulldozer. The neighbors were invited to share in Haruzō's prosperity, and then found themselves invited back less than a week later for a second celebration after Haruzō's son crashed the car on the by-pass into town. Gossip doesn't relate how the accident occurred, or if the boy was drunk at the time, but Haruzō has bought a new, and identical, car.

One good reason for sharing one's fortune is to stifle criticism and gossip. In rural Japan people hold very strongly to the ideal that says the individual should always subordinate his interests to those of the group—the household, hamlet, youth association, pear growers' cooperative, or fire brigade, according to the context. The man or woman who sticks out from the rest tends to be hammered down like a protruding nail. I saw this for myself when the owner of a large garage in Fujioka built himself a luxurious home. Daisuke asked me to help on the day of the beam-raising ceremony, and it was clear from the hints dropped during the course of the day that the garage owner's extravagance was alienating him from the community in which he lived. Anyone who indulges in conspicuous consumption beyond a certain norm, therefore, is likely to find himself the subject of considerable backbiting. A few bottles of *sake* and platefuls of expensive raw fish can work wonders in silencing the most agile of tongues—temporarily, at least.

Other occasions that local people regard as a matter of good fortune, and consequently of celebration, are a man's forty-first and sixty-first birthdays. A few days ago Inoshige completed his first forty years, and today he is holding a celebration to which he has invited the whole of Amagase and several friends from neighboring communities. At first Inoshige had planned to borrow the school playground and involve everyone in a game of softball, but one or two of the older men, like Terukichi and Noboru, Daisuke's uncle-cum-father, objected. This was a traditional celebration; it should be celebrated in a traditional manner. Without Inoshige's having very much say in the matter, it was arranged that all the men of Amagase would practice some archery. The others could come to the party afterward.

For some reason or other, the men of Amagase have taken to this sport. Daisuke gives his story of its origins as we tramp up the path that leads toward the Otomai pass.

"In the old days there wasn't much to do here in the way of entertainment, and all we did was work. You'd get the occasional theatrical troupe coming up the valley, and they'd set up a puppet show in the yard of one of the bigger houses in the hamlet—Haruzō's place, generally. And we'd all gather to watch. It was good fun for the kids, but the troupes stopped coming after the war."

Daisuke stops to light a cigarette. The archery range is just ahead of us, and we are early.

"There was also a lot of gambling with flower cards [*hanafuda*]. You know, the ones the children play with over the New Year. The story I heard was that a policeman was tipped off about a game in progress up in Noda. He came all the way up the valley on foot from Fujioka to investigate. There was an old hut the Noda men used to use on the other side of the river, but the policeman caught them, all the same. So what did they do? They killed him. Don't ask me why. History doesn't say much about what makes people do things. Anyway, it was snowing hard, and the Noda men disposed of the body, burying it somewhere up in the mountains, and all traces of what had happened were soon covered up. The police in town had no idea where their single representative in Fujioka had gone, and there were no tracks to follow. They never did find out what happened. And it's said that archery was started after this incident to avoid further trouble."

Daisuke pauses, looking out across the valley. "Not that the story makes very much sense. Archery is practiced by people living up in Ichinotsuru. And by us here in Amagase. There have been one or two people in other communities who have participated in contests. The funny thing is, I've never known anyone from Noda to let loose an arrow. That's the one place archery has never been practiced."

There are voices behind us, and we are overtaken by Haruzō, Inoshige, Terukichi, and a few others—including our *shigin* teacher, Harimoto, who, as priest from the shrine down in town, is an honored guest at this occasion.

"I was just telling Būchan here about archery."

"Quite right, too," says Haruzō proudly. "We've a fine tradition in Amagase, you know. In the old days some of us used to walk miles just to get to archery contests."

"I remember Terukichi's father coming down to the shrine many years ago," says Harimoto. "Like a wizard, he was, the way he shot his arrows."

"Ah! Hamakichi! Now he was the best archer we ever had."

"But he never bothered with any of those certificates and things, did he?" It is Katō Michiya chiming in, the man who works down at the valley post office and whose son is in Alyosha's class at school. "Not like Haruzō's father, who had to go all the way to Kyoto just to get his grade-three papers. Didn't you do the same, Haruzōsan?"

Haruzō places his bow down on the floor of the hall at one end of the archery range. "No. I only got as far as the first grade, and that exam we can take in the prefectural capital."

"You should follow in your father's footsteps, Haruzōsan," Terukichi encourages him. "Nobody seems to care as much these days as they used to. Do you remember when it rained, how we used to practice our archery? In the rainy season we could go on for days on end. But not now. Nowadays everyone is too busy making money to enjoy themselves."

As Terukichi takes hold of a broom and begins sweeping haphazardly around the floor, Inoshige whispers in my ear, "Terukichi's a fine one to talk when he can't even draw a bow. It's ironical that a man with a withered hand should always be the first to suggest that we do archery on occasions like this."

Inoshige goes to set up the targets, four in all across the range, at about 60 paces from the hall. Then everyone lines up and bows to the god whose image is on the southern valley side of the building. After bowing three times, the men clap their hands twice and bow twice more. As the oldest man present, Noboru says a few words in greeting, and Inoshige a few words more. As the honored guest, Harimoto is asked to make the ritual opening shots. He narrowly misses the target both times.

Then the firing order is drawn up according to household membership, with Haruzō, Noboru, Saihito, and Daisuke lining up first because theirs were the top two houses coming down the hillside. Behind them, four more men take their places, including Inoue Torakichi, whose younger sister, I have just discovered, is Hanako, my landlord's wife.

The rest of us cluster around a hibachi that had been lit soon after our arrival and, as people take their turns in firing, some *sake* is brought out. There is a chorus of approval when Inoshige hits the target with his first arrow. And does the same again with his second. As he steps back from the open front of the hall, Harimoto is the first to congratulate him.

"Now that's what being forty-one is all about." He hands Inoshige some *sake*.

"That's what Ayako told me the other night when I was too drunk to satisfy her in bed," replies Inoshige, clearly determined that his birthday celebrations should not become too serious.

Terukichi's son Umao, a taxi driver, has found a strip of corrugated iron on which to toast some dried fish.

"Michiya! Where are you?" Terukichi calls loudly. "It's your turn."

"Already? On my way." Michiya gets up and looks for his arrows. Then he takes his place at the front of the hall, sets his feet wide apart, and standing square to the target, draws his bow. Arms trembling slightly at full stretch as he tries to control his aim, Michiya eventually looses an arrow that flies straight through the air and hits the center of a target with a dull thud. One or two men begin clapping, but Terukichi points out that Michiya has hit the wrong target. The *sake* is clearly beginning to have its effect.

Eventually it is all over. Each participant has fired two arrows ten times, and the winner is Haruzō with a total of eleven out of twenty possible hits. Michiya is given the benefit of the doubt over his use of another archer's target, and ties for second with the priest Harimoto with nine hits. Inoshige is out of it, having faded badly toward the end of the competition, overpowered by the effects of alcohol.

Next, two gold-papered targets are set up. These are very small cross sections of bamboo stem, about the size of a large fist. It is explained that the first person to score a hit will be the winner of this special contest. Because the order of shooting is determined this time by age, the older men are greatly favored—especially since they are allowed not one arrow, but two. Noboru comes very close with his first arrow. Haruzō comes even closer, and his arrow clips the very edge of the bamboo target, but does not pass through the hollow center of the bamboo stem. So despite a great roar from those assembled, his shot is not deemed a hit by Harimoto, who is acting as umpire and is standing halfway down the range, the better to see the arrows. Four more men line up, the youngest of them being Daisuke, who comes close with his first arrow and then lets loose a second that pierces the target at four o'clock of center. There are shouts of surprise and approval as people begin stacking their bows away. Daisuke has scored only two hits all afternoon, and everyone is clearly pleased that he has rediscovered his "carpenter's eye."

After the prize-giving ceremony, in which everyone is given a large tin of salad oil, we all file back down the hillside to Inoshige's house. The sliding screens separating the *kotatsu* room from the guest room have been removed, and low tables are laid out in a U-shape around the room. The oldest men—Noboru, Terukichi, Harimoto, Haruzō, and Torakichi—are seated at the top of the room, with their backs to the raised dais (*tokonoma*) and the ancestral shrine beside it. The rest of us take up our positions according to age along tables lining each side of the room. Other guests have arrived—Wada Tatetarō, Yamaguchi Takeshi, Kajiwara Katsuhisa, Noda Moriyuki, Kajiwara Buntarō, Kajiwara Tōsuke, and one or two others—and I find myself sitting between Katsuhisa and Terukichi's son Umao. Below us sit the women, also in age order.

Once we are all kneeling formally, with Inoshige at the foot of the room facing us, Noboru gives a little speech.

"Today is Inoshige's forty-first birthday party, and this is something that has been celebrated for a very long time here in Amagase. Of course, people have forty-first birthdays in other hamlets in this valley, but our hamlet, I like to think, is rather special because of the way we celebrate. For as long as I can remember, we have made it a custom to have an archery contest on special occasions. I had one when it was my birthday some years ago now, and then Terukichi here had his. And so it's gone on through the years until today, when it's Inoshige's turn. I don't know why we do it this way, but the important thing is that we do. Perhaps it's got something to do with a man's becoming head of his household when he turns forty years of age. I don't know. What I do know, though, is that people in Amagase are always going around counting one another's ages and trying to calculate when the next celebration is going to be. By my reckoning, Michiya here is next in line, and we've only got a couple of years to wait. After that, we've got Saihito and Umao in their mid-thirties now, so it looks as if we've got plenty of celebrating to do over the next few years. This is a good thing."

Noboru finishes amidst some laughter and applause, and Inoshige bows to us all.

"Thank you very much, Noborusan. Today, as you know, is my forty-first birthday, and you have been kind enough to help me celebrate it up at the archery range. Some of us had a little trouble aiming straight. And some of us aimed rather well at other people's targets." He grins at Michiya. "But I think we all had a good time, and that is what matters. All the same, I think we should note that it was the older men amongst us who generally managed to shoot straightest, and I hope that this will be a lesson to us youngsters and make us try harder in the future to follow their good example. And now I ask you to join me here for a little refreshment. I apologize for the poor quality of the food, but ask you to forgive us and hope that you will show no restraint in whiling away the next few hours here."

Noboru now begins to sing a congratulatory song (*utai*) called "Takasago," in which we all join before drinking one-third of a cup of cold *sake*. Inoshige sings the traditional reply, "Shikai nami," and we drink another mouthful of *sake*. Then Harimoto, who is kneeling beside Noboru, is asked to sing the final rejoinder, "Chōsei no ie ni kōsō," after which we drink up the rest of the *sake* in our cups.

The women then get up from where they are kneeling and begin pouring warmed *sake* for all the guests. Once everybody's cup is filled, Noboru proposes a toast.

"*Omedetō gozaimasu*. Congratulations!"

We all raise our cups in the air and call in unison, "*Omedetō gozaimasu!*" Then we drain the *sake* and settle down to more serious drinking.

And *sake* drinking, as I have learned over the past year, is a very serious business indeed, for it is on occasions like this that community matters are brought out into the open and discussed—even fought over at times. There are several stages through which formal parties like this one tend to pass. In the beginning you sit cross-legged on the floor, picking with your chopsticks at the food laid out before you—raw fish, raw chicken, fish soup, a potato salad (Ayako's first putting to the test of what she has learned in Kyōko's cooking classes), Misae's boiled vegetables, seaweed, and so on. But the more important stage—the *sake* drinking—soon follows. You allow your cup to be filled by those sitting alongside you, and you yourself fill the cups of your neighbors, for it is impolite to pour your own *sake*. After a few minutes, men will give you their own cups to drink from, and these you should always return after draining the *sake* in them. As time goes by, you find yourself receiving cups from men seated farther away and eventually it becomes more convenient to stand up and take the cup to a man, rather than have it passed down to him hand to hand. This custom enables men to move around the room, and the initial order of seating people by age soon breaks down as small drinking groups are formed here and there at the low tables. From this point on, serious debate can take place, and men will use the custom of exchanging cups to make a beeline for somebody they want to talk to about something. It is then that the important conversations will take place, for it is only under the influence of *sake* that men find themselves able to say what normal etiquette requires that they refrain from mentioning. Not only this, but everything that is said is remembered by those involved, and the information gained during a *sake* party is then used in the course of everyday community affairs.

But this evening there is to be no quarreling. People are here to enjoy themselves, and anyway there are too many outsiders present for the people of Amagase to start quarreling among themselves.

"This isn't the way we used to drink, you know," says Haruzō, with whom I soon find myself sitting and exchanging cups. "In the old days it wasn't proper for young men to pass cups up the table. Instead, they had to wait for their elders to offer them cups first. Only then could they make the exchange. Nowadays, though, things are different. Young men like Umao there quite happily rush up to the head of the table and exchange cups with old men like Noboru. It's not the way things should be done. People don't have so much respect for the old nowadays."

"You're right, of course, Haruzōsan," puts in Tatetarō, slapping the older man cheerfully on the back. "But today it doesn't really matter, does it? After all, we're only here to have a few drinks and enjoy ourselves."

"That's true. It's Inoshige's celebration. But still, I was just pointing out to Būchan here that it's not right—"

But I never hear the end of that sentence, for I make use of the cup-exchanging custom to get up and cross the room to where a more cheerful group is seated around Inoshige.

"Inoshigesan!" I call out, raising my cup toward him balanced properly between thumb and forefingers as I have learned. "This is a good party. Congratulations!"

"On what? On being a bit balder than last year?" he inquires with a grin.

"Now that you mention baldness, what about Būchan here?" puts in Buntarō. "I've noticed he's getting a bit thin on top recently."

"Yes. That's what comes of trying to be a scholar."

"Well, you know what we say, don't you?" It is Katsuhisa, looking more benign than ever. "In Japan we say that the mark of a good teacher is that he is bald. You've got hope yet, Būchan."

"In which case, you've got none at all," says Michiya, whose own black hair stands up thick as a field of wheat.

"And that's why you became a postman, not a teacher," retorts Inoshige.

"There are too many teachers in Japan. They say that you can climb any mountain and throw a stone in any direction from the top, and you're guaranteed to hit a teacher. That's the kind of place we live in."

"Really? I never knew there were so many bald people around."

I suddenly find a *sake* cup being thrust toward me. It is the Shintō priest, Harimoto.

"You didn't shoot any arrows today, Būchan," he begins reproachfully, but knowing that it would not perhaps have been appropriate for me to join in the serious part of Inoshige's birthday celebration.

"It would have been difficult," I reply, learning the country art of having an excuse ready at all times. "I'm left-handed, so I could never have worn those leather gloves people doing archery use."

"So you're left-handed, are you?" Harimoto looks interested. "There are rules about left and right, you know, according to Shintō beliefs. When you're eating, for example, a bowl of rice should be placed on the left of a tray and soup on the right. And when you're drinking, you should hold your *sake* cup in your left hand."

"Is that so, *sensei?*" Katsuhisa, himself a *sensei* (teacher), honors the older man by using his title. "I wonder why that is."

"Easy," comes the reply, as Harimoto downs another cup and passes it to Katsuhisa. "Because you use your chopsticks in your right hand."

"Unless you're someone strange, like Būchan here."

"Are you left-footed, too?" Harimoto asks. "When you start moving forward in archery, you're supposed to start with your left foot, you know. When kneeling, a man is supposed to cross the big toe of his left foot over that of his right. A woman kneels the other way around."

Harimoto's attention is distracted by a newcomer, and I have a chance to look around. The party is in full swing, and the men have broken up into three main groups. One at the top tables, where Noboru, Terukichi, and Haruzō are more or less holding court; a second in which I myself am sitting; and a third at the far end of the room, where most of the women are gathered. I decide to see how Kyōko is surviving this initiation into valley entertainment.

"Būchan! Būchan!" Misae's sunburned face crinkles with merriment as she pulls me down to sit beside her and then cuddles up with her arms around me. "Are you busy tonight?"

"I'll be busy drinking *sake* tonight," I reply, offering my cup. She downs some of the *sake*, but pours the rest with a neat twist of her wrist into an ashtray nearby.

"You shouldn't do that," I reprimand her.

"I know I shouldn't, but I'm drunk," she replies.

"You've learned a lot, Būchan." Daisuke is grinning at me from the other side of the table.

"Only from bitter experience," I answer, and tell them how I nearly died of drink during the first few nights I spent in Kamayama. As a newcomer, I had been feted by the local potters. Unused to taking in quite so much alcohol at quite such a speed, my head had soon started reeling from the effects of the *sake*. What I couldn't work out at the time was how the others seemed to put away just as much *sake* and yet remain fairly sober. And then the light dawned. The potters kept large ashtrays by their feet and, having accepted a cup, they would take a sip before discreetly pouring away the rest of the *sake* and returning the cup empty. Somebody could have done a thriving business in recycling alcohol.

"Hey, Būchan! What are you doing down here?" It is Takeshi, my landlord. "Is the house still standing?"

"The house is standing, but the bath's got a leak in it. Water drips into the firemouth, and it's hard to heat the water properly."

Takeshi listens with a serious face, but then brightens up suddenly.

"That's bad," he says, flashing me one of his toothiest smiles. "I thought your name was Moeran, and *moran* means 'doesn't leak' in Japanese. And yet here you are with a leaking bath. That's not the way things should be."

That pleases everybody, and the joke has to be repeated for the benefit of Tatetarō, who has just joined us. Daisuke, however, has some advice for me.

"Know what to do? Heat the bath up without any water in it. Then pour the white of an egg on the crack. If you leave it for twenty-four hours, it'll stop the bath from leaking any more. And then you'll live up to your name again, Moeran."

Somebody at the top of the room starts singing a folk song, and soon most people are joining in. Ayako goes out of the room and comes back with a cassette recorder and microphone, which she plugs in. Inoshige takes it and stands up, somewhat unsteadily. Then with *sake* cup in hand, he sings one of his favorite Shimazaki Tōson poems. He is in good voice, and his interpretation is much appreciated.

"Now it's Būchan's turn," calls out Harimoto, clapping his hands loudly and grinning red-faced in my direction.

"Yes, Būchan. Give us a song!"

I have no alternative but to stand up and give everyone my stilted rendering of the *shigin* song "Tsuki wa kiyoshi" ("The Moon Is Clear"). I am just able to make the high notes near the end, and there is exaggerated applause as I sit down and Takeshi staggers to his feet to sing "You Are My Sunshine." Again I am called upon to do our duet act, arms around each other's shoulders. We have entered a new stage in the party, where singing begins in earnest.

In order to avoid drinking too much *sake*, I take the only permitted route of escape—to the bathroom. Looking as inebriated and bleary-eyed as possible, I stagger across the room and out into the quiet of the corridor. From there I am able to slip outside for a few minutes of fresh air, and my head begins to clear. Before long, however, Michiya comes lurching out through the doorway. We stand together by the river, urinating, before heading back for the party, where the singing is still going on as Umao struggles tunelessly through a modern pop song.

Noda Moriyuki, who frequently works with Buntarō and Tō-suke up in the mountains in a forestry team headed by Inoue Tora-kichi, is setting out to entertain people with a story.

"There was this young man in Keibaya," he begins. "He was so miserable about some girl who'd stood him up that he decided to commit suicide. So he climbed up one of those steep hills where all the tourists go and jumped off the edge. Whooooo!" He imitates the falling man. "All the way down two or three hundred feet. Right into the middle of the thatched roof of a farmhouse that happened to be situated there at the bottom of the precipice. And because it was thatch, he just stood up, jumped off the roof, and walked away."

"Wow! That is unusual," says Buntarō. "If only that had happened to poor Akihito."

"But you haven't heard the end of the story yet," Moriyuki silences him. "The old lady whose house it was was out in the garden digging her vegetables. She heard something, looked up, saw the young man crash into her house roof, had a heart attack, and died."

Everybody bursts out laughing at Moriyuki's joke.

"That's a good one. By the way, where's your old lady, Moriyuki-san? I haven't seen her this evening."

"Ah!" says Moriyuki knowingly. "There's a story about that, too."

"A story? What story?"

"Well," Moriyuki says with a boyish giggle, running the three middle fingers of his right hand across a row of gold-filled teeth, "it's this kind of 'story,' *hanashi*. She's got no teeth, *ha nashi*, because she was at the dentist's all day."

Everybody laughs again. "A toothless story! Did you hear that?"

"It might feel a bit different when she gets hold of you tonight," Buntarō says. "But at least you can relax. She won't be able to bite off your prick now."

"Better make sure first. Give her a sweet potato and see what happens," warns Tatetarō, brandishing a long potato that happened to be on the table beside him.

"Hey! That's a big one!"

"Too big for me," says Tatetarō, trying it on for size and shaking his head. Then he thrusts it into my crotch. "It'll probably fit Būchan, though."

"Can I make it bigger for you?" Misae begins stroking the potato as Tatetarō waggles it gently to and fro.

"It's quality that counts. Not quantity!"

"This fellow's got his head screwed on," roars Tōsuke, his voice—like everyone else's—getting louder as the drinking continues.

"You want a prick that talks to you, Misae." Buntarō picks up the microphone, which is lying on the tatami mat nearby, and begins pounding it against his penis.

"That's not much of a noise," shouts Moriyuki, as Buntarō begins to unzip his fly. But Misae grabs the microphone and taps it against her breasts with much greater effect.

"Hey, Misaechan! Let me help!" Buntarō, his fly wide open, half falls on Misae and begins thumping the microphone against her ample bosom.

"Feels good, doesn't it?"

Moriyuki, determined not to be outdone, unzips his fly, too. But after the three of them have beaten out the rhythm of Tōsuke's drunken song on various parts of their anatomies, Misae is declared the winner—much to the chagrin of the two men.

Daisuke, overcome by the effects of the *sake*, has quietly fallen asleep—a bit like the dormouse at the Mad Hatter's tea party. Buntarō thinks it would be a good idea to record his snores for posterity, and this he proceeds to do, much to the merriment of all. Just as we are beginning to tire of his antics with the microphone, the door is thrown open and Inoshige, who slipped away without anyone noticing, dances into the room with an enormous top hat over his head and shoulders. He has stripped to the waist and somehow managed to place his arms up inside the hat. Ayako has tied a stick across the lower part of his back and clothed it with a pair of trousers. On each end of the stick she has fitted a glove, so that Inoshige looks as if he has arms and hands stretching out from just above his waist. Ayako has used her makeup to paint two eyes just below Inoshige's nipples and a red-and-black mouth across his navel.

His appearance is greeted with great mirth and, as he belly-dances around the room, people roar with laughter and approval.

Daisuke, awakened by the noise, rolls on the *tatami* in hysterics. Buntarō, his fly still open, thrusts his hand inside his trousers, pokes one finger through, and begins waggling a large beer bottle on it. Moriyuki folds up a thin cushion between his legs and wiggles his way toward Buntarō, thrusting the hole made by the folded material provocatively toward the twitching beer bottle. The two of them proceed to act out a coital dance while I—as ordered—take photographs for posterity.

Alas! I was either drunker than I thought or laughing too hard. When I have them developed a week later, all the prints are hopelessly out of focus.

11 Scattered Blossoms

On such a springlike day as this,
When the light suffuses
Soft tranquility,
Why should the cherry petals flutter
To the earth so restlessly?

—*Ki no Tomonori*

24 Spring is a busy time of the year. The fields have to be plowed, then flooded in readiness for the transplanting of the rice plants during the rainy season. The pear trees have to be pollinated and fumigated, and the marble-sized pears covered with little paper bags to protect them from the insects. Every time it rains, the oak mushrooms have to be gathered from where they grow in the forest shade and then dried, first in the sunshine, later in wood-burning ovens.

Still, it is not all work. There are softball games and the valley's marathon-relay race, in which the four villages making up the valley population compete against one another. Each team has ten members, drawn two by two from each of the age groups between ten and fifty. Each village fields two teams, whose runners start at the North Oni Primary School and proceed up the valley to Ichinotsuru, where they turn around and run all the way down to the South Oni school, before turning around yet again and racing back up the hill to where they started. Much to everyone's surprise, Yashiki manages to come in a creditable second to Suzuka village.

The school year itself begins in April, and this means that a number of farewell parties and celebrations take place in the valley at this time, as children graduate from one school and enter another and as teachers themselves take up new appointments. The North Oni Primary School headmaster, Fujita, has been transferred this year to a larger school in town. This is seen to be a deserved promotion, but there is slight anxiety among parents as they wait to learn who will take his place. He has been an unusually popular headmaster.

Rumors about the new headmaster, whose name is Hageyama, precede the arrival of the man himself. This is a small world, and there is always somebody who has a relative somewhere who knows the person you wish to ask a favor of or, as in this case, are merely inquiring about. Already people are suggesting that Hageyama will not be as good as his predecessor. The phrase that is used is stronger than this: *"ningen ga dekiteinai"* is the way Katsuhisa puts it. Literally translated, this means "he is not a proper human being" and refers to a man's spiritual development.

Katsuhisa himself has been talking of giving up his job as a teacher. After all, his family owns enough forested mountain land for him to be able to keep his mother, wife, and three children alive and well. He doesn't really enjoy the hassle of teaching at a large high school in town; so why bother at all?

"It's not the kids I mind so much," he says one day, as we inject dead tree branches with oak mushroom bacilli. "It's all the bureaucracy involved. I don't know what it's like in England, but here in Japan the education system is a mess. It stifles the children entirely. About the only time they are given a chance to show their enthusiasm is when I take them away for weekends up in the forestry lodge on Mount Toyama. I wish I could stop really." Sighing gently, he gazes longingly up at the ridge above Amagase. "Then I'd spend all my time planting different kinds of trees and shrubs. I've got a nice little hut of my own way up in the hills there, you know. On a small plateau among the cedar forests. I've cleared the area and am planting my own trees—a few maples here and there; some oak trees; and various kinds of pine. When I get really pissed off with something, I get in my rusty old truck and bump my way up the mountain track beyond Haruzō's place. There's a place I can leave it, just beyond where Aso's boy had his accident, and from there I walk on up. You must come sometime. We can take the children and have a picnic up there."

He squats down in the long grass and whittles himself a new toothpick.

"Yes. It'd be nice if I could stop teaching. Financially, though, it's a bit difficult at the moment. You see, my grandfather had a mistress who bore a son by him. He died soon after the boy was born, but my family had to help look after him. My father acted as guarantor for this 'uncle' of mine when he borrowed money to set up a small business. That's the way things are done around here. The banks lend you money, provided you can get someone to act as your guarantor. Of course, because it was his stepbrother asking for security, my father could hardly refuse. That is what kinship relations are all about. But my 'uncle' eventually defaulted on his payments, and two years ago we found ourselves suddenly landed with a multimillion-yen loan. We've been paying it back, month by month, ever since."

He smiles and tries out his new toothpick. "No, I guess I'll have to carry on teaching for another year or two. Maybe then I can quit. In the meantime, I'm being transferred, you know, to a school in a town near the prefectural capital. It's about an hour and a half's drive from here. The only good thing about the appointment is that I'll be out of sight of my mother all the week. By the time I get home in the evenings, she'll have closeted herself up in her room at the back of the house, and all will be quiet. I feel sorry for Misako, though."

Misako herself is almost exactly the opposite of her mother-in-law in temperament. Yuki will do her best to ignore people outside the house and will always turn away when she sees someone approaching her in the fields. Misako, on the other hand, mixes happily with the other women, and her frankness has made her popular with many of her husband's friends. Perhaps "friends" is the wrong word to use, for the people of Mon have always been landlords, people with money, and rich people could never truly be "friends" with plain farming folk. Even today, when everybody has his own land to farm, Katsuhisa is looked upon slightly askance. The fact that he is a respectable teacher, of course, also serves to set him apart from other men in the valley. But he is not one to put on airs, and people like him for that.

What astonishes me is how people here, despite group ideals, will act in ways that are to my mind extremely "individualistic"—in the worst sense of the word. Katsuhisa's "uncle" is a case in point, and it is not the first story of its kind that I've heard here. This paradoxical relationship between individual actions and group ideals I have noticed at work in other spheres of life. The household, for example, is supposed to exist over and above the individual family members it embraces. Rather like the English royal house of Windsor, the household continues through time, regardless of the fact that its members may die. Property and land, therefore, belong to the household, and to its ancestors, and not to the individual. But I have noticed that, within the household system, each individual's activities are strictly defined. Misako, for example, is allowed to go into what she calls the "pickles store" around the side of Mon. But she is strictly forbidden from entering the main storehouse with its wealth of family heirlooms—armor, dyed fabrics, lacquerware sets, and so on. These are considered by Yuki to be "her" property, and any request to see them has to be made directly to the older woman, and not through Katsuhisa or his wife. It seems strange that an individual should have such command over what are strictly speaking household belongings. Even Katsuhisa, who is household head, has a hard time gaining access to things in his mother's care, and there are some things, he admits, that he will probably never find out about until Yuki dies. "Still," he tells me with a smile, "it's little things like that that keep her happy. Why upset her more than is necessary?"

At Inoshige's, life is made both easier and more complicated by the fact that Misae is living with the family. She has taken over almost all of the farmwork—weeding the rice paddy, growing vegetables, and so on—thereby leaving Ayako to help her husband mix the clay and decorate his pots. But Misae also does the washing and prepares certain kinds of food, such as *gameni*, and it is this that complicates things, for the household cooking is really Ayako's job. Precisely because Misae does certain household tasks, she controls everything to do with them. In making red bean rice-cakes, Misae always squashes the beans, even though she knows that Ayako and the children prefer them whole. When the children's clothes get too small, Misae passes them on to her own grandchildren, never to Ayako's nephews or nieces. Yet it is perhaps because nobody does interfere in others' work that things go so smoothly. Ayako is certainly not one to complain as she makes Den put on nappies (washed by Misae) every night before she goes to bed. The old lady, true to form, never says a word of thanks to her daughter-in-law. All she can mutter is, "It'll be your turn soon."

Once Ayako got so fed up with Den, who loves to grumble about Misae, that she sat down with Inoshige one night and told him all the impossible things the old lady was saying and doing. Inoshige heard her out. Then in a perfectly calm and serious voice, he said, "Right! If that's the way things are, I'd better kill her now before she causes any more trouble."

Ayako knew from his face that he meant what he said. She has made sure never to complain to him again.

25 One day we are awakened by a telephone call from Takeshi. May he come up and see me? It is half past six in the morning.

We just have time to eat breakfast before he arrives. Sliding open the door noisily, he takes off his cap and bids us a nervous good morning. Then he climbs into the *kotatsu*, while Kyōko serves him tea.

"It's my daughter, Emiko," he starts to explain. "You know she was chosen to go as representative of the town's Youth Association on a trip to India and Kuwait?"

We had heard this from Takeshi a couple of weeks earlier and had been duly impressed.

"Well, she's gone off to Tokyo on the first stage of her trip, and I thought I might fly up to the capital to see her off. How do I get on an airplane?"

I inadvertently swallow rather more of my coffee than I had intended.

"How do you get on an airplane? Why, Takeshisan, you buy a ticket!"

He looks surprised. "Ah!" he says, scratching his head. "A ticket!"

"Yes, a ticket."

"And where do I get one of those?"

"From a travel agent. Or else you can phone up the airline company at the airport and make a reservation."

"But how do I come back if I don't know when I'm coming back?" he asks, slightly agitated.

I tell him to calm down and say all that again. It appears that he is referring to the problem—to him unsolvable without help from me—of buying a return ticket and of having to confirm his reservation after his arrival in the foreign land of Tokyo.

"I've only been to Tokyo once before, you know. But that was twenty years ago and things have changed now. Where do I stay when I get there?"

"In a hotel, I suppose."

"Which hotel?" he asks. "Where do you stay?"

"With friends usually."

"I suppose I can't stay there, too?"

"Not really," I say, doing my best not to offend him. "They don't speak any Japanese, so it would be hard to communicate with them."

Eventually he takes his leave after I tell him where to find a travel agency in town.

Later, in the afternoon, I see him working in the orchards. It is a busy time of the year for him, too, for he has to pollinate all the pear blossoms to ensure a good crop. So he and Hanako are working methodically around the orchard, going from one tree to the next, cross-pollinating the flowers by hand.

Around about tea time, he slides open the door again and stands there cap in hand, shifting nervously from one foot to the other. We finally persuade him to step up into the main room, so he puts his cap on his shoes in the hallway and joins us in the *kotatsu*.

"It's about my trip to Tokyo." He laughs loudly in that curious way he has when nervous or embarrassed. I ask him whether he managed to get a ticket all right.

"Yes. Thank you. It was very easy. I hadn't realized." He gives us a sheepish grin before continuing. "You see, my Emiko is leaving for India by ship." He pauses.

"Really?" we encourage him to continue.

"Yes."

"By ship? That *is* unusual."

"Yes. And you may not believe it, but I've never seen a ship in my life."

"So you're going to Tokyo to see a ship?"

"That's right. If I see Emiko off, I can go on board. She'll show me her cabin and around the ship."

It is touching to see a grown man so excited. I tell him a little about the few ships I have been aboard. "But Emiko's ship will be much bigger. I've never been on one like that." It is an art trying not to hurt a person's feelings, and I am afraid that my attempts at diplomacy will be misinterpreted as insulting conceit.

We talk about this and that, until Takeshi asks whether the bath is still leaking. I tell him that Daisuke's advice about the white of an egg appears to have done the trick. Then, since we are talking about the house, I ask him directly about something that Kyōko and I have been discussing for several days.

"Takeshisan, I don't suppose you would consider selling us this house one day, would you?"

He pauses and looks at me, scratching his cheek. "Oh! So you want to buy this place, do you? You must like it here in this valley."

We assure him we do.

"Other people have wanted to buy this house, you know. Somebody once offered me half a million yen for it, but I refused." He grins his toothy smile and looks at me sharply. "The best thing for you, Būchan, is to pay rent. After all, thirteen thousand yen isn't much, is it?"

"It adds up, though, over the years."

"That's true, it does. And I can use that money to send my boy Reisuke to agricultural college in the prefectural capital. Which is why, incidentally, I'd be grateful if you didn't say anything about paying rent when you fill in your tax returns. I need to save as much as I can."

He pauses to allow me time to wonder at his planning of the future.

"No. To be frank, if you want to buy this house, you're going to have to pay a lot of money for it. After all, you have to consider my position as well. If I sold you this house, I'd lose my personal contact [*tsukiai*] with the people of Ōkubo. The nice thing now is that I don't just take money from you. I come up here and give you a few pears or vegetables from the garden. And I empty out your cesspit once a month. But if you bought this house, I wouldn't be able to do things like that anymore." He pauses to make sure that we understand the logic of his argument. "That's why it's better for you to rent the house. Of course, you could rent the land and build yourself a new house if you wanted. I'd have no objection to that. But you'd have to pay me at least fifty thousand yen a year rent."

Inoshige chuckles when I tell him what Takeshi has said.

"Well, well. I never would have believed it. As I told you before, you never know what is going on in that man's mind."

26   The spring flowers come and go in such profusion: violets (*sumire*), rape (*na no hana*), peach blossom (*momo*), sappan (*suō*), forsythia (*rengyō*), kerria (*yamabuki*), mountain cherry (*yamazakura*), and now the azaleas.

"*Yamazakura* is a word we use for 'buck-toothed,'" says Katsuhisa as we scythe the grass along the wall below his house. "Why? Because with ordinary cherry trees the blossoms [*hana*] come out before the leaves [*ha*]. But with *yamazakura*, it's the other way around, with leaves before the blossom. But *ha* is a homonym for teeth and *hana* one for nose, so 'leaves coming out before the blossom' can also mean 'teeth sticking out before the nose.' That's why *yamazakura* means buck-toothed."

The *yamabuki* I recognize from a popular song by Sen Masao, which is played constantly over the loudspeaker of the truck that winds its way up the valley three times a week, filled with groceries for sale to wives who have no time to go down to the town to do their shopping. All around the house the valley echoes with the tremolo of "Kitaguni no haru" (North Country Spring):

> Let us return
> To that land of our birth,
> Let us return.

We have no need to return, for this is our home now. *Asking for nothing, wanting for nothing; my body like a drifting cloud.*

27   Kumao has arranged for his son, Eisuke, to be married, and today three of his relatives go to collect the bride's dowry. This is known as *nitori*, "getting the goods," and is carried out by members of families related to the groom.

Before nine in the morning, then, Jirō, Michiya, and Yasuji, the barber who lives next door, gather at Kumao's for a meal and the usual celebratory cold *sake*. As we prepare to leave, Fumiko presents us with yellow headbands and some yellow streamers, which we tie to the antennas of Jirō's and Michiya's trucks. Then we climb in and leave for the bride-to-be's home, some 40 miles away.

It is a pleasant drive up into the mountains in the center of the island. We pass a large dam and reservoirs, then go on through attractive hot-spring resorts before eventually coming out onto a wide plateau that somehow reminds me more of central Europe than Japan. There is more space here, perhaps because the mountain slopes are bare, not forested.

"They raise cattle around here, you know," says Michiya. "It's nice, isn't it, having so much pasture land. You don't get that hemmed-in feeling you have sometimes from cedar forests. But it gets really cold here in winter. The snow piles waist-high."

Eventually we reach the bride's house, a lovely thatched building right beside a mountain river. We get out and walk around a bit to stretch our legs. A woman shows us into the house and we line up, kneeling formally, waiting for the bride's family to come in from the fields and cowshed. Eventually, having assembled, they all file in and kneel before us.

"Good morning."

"Good morning."

"We've come to collect the bride's goods, so please be so kind as to arrange things."

Tea is served and a desultory conversation ensues. The bride's family is polite but distant, perhaps even slightly hostile. We have, after all, come to take away the wealth invested in the household head's daughter. Finally, though, we manage to obtain permission to load up our trucks. We put on our yellow headbands and go outside into the warm sunshine.

"I thought they were supposed to give us red headbands," mutters Jirō, as senior representative of Kumao's family slightly uneasy about the way we have been received.

"Maybe the custom's different around here," suggests Yasuji.

"I suppose it must be. Oh well, let's get to work!"

It doesn't take too long to load up the vans—a few pieces of furniture, some kitchen equipment and bedding, and a few boxes full of clothes and linen. Having secured everything with ropes, we prepare to leave. But the bride's father suddenly relaxes and starts insisting that we stay to eat something. After one or two protestations on our part, we are shown back into the guest room, where a magnificent display of food awaits us on a table set before the ancestral shrine—itself especially bedecked for the occasion. *Sake* is served and the "Takasago" is sung by Jirō. This is followed by a long, rambling conversation, which revolves first around the weather, before shifting to a discussion of the general climatic conditions in our respective valleys, the nature of the snow here and there, the height above sea level of the bride's and groom's houses, the relative coolness of the summers, and so on. I sense a certain verbal dueling at work here as each party tries to make its own locality out to be the better place. Ōkubo loses out over the quality of the river water and the size of the fish therein. It also yields to the bride's community in the competition for summer coolness and height above sea level. But it wins hands down on relative warmth in winter and on the quantity and quality of its cedar plantations: 4–3 to the bride.

The discussion turns to hamlet activities, where Yashiki village's devotion to softball, archery contests, and marathon races arouses much appreciative comment: 5–4 to the groom. However, a local runner from the bride's community is highly commended for his participation in a recent prefectural race at the age of forty-three. The verbal sparring ends in a 5–5 draw.

Next we discuss cedar trees and which types suit what kinds of soil, before moving on to land yields and cattle fodder. After all this has been gone over, we finally get up to leave. As we stand outside admiring the river and our host's cows, we are given *hikidemono*, departing gifts of sweet bean cakes. Then we get back in the trucks and drive off.

An hour and a half later, we arrive back in Ōkubo. Everything is unloaded, and Fumiko serves us tea. She and Kumao clearly want to know everything that happened and eagerly question us. Were we served a proper meal? Did we receive *hikidemono* gifts? Were there any other relatives there? If so, what were they like? Jirō and the others fill in all the details of our visit, and the generally agreed opinion is that the bride's father is a man of substance (he is running for election to a position in the local Agricultural Cooperative), and that this is a family of good people. What surprises me here is the way in which Jirō, Michiya, and Yasuji between them piece together chance remarks about land holdings, timber-marketing methods, cow fodder, head of cattle, and so on, to create a total picture of the other household's financial position. There was more method in their verbal sparring than I had thought possible.

The wedding itself is held a few days later—a fairly quiet affair in which two people from each household are asked to attend the reception at Kumao's house. Yet another hangover.

28   One afternoon, I come across Takeshi skinning an adder that he had caught in the orchard.

"I nearly stepped on it," he says, waving it in my face. "They're poisonous, you know, so you'd better warn Alyosha and Maya about them. They used to say in the old days that, if you saw an adder, you should trace a circle around it in the dust with your foot, then go and get a stick to kill it. And when you came back, the snake was supposed to be there still, waiting to be killed." Takeshi barks out his strange laugh, as he scratches the back of his head with the handle of his knife. "It never was, though."

After he finishes skinning the adder, he hangs the flesh out to dry from the roof of his toolshed near our house.

"It makes you really strong," he grins. "You should take some to please your Kyōkochan when you go to bed at night."

But snakes can cause trouble, even though they may be used as aphrodisiacs. There was a break in the electricity the other day, and Kyōko telephoned the company to find out what was wrong. She had been in the middle of baking bread in an oven that works off a tank of propane gas but is thermostatically controlled by an electric fan. Once the electricity went off, so did the oven—automatically.

"Ah, yes!" said the telephone operator at the electricity company's office in town. "I'm afraid that, at the moment, there's a snake loose in the power station's water tank. Please bear with us awhile."

We can only sympathize, for we ourselves have a five-foot-long snake living under the house. This morning Ayako saw it when she dropped by to see Kyōko.

"If you see a snake like that," she told us, "it means it will rain."

Sure enough, a couple of hours later, the first torrential rains of the monsoons begin.

29 "Have you noticed how in Japanese we often distinguish between plants that give food and the food itself? Between edible and inedible states?" asks Katsuhisa one day. (Katsuhisa, always the teacher, has taken it on himself to school me in all things Japanese.) "I suppose rice is the best example of this. When the ears first come out in the paddy fields, we call rice *ine*. Before that, it is just plain *nae*, a word for plants in general. Then, when the rice is ripe enough to be harvested, we refer to it as *kome*. And *kome* is the word we use when it is cut and hulled, although there's also *genmai* for un-husked rice. *Gohan* is for cooked rice and, by extension, a meal. *Mochi* is a different strain of rice—small-grained and very white.

When people want to distinguish ordinary rice from *mochi*, whether ripening in the fields or just harvested, they call it *uruchi* instead of *kome*. Difficult, isn't it?" he says with a laugh. "I suppose it's because rice is part of our staple diet that we have so many words for it. I suppose you have the same sort of thing with bread or potatoes. Or are you less complicated than us?

"Another food that is distinguished between its raw and dried states is the 'oak mushroom.' Mushrooms growing on the tree logs are called *naba*, but when they're dried they turn into *shiitake*. But that's only in this part of the country. In other parts of Japan people use different words, so I'm told. One of my fellow teachers, whose wife comes from Kawasaki, says that in the Kantō area, *katsuo* refers to the live bonito, *katsubushi* to the dried fish, and *namaribushi* to the fish when it is about to be dried. I prefer to eat and never mind about the words."

All the same, food in the country is not that important. That is to say, the consumption of food hardly matches up to people's emphasis on its production. It is not something, for example, that people willingly spend money on. The daughter-in-law of Katō Tamaki, whose baby was severely burned recently when he fell in the *kotatsu*, has been told by her mother-in-law not to spend more than 1,000 yen a day on food for the family. Preferably, she should keep her expenditures down to 20,000 yen a month. This works out to little more than $100 a month for four adults and one other child besides the baby. It also means that the cost of the cooking classes she attends at the Valley Coordination Office every week eats up fully one-fifth of the household's monthly expenses.

The Katō household's situation is by no means extreme. Hideko up the road says that this year the winter vegetable crops were poor because of the extreme cold over the New Year. As a result, she must make do with daikon radishes, turnips, and Chinese cabbage, supplemented by sweet potatoes and ordinary potatoes, both unaffected by the weather. No farming household buys vegetables at any time of the year. What you don't grow, you don't eat.

Yuki, Katsuhisa's mother, leads a somewhat different style of life. In the past, the Mon house always had servants to do things, and even now Yuki refuses to work in the rice paddy. So people are hired throughout the year to till the earth, transplant the rice seedlings, weed the fields, and finally harvest the crop. This labor costs the household about 100,000 yen a year. Since the family consumes something over 660 pounds of rice in that time, it works out just as cheap—or expensive—to buy rice at the standard price of 145 yen per pound. In fact, it probably costs more to grow it, for Yuki spends 30,000 yen on dried ground fish to be used as fertilizer. This, together with the fact that Katsuhisa refuses to allow Yuki to use insecticides, gives the rice an especially good taste, but that is the only advantage to be gained from growing one's own.

Yuki's peculiarly un-farmerlike attitude can also be seen in the way she insists on using all her unirrigated fields to grow vegetables. But she never bothers to thin them when they start sprouting, which means that they never grow to a decent size. In the end her family eats some of the vegetables, but Yuki lets most of them go to rot. I suspect that she lets this happen not because she is lazy, but because she does not see herself as a farmer's wife. Her lackadaisical attitude is proof to her, and a reminder to others, of her household's status in the neighborhood.

30   Almost every morning now, some of the men will gather down at the school playground at six o'clock to practice softball for an hour or so before breakfast. When the monthly village holiday comes around, everyone gathers for a proper game. Men are paired off according to approximate age and are made to do *janken*, the paper-stone-scissors finger game, to decide who will be on which team. There is great excitement and some hilarity as the *janken* losers eventually turn the tables in the last innings and win 17–16. People decide to have a second game, but eventually give up when the score is 15–15.

The real purpose of all this practice is to prepare a team for the town's annual early-morning softball competition. This year Ya-shiki village has been matched against Shimoide ward, and during the course of the next few weeks the valley is flooded with rumors about how good the opposition is.

"It's the pitcher we've got to worry about," Inoshige tells me seriously. As a forty-one-year-old, he usually finds himself the clean-up batter, hitting in the important number four position.

"They say the woman who pitches can throw curves, sliders, the lot. We haven't got anybody on our team who can do that—not even Tōsuke on a good day. And there's something else, too. Because she's a woman, she's allowed to stand three feet closer to the batter. It's not really fair. A lot of the women around here are as tough and strong as the men."

That may be a slight exaggeration, but the erratic nature of Tō-suke's pitching is certainly not. There is a further problem in that each team has to field two women, and Yashiki has nobody who is willing to play.

"We may have to call on your Kyōko," warns Buntarō, whose own wife, Hideko, has implied that the game will be played at "that time of the month" when a woman can't run around very much.

"Women always have an excuse when they need it," mutters Ino-shige so that Ayako won't hear. "And the trouble is you can't very well verify the situation, can you? I wish we men had periods, too. Then nothing would ever get done in this world."

Eventually, Misako is persuaded to join the team, along with Te-rukichi's unmarried daughter, Michiko. The rest of the team is made up of the usual division between age groups. The dreaded day comes and everybody duly wakes up on time to gather down by Kuroda Takayuki's *sake* shop in Inekari. It is only just half past five and in the gloom of a cloudy dawn most people have already given up hope of winning the game.

"Fancy having to face a woman pitcher at this time of the morning," complains Buntarō, adjusting his black-and-green cap. "It's hard enough just looking at the wife."

We drive down to the main sports ground in town, where we line up in front of the opposing team from Shimoide, doff our caps, and chorus "Good morning!" before running back to our team bench. We do our best not to show our apprehension as our opponents take the field. The dreaded female is nowhere to be seen. Instead there is a young pitcher in his early twenties, whose very first ball Buntarō, much to his own surprise, hits straight over the head of center field for an in-park home run.

"*Chōshi ii zo*. We're in good form. Who said we weren't going to win?" Inoshige looks happier.

But the next three batters are quickly out, and Shimoide proceeds to hit everything Tōsuke throws at them. That is, everything close to the plate. It is one of his more erratic days and, what with walks and errors, he soon allows Shimoide to mount up an impressive score. One ... three ... six ... eight ... eleven ... thirteen runs in the first inning alone. At last, the Yashiki team manages to get the other side out and comes back to its bench looking somewhat crestfallen as Inoshige takes up his stance at home plate. The first ball comes zooming in.

"Stri-i-i-i-ke!" shouts the masked umpire, in what sounds like an imitation of one of Mifune Toshiro's more bloodthirsty samurai war cries.

Inoshige takes a step back, adjusts his cap, hitches up first one pant leg, then the other of his skin-tight uniform, raises the tip of his bat in the air, and faces the pitcher. The next ball is low and outside the strike zone.

"Ball!" calls the umpire, swinging his body away and turning his head sharply to one side.

Inoshige goes through his little ritual of adjusting his uniform and cap. He looks very professional as he squares himself up once again, feet slightly apart in the ashen dust of the batter's box. The pitcher throws a slower ball. Inoshige swings at it, makes contact, and sends it shooting high in the air toward right field. One of the two women on Shimoide's team is fielding there, and as she dithers, taking now two paces forward, now two paces back, we just have time to comment that this looks like a hit. Inoshige might get to second base if the ball drops over her head. If it does land within reach, she's bound to drop it.

And drop it she does. The trouble is that, instead of falling to the ground, the ball bounces out of her glove and into her bosom, where it lodges securely between her heaving breasts. Inoshige is out.

This is the ultimate shock. Somehow, a rumor begins floating around the bench that the Shimoide pitcher is in fact an "expert," a high school coach. The batting disintegrates. Yashiki takes the field, and Tōsuke walks more batters. Eisuke is called in as a relief pitcher, but it makes little difference. More runs are scored against our team, and the game is brought to an end after five innings, but not before Daisuke has the distinction of scoring a single, and Misako nearly makes it to first on a bunt. Unfortunately her legs are just too short, and she is out before she touches the base.

As for the final score, everyone is agreed that it is a mammoth total, but nobody is quite sure whether Shimoide has scored 20, 22, or 25 runs to Yashiki's one.

"At least we don't have to get up early anymore," sighs Inoshige over an eight o'clock beer back at Takayuki's *sake* shop.

31   The midday calm is broken by the voice of twelve-year-old Ryūichi shouting at Alyosha from the other side of the valley in Takao.

"Are we going fishing?"

"Ye-es," shouts back Alyosha, standing on the veranda and cupping his hands to help direct his voice.

"Shall I come up now?" comes back the reply.

"No. Wait a few minutes. I'm still having lunch."

"Okay. I'll see you up by the Todoroki bridge."

But the conversation is not quite as straightforward as my writing it down would make it appear. The distance between the two boys is such that it takes about three seconds for the sound of their voices to carry across the valley. Between every exchange, therefore, there is a five-to-six-second silence—long enough for Alyosha to wonder aloud, "Perhaps he hasn't heard me?"

Impatient, he starts to repeat one sentence before Ryūichi's reply comes echoing across the valley, and for a while there is confusion as half phrases are caught, not understood, and queried.

When he finishes his lunch and gets ready to leave, Kyōko tells him to wear shorts instead of his green track pants.

"But I can't do that. I wear green so that the fish won't notice me."

Like Winnie-the-Pooh, he also wears a blue sweater and pretends to be part of the sky and the grass. Delusions start at an early age.

Come home then, my boy, when the temple bell booms out. Then you will know it is time for supper.

32   Just as the passing of spring is measured by the flowers, so is the passing of summer measured by the insects. In June the fireflies light my way home through the evening mists. Early in July the twilight cicadas (*higurashi*) echo in the bamboo groves around the house. Then come the dragonflies (*tombo*), hovering and swooping across the fresh green rice, where the frogs keep up their ceaseless chorus. And with midsummer come all sorts of cicadas (*semi*), bees, and fearsome-looking armor-plated beetles. The children go out in the early morning to shake the oak trees and make the beetles fall down before they are fully awake. They put them in glass boxes filled with sawdust and impassively watch their captives fight and claw one another to death.

The horseflies suffer no less painful an end. Flying silently but slow enough to be whisked up in the cupped palm of a man's hand, they may have their heads burned off with the end of a lighted cigarette or else their wings are pulled off and they are tossed to the ground, there to thrash around ineffectively until snapped up by a passing chicken, cat, or dog.

Around the middle of August we start to see a red-colored dragonfly.

"That's called a *shōrosama*," explains Katsuhisa as he heaves a crate of beer into the back of his rusty old truck. "We use the word *shōro* around here to refer to the ancestors. I guess we call these dragonflies 'ancestors' because they make their appearance just before the midsummer *o-bon* festival, when the ancestors come home for the weekend. At least, that's what we like to believe."

We drive off down the hill, turn up the valley road, and make for Inoshige's. Kuroda Takayuki, the *sake* shop owner, is loading his van with crates of beer and juice.

"This is a really busy time of the year for people like Takayuki. This and the New Year. Everybody puts in orders for their seasonal gifts, and he delivers crate after crate of *sake* and beer to houses all over the valley. I hear he's even bought a short-wave radio so that Mieko, his wife, can keep in touch with him when he's out on his rounds."

We turn off and head up the hill for Amagase. "This is the time when those two get really happy," Katsuhisa continues. "People feel bound to pay their debts, so Mieko is kept busy toting up all the accounts she's put down in her ledger. You know, all the bills run up by men who drop by the shop on their way home from working in the mountains and who never carry cash on them. I do it myself, too, sometimes. You'd be surprised at the way a few drinks here and there can add up over a six-month period."

We pass Terukichi's son Umao wheeling a barrow of juice and beer across the swaying footbridge to Michiya's house on the other side of the river. Everybody is giving everybody else presents, thanking them for past favors, soliciting them for the future.

"I suppose you could say that by giving people presents we are reinforcing our personal networks and paying people back for the kindness they have shown us over the past six months. A fulfillment of obligations, really. But at the same time, it acts as a kind of safety device. By giving people presents we are also asking for their coop-eration in the future. In a small country valley like this, that makes sense. You never know when you might have need of help from those living around you. It can all get out of hand, though. Some people just pass their gifts around every six months without even bothering to open them. I've heard it said that if you wait long enough, the present you give your next-door neighbor will come back to you unopened from someone living in the nearest town."

We pull up and park at the side of the road below Terukichi's noodle shop. There are several hikers who have come down from the mountains and are looking across the road toward where Ino-shige and Ayako are unloading the kiln. Katsuhisa slides the crate of beer off the back of his truck, and we take it up to Inoshige's yard.

"That's very kind of you, Katchan," Ayako says, slipping the towel off her head and bowing to him in thanks. "You didn't have to worry yourself about a present for us, though."

"Well, it's just a small token of thanks," Katsuhisa bows, a little more formally than usual, as Inoshige comes across the yard.

"It's nice of you to drop by, Katchan," he says. "Step up and have some tea."

We know one another well enough not to have to go through the usual masquerade of polite refusals that etiquette generally de-mands. Inoshige picks up the crate of beer and carries it into the main room. The ancestral shrine has been especially decorated, and a number of gifts are piled in front of it. To these Inoshige adds Katsuhisa's beer.

"Haven't you noticed before how we always place presents before the ancestors? Well, most of the time, at any rate. We did it when you first came here and gave us that pretty linen cloth from Ireland.

We had to show it to the ancestors before we could use it. You may not have noticed, though, because there was just the one gift. But at a time like this, when everybody is giving everybody else presents, we have to put them all in front of the *butsudan*, or else people will be offended. In the old days, if you went to a landlord's house, you'd find presents piled right up to the ceiling."

"That's true." Katsuhisa has from somewhere produced one of his ubiquitous toothpicks and uses it to spear a pickled plum. "My mother is still very proud of her position, and she takes pleasure in measuring the amount of gifts we get."

"Is that so? Then I must give you something to add to her collection," Inoshige smiles. "Why don't you help yourself to a pot that you like. It should last longer than a few bottles of beer or packets of noodles."

This time Katsuhisa does protest, but Inoshige insists on giving him a large plate. Yuki is delighted, of course, and adds it to the voluminous pile of gifts in the small four-and-a-half-mat room set aside solely for the ancestral shrine.

"I wish I could use it for dinner tonight," sighs Misako. "But you're not allowed to. Presents must be kept unopened until the first day of *o-bon*."

33 The days get even busier. The *tatami* maker comes up the valley taking orders. Katsuhisa arranges for new mats to be put in his study, and Kumao decides to change the mats in his main guest room (one should, after all, spend money to impress the bride). Then Masaki, next door, orders some new mats, and Munetoshi, not to be outdone, follows suit. The *tatami* maker does well in Ōkubo.

"That's the way things always are," says Michiya, when we meet by chance at Takayuki's and share a bottle of beer together. "People never like to do things on their own. If somebody wants to buy a piece of land, or plant a few pear trees, or add an extension to his home, he'll always try to get somebody else in his community to do the same. You must have noticed the effect of this mentality when you drive around the country."

Michiya is right. You can pass vast stretches of grape vines along the main road to the prefectural capital. Two or three miles later, these are replaced by pear orchards, and there isn't a grape vine to be seen. A bit farther on and everybody living in the next village seems to have gone in for garden shrubs. After that, all the fields are lined with vinyl storehouses for market produce. You rarely find variation within any single area. What one farmer does, all the others seem to want to do too.

"It's hard to know how or why things get started the way they do," continues Michiya. "In the Oni valley, so far as I know, Yamaguchi Takeshi may have been one of the first to turn to growing pears. But I don't remember whether he was *the* first to do so. In fact, I rather doubt whether you'd ever find anyone willing to admit that he was the first. In the end, all you'll be able to say is that the Agricultural Coop encouraged the change from rice paddy to pear orchard. But whether it was one man who took the first plunge, or whether a few relatives or neighbors made up their minds to try it together, is hard to say. Community restraints being what they are, I'd guess that several people decided to make the change together. But given the fact that we Japanese tend to take orders from above rather readily, I suspect that the change was initiated by the Coop. It's difficult, as I said, for anyone to do anything entirely on his own. Unless, of course, he somehow manages to frame his actions within what are seen to be community interests. Haruzō is good at that when it comes to building new roads."

Michiya is one of the few men I know in this valley who seems able to detach himself from what is said and done here and to comment upon it all with reasonable objectivity. It is perhaps not surprising to find that he is the valley's only fee-paying member of the Japanese Communist Party.

"People are always talking about '*minna to issho*,' everyone together. You can see how this togetherness works in the way people are overtaken by fashions. One moment we're spending hours shut up in an unhygienic bowling alley; the next we're playing the latest variation in pachinko. As far as I can see, we'll soon be doing rock-and-roll dancing in front of our equivalent of the Meiji Shrine— Tenmangū. All the old people around here are currently into gateball, which is a variation of what you call croquet, or so I gather. I doubt whether it will last that long, though. Everything has its boom, followed by collapse. Things somehow seem to accelerate

until they are out of control. Like the boom in folk-craft pottery
that you're studying up in Kamayama. But once you get a boom,
you get overproduction; supply exceeds demand, and you get another kind of boom—that of financial disaster. People turn all together to something new, and the same old cycle goes on." He
chuckles and wrenches the cap off another bottle of beer.

"Perhaps you foreigners are right when you accuse us of being
like lemmings or robots. But remember. This pattern of production is perfect for those interested in the promotion of industrial
capitalism. For this way of life, it pays to have mindless 'all-to-
gether' people. The government is clever, the way it promotes un-
critical thought through an examination system that demands
nothing more than rote-learning."

He grins, and the furrows deepen in the freckled skin around his
eyes. "Not that there are many people in this valley who would
agree with what I think. So don't take it too seriously."

34   In the week before *o-bon* the valley begins to be filled with
unfamiliar faces—the faces of people who have come back to their
birthplace for the ancestors' festival. Masaki's two brothers and
their families arrive late one afternoon and, in no time at all, their
children and ours are playing hide-and-seek in the orchards.

"In the old days," muses Inoshige as we watch the children from
the veranda of the house, "*o-bon* was fixed by the lunar calendar. It
used to fall right on the night of the full moon. But not now." He
jerks his head toward where the crescent-shaped moon hangs
clearly lit by the setting sun. "On the first night of *o-bon* we used to
play hide-and-seek (*onigokko*). It was about the only time of the
year when young girls were allowed out of the house after dark.
Amagase hamlet formed the bounds of the game, but of course
there weren't that many places to hide, and anyway everybody
knew them pretty well, so it wasn't difficult to catch someone.
When you did, you then had to guess who you had caught. That
was where the fun began. If someone was hiding in a dark place like
my old kiln, it could be tricky trying to work out who it was, but
you were allowed to feel your captive to get a clue." He chuckles as
he savors the memories of youth. "That gave us a chance to feel a
young girl's breasts or bottom, as we tried to make her giggle and

reveal her identity. After a while, we boys soon knew which girl was which, just from the feel of their bodies. What was really disappointing was when I caught another boy. I'd purposely get his name wrong, though, just so as to be 'it' again and find a girl."

Buntarō, who was passing along the road below our house, comes up to join us.

"It's nice to find this part of Ōkubo so lively again," he says, gulping down his beer thirstily. "That's the way *o-bon* should be."

"Yes. I remember when my father died, we had something like twenty-seven relatives sleeping on the floor."

"Twenty-seven? You *have* got a large family, Inoshigesan."

"Yes. There was Misae's daughter and her two children. Her son and his wife and children. My eldest sister, the one who's just died, and her husband. My younger brother and his wife and children. One of my elder sisters who had come down from Tokyo with her boys. There were so many kids running around the house, old Granny couldn't work out who they all were."

"Yes. When we were over there yesterday afternoon, she was muttering to me about two rather large great-grandchildren of hers she had seen playing with Shigeki and the girls. 'Who are their parents?' she kept asking. 'Which of my children produced those tall boys?' It took me a few moments to realize that she was referring to Alyosha and Maya."

Next afternoon, a Saturday, families go to meet their ancestors and there is a procession of people passing Mon, Katsuhisa's house, as they go to visit the temple where the ashes of the dead are housed. I accompany Katsuhisa and his mother when they slip across the road to the temple. We go up the steep steps to the main hall and, throwing ten yen on the *tatami*, bow before the main ancestral shrine there. Then Yuki gets fresh water for the bunch of flowers she has brought with her and places them in a small jar in front of the wooden memorial to members of the Mon household. Katsuhisa lights an incense stick. Then mother and son place the palms of their hands together, their fingers entwined with beads, and pray.

After this, they climb more steps behind the temple to the two-tiered pagoda where the ashes of each household's dead are kept.

Again they pray before the ancestral shrine there, before making their way among the boxed cupboards that stand in rows like some library card catalogue. Katsuhisa opens one of these boxes to reveal a number of little white bags standing on its shelves.

"Here they all are, you see, living happily together. That's the way things should be," he says. After a moment's reflective gaze at the ashes of his ancestors, he locks the cupboard door and leads me off to the priest's residence, where we are served *shōchū* (distilled potato spirits), together with dried fish in vinegar, seaweed, and sweets.

"It's easier now with people being cremated. Somehow, it doesn't make death quite so hard to bear." Yuki uncharacteristically begins to reveal her feelings. "In the old days when somebody was buried, there was so much emotion. The eldest son had to begin scooping the earth onto the coffin. Then other close relatives each took handfuls of earth and threw it into the grave. We'd cry a lot then as the rest of the community residents would shovel in the earth. I hated the way the coffin gradually disappeared from sight. Now there is only the dry feeling of the crematorium. And there is nothing to remind us of the dead except for a small bag of ashes, which normally we never see. Not like the old days, when there were always the bones to bring back memories."

We are served tea and soon depart. Yuki, fortified by the *shōchū*, warns me to watch my step.

"It's bad luck to slip and fall down on your way home from the temple," she says. "When I was young, the path up to the temple where I was brought up was uneven and winding, and one of us children almost always tripped and fell somewhere. Whoever it was then had to go back to the temple and go through the whole process of welcoming back the ancestors again. Nowadays things are better, although Norihisa did trip over last year, didn't he, Katchan? I made Misako take him back to the temple. There's no point in tempting fate, is there?"

Back at the house, Misako is preparing a large basket of fresh fruit and vegetables, together with a plateful of rice dumplings. "We mustn't let the ancestors go hungry while they're home," she says with a slightly embarrassed giggle. "Today they get round dumplings, but on Monday when we see them off again, we give them sausage-shaped dumplings. Why? Because the long ones are easier to throw over their shoulders. The ancestors can then chew them on their way back to wherever it is they go."

Later on in the evening everyone in Yashiki village gathers for the *bon* dance. "This is something we've done for longer than anyone in the valley can remember," says Buntarō who, like all the other men, is wearing a dark-hued cotton robe. We lean against the bridge railing by Inekari's shop, where the breeze from the river is pleasantly cool. "In Ichinotsuru and other hamlets, the *bon* dance is quite new. Some of the wives and mothers of men who were killed in the war decided that the dead ought to be remembered. That's why they started the *bon* dance there. But here in Yashiki we've been dancing for ages."

"That's right, Buntarō." It was Munetoshi, glad as usual to fill me in with some facts. "We always dance in the yard of a house where a death has occurred during the past year. That's why we're starting down here. Takayuki's father died in the early autumn last year. And then Aso's Akihito had his accident, so we'll be going up to the house we call Naka to dance."

"And then there's Inoue's boy. You're not forgetting him, are you?"

"Ah, yes. It had almost slipped my mind. That was a strange case, wasn't it? Were you here then, Būchan? No, it was before you came."

"You see the house down the alley between Inekari's and Kuroda's two shops?" Buntarō points across the river. "Well, there was a boy there who'd just left school when he met up with a girl in town."

"She was working in a bar of some kind. A hostess, she was."

"Yes, she must have been. Well, they were having an affair. You know, the usual quick visits to one of those love hotels along the riverbank."

"And it turned out that she was somehow involved with a gangster."

"You can imagine what happened when *he* found out. Began threatening the Inoue boy."

"And demanded compensation, the way these gangsters always do. I don't know how much, though."

"Nor do I, but it must have been a lot to make him do what he did."

"That's true, Buntarō. Well, anyway, the boy came back home one night, parked his car by the kindergarten up the hill there, and committed suicide."

"The way he did it, though! Coming all the way back to kill himself right in front of his parents."

"You know what he did? He fixed a piece of rubber tubing onto his exhaust pipe, fed it back inside his car, and closed the windows and locked the door. He sat inside, started the engine, somehow rigging the accelerator pedal so that it stayed down. He was found dead the next morning."

"Poor lad!" Buntarō exclaims sympathetically.

"But it seems that one good thing came out of it all." Munetoshi lowers his voice and glances round to make sure that nobody is eavesdropping. "Have you heard about the insurance?"

"No. What insurance?"

"Apparently, old Inoue had some family policy. It's said they are due to collect quite a lot of money."

"Really? Well, I never."

But I am to hear no more gossip, for people are beginning to form a circle nearby, fanning out across the bridge, men and women together. It has been decided that we will start by dancing here for the Inoue boy and Takayuki's father. Then we'll go up to Aso Masaki's house.

Tōsuke, Michiya, and Ibata Haruo are the three main singers.

"Normally, Takayuki himself joins in, but this year, of course, he can't," explains Munetoshi as we begin to move slowly clockwise, dancing the slow steps of "Shianbashi" (The Bridge of Reflection), fans beating out the rhythm under the starlit sky:

> Gathered, gathered,
> The dancing children gathered
> From the autumn ripening harvest,
> How well they have gathered.

It is warm, and the cool breeze coming down with the river is not enough to stop us from perspiring gently as we dance. Tōsuke, Michiya, and Haruo begin to get into their stride now as their voices ring out in the night:

> Only a child excels his parents,
> Like the bamboo shooting up,
> Seven knots for the parents,
> Eight knots for the child.

And so we dance on, slowly, rhythmically, occasionally joining in with a chorus of this beautiful song whose tune has come, it is said, all the way from the fief in the north of Japan ruled by the Satake clan lord. How it got so far south nobody knows. But the words, surely, can only have come from this island:

> You and I are like the ink on the stone;
> The more we grind together,
> The greater the flush of our love.

After more than half an hour, we finally stop to refresh ourselves, gulping down the beer and juice that are served to us. We squat in the road or rest against the railing of the bridge, laughing and talking, before moving down the road toward the turning up to Ōkubo. The children run among us, weaving in and out, laughing and screaming as they scamper around in the dark. Some of the older boys set off fireworks; others light sparklers, which they wave in the air. Summer is the season for fireworks.

We reach the top of the long slope and turn off down the road to Masaki's house. The doors and windows have been thrown open, as they were at the funeral, and the ancestral shrine has been especially decorated with all sorts of lights that flicker gently within their paper shades. Tōsuke and the others position themselves under the lamp outside the front door and start to sing once more:

> Whenever the seventh month
> Brings with it the ancestors' return
> I start to dance to meet my loved one.
>
> In memory gazing at her photograph
> Why does the photograph not say anything?

We dance onward, ever on, stepping around the ring that we have formed, breaking one pace back, turning one step into the center of our circle, clapping hand on fan, bending, swaying, raising the fan high. Our feet grow tired, unused to so much dancing in wooden clogs (*geta*). Masaki, kneeling on the veranda of his house where his whole family has gathered to watch the villagers celebrate his son's return, invites us in for refreshments. We step up and seat ourselves cross-legged at the long row of tables. Never has beer tasted so refreshing, its coolness bringing perspiration to the brow and nape of neck.

Eventually we get up and step outside into the night. The children are setting off more fireworks. One of the dogs barks from the safety of the orchards above the house. Men and women gather themselves together and slowly make their way down the path to the track that leads back down the hill, talking and laughing loudly as they disappear into the bamboo grove. Then there is only the sound of their voices and of their wooden clogs rasping on the hard earth. *Out of the dark along the path of darkness we must go. Shine on us from afar, moon of the mountain ridge.*

35 While the ancestors are home between the 13th and 15th of August, everyone celebrates.

"When my father died," says Inoshige, "and we had all those people here to stay, we got through five bottles of *sake*, fifty bottles of lemonade, and ninety bottles of beer."

During the drinking sessions, stories of the dead are told, and younger men are advised about how to treat the old. Takayuki is told to look after his mother; she has had a hard life. Inoshige recalls how once he told Inekari Gorō to take care of his grandmother, who was ill at the time. Gorō's uncle, who was there with them, said his nephew didn't have to bother. But Inoshige insisted. All Gorō had to do was poke his head around the door of his grandmother's room every morning and evening to make sure she was all right. In this way he could gauge how close she was to death and would be able to keep relatives informed. Gorō acquiesced. The next morning his grandmother was dead.

The young wives go back to their homes at this time of the year. Eisuke's new bride goes to see her parents, as does Hideko, who takes her children with her. Buntarō looks slightly despondent.

"It's so quiet," he says," with just me and my parents at home. I don't like it. I don't like it at all."

Katsuhisa takes Misako and the children off to her family for a couple of days. Inoshige goes to spend the night at Ayako's little thatch-roofed cottage on the edge of town. Those who visited the valley for *o-bon* begin to return to their workplaces in Tokyo and Osaka. After the bustle of the festival, everything is suddenly rather empty.

Life is measured by *o-bon*. The horseflies get fewer; the pears taste crisper; the weather becomes cooler.

36   The most common form of greeting at this time of the year is "It's got cool, hasn't it?" (*Suzushiku narimashita nē*). This, of course, has its spring parallel, "It's got warmer, hasn't it?" I suppose a statement of the obvious cannot be interpreted as threatening behavior by acquaintances when they meet on the road. "Well, this is a rarity" (*kore wa mezurashii*) used to strike me as rather an impolite way of initiating a conversation, but it is commonly used by acquaintances who have not met for a while or who meet in an unusual situation.

Another phrase used to greet people is the direct question, "What are you up to today?" (*kyō wa nan no kotsu desu kai*), which is how Hideko addressed us when she saw us wandering through the pear orchard hand in hand the other morning. She found it hard to believe that a man and his wife could find the time to take a stroll.

The most frequently used greeting of all, though, is surely the one that emphasizes ongoing relationships between people: "I'm indebted to you for the other day" (*kono mae o-sewa ni narimashita*). This phrase is also used to initiate what are seen to be relations of indebtedness, or give-and-take, as when people gather for a PTA meeting, a village outing, or the hamlet's monthly get-together when taxes, insurance dues, and television license fees are paid. "*O-sewa ni narimasu*" are the first words spoken by anyone joining this sort of gathering.

I have noticed, too, that a person will use the phrase on behalf of another member of his or her household. Umao, for example, spent the evening drinking at Inoshige's the other day, and the next morning first his mother, then his wife, Taeko, and finally old Teru-kichi himself, one after the other repeated "*Yūbe, o-sewa ni nari-mashita*" to Ayako, Misae, and Inoshige when they met them during the day. Greetings are made not simply to individuals, but to whole households. They leave very little room for creativity or manipulation of the set order of social relationships among people here in the valley.

"All the same, greetings are much freer than they used to be," Haruzō assures me, when we are caught in a sudden downpour and find ourselves sheltering by the Tenmangū shrine above the school. "In the old days young people were expected to greet their elders. Women were expected to greet men, and poor tenants their rich landlords. Those were the three main rules. What's more, inferiors were expected to stop dead in their tracks and bow deeply while exchanging greetings. Nowadays that sort of thing never happens. People just continue whatever it is they're doing at the time and nod their heads. It just shows that differences in age, sex, and wealth have stopped having so great an influence on the way we behave. That's democracy for you, I suppose."

Younger men may be glad that a notion of "democracy" allows them a voice in village affairs. Poorer men are doubtless delighted not to have to submit openly to the authority of the rich. But men, of whatever age and social status, feel that women are particularly lax in their manners.

"In the old days we thought of women not just as being of a different sex. They were a different *species*," Haruzō continues, as he settles himself with his back to a pillar. "When a woman gave birth to a boy, there was always plenty of celebrating. But if she gave birth to a girl, people ignored the birth entirely. You'll see for yourself soon, when Taeko has her next baby. Poor old Terukichi doesn't know what to do. Three grandchildren and all of them girls. If that had happened a few years back, people would have started blaming Taeko for bringing a girl instead of a boy into the world. Nowadays people just sigh in disappointment and give Umao drunken advice on how to father a son. Do you know, that fool Inoshige suggested that Umao stand Taeko on her head and then stick his prick into her. I've never heard anything so crazy in my life. That's what *sake* does to a man."

Considering the fact that greetings are so uncreative, it is perhaps not surprising to find that there isn't much to be found in the way of verbal abuse. This is partly because social relations are too close-knit to permit open defamation of character. Gossip is acceptable because it is behind a person's back. But insults are too direct for comfort. In the country you cannot swear at someone who has just backed his tractor into your car because there is every likelihood that he is related to somebody you happen to know. This valley is terrifyingly small. A chance remark, an ill-directed smile, a failure to respond to someone in the accepted manner—all these may well be reported back to one's immediate circle of friends or neighbors from as far away as the prefectural capital.

So you don't knowingly insult people. This is not the case in cities, of course, where men will revile one another in those passionate flare-ups that often follow traffic accidents. All the same, even these remarks are somewhat limited, for the Japanese do not make use of that kind of defamation of sexual character to which we in the West are accustomed. Rather, they seem to prefer to insult your intellectual capabilities. "Go bang your head against a wall of bean curd and die!" (*tōfū no kabe ni atama o butsukete shinde koi*) is one nice phrase I've heard. Only an idiot would hurt his head on such a soft-textured food.

"Sometimes you'd get people with rhythmical chants made up about their names," says Inoshige as we squeeze into a kiln chamber with a long tray of glazed teacups and start lining them up on the shelves. "My friends used to have one for me when we were kids. How did it go now? Ah yes.

> Bushy Shige's hair in his nostrils
> Tripped him up and over he fell.

But then everybody had some chant or other like this, so you can't really call it abuse. All children like to pick on each other's physical features, after all. If your belly-button stuck out like it often did in the old days, you were called 'debeso' [Protruding Navel]. One of my teachers at school was called 'deba no kami,' the buck-toothed god, but we never used that nickname to his face. Always behind his back. Poor fellow!"

We put the last two cups on the kiln shelf and ease our way out of the chamber. "The only word that people used in abuse that I can remember is the old word for 'you,' *kisama*. It's written with very high-flown honorific Chinese characters. But for some reason or other the word has come to be used pejoratively. Daisuke's grandfather used to curse his wife and call her '*kisama*,' much to her delight. Why? Because during the feudal period only samurai were allowed to use the word. Daisuke's grandmother felt that she had really gone up in the world and used to thank her husband for calling her by such an exalted term!"

Katsuhisa has only one comment to add: "I remember when I was a teenager, reading about that novel *Lady Chatterley's Lover*. There was a great furor when it first came out because it was full of swear words. Yet you tell me that in England some people speak like that all the time. It makes you wonder what all the fuss was about, then, doesn't it? Here in Japan things are the other way around. We don't use much abuse in our everyday speech. Instead, you'll find that most of the commonly known words and phrases, together with a few of the less common ones, originated in the works of our famous novelists. And yet *they* never have difficulty publishing their work!"

37 There is a nice phrase used here in the valley to describe the process of growing old. They say that someone's "back got bent from early on" (*hayaku kara koshi ga magatteru*). This depicts perfectly the image I have of Tōsuke's old mother walking along the edge of a field, her torso almost horizontal to the ground, unable to straighten up after years of bending among the rice plants.

Sometimes I am surprised at how localized the Oni valley dialect is. Yesterday Kyōko phoned a friend in town and said that she was about to "go down" (*kudaru*), meaning leave the valley for the town. The friend had to ask what she meant. Town people do not use the word *kudaru* unless they are referring to coming back from a visit to the capital. To "come down" from Tokyo, yes, that made sense. But who ever heard of anyone "coming down" from the Oni valley? We who were born in two of the largest cities of the world are now regarded as country bumpkins.

38 Terukichi has decided to add an extension to his noodle shop, jutting out above the Amagase stream. It seems as though there are enough hikers to warrant the expense, and he is going to start a family inn. Daisuke, the carpenter who helped repair my house, was asked to do the job and has laid the foundations. Today Harimoto, the Shintō priest, comes up to perform the roof-ridge-raising ceremony.

Before he starts the ceremony, he places four bamboo rods in a square and strings rope made from strands of rice straw between them. Then he cuts a number of paper streamers, which he hangs from the rope, four on each side of the square. In the middle he places a small evergreen bush from which he hangs one much larger paper streamer. Terukichi has laid out food and *sake* on two shelves—bream, rice, and *sake* on one, and dried fish, fruit, and vegetables on the other. On the second shelf he has also laid out a dish of salt and confetti-like paper squares to be used in the ceremony.

The ceremony itself is fairly simple. Harimoto faces the area where the extension is to be built, claps his hands twice, bows twice, and intones a prayer. After this he bows twice, claps his hands twice more, takes some salt and paper from the dish on the shelf, and throws it into the air. At the same time, he utters a loud "O-o-o-o-o-om!" This is followed by more handclaps and bows as he waves a bamboo stem with fronds. Small fronds with paper streamers are then given to everyone present at the ceremony (Terukichi and family, together with Daisuke and his apprentices). Each in turn comes forward, places the frond on one of the dishes on the lower shelf, and claps his or her hands twice. Harimoto then scatters salt and paper twice over the foundations of the extension, while Daisuke pours *sake* into each of its two sections. After that everyone drinks cold *sake*.

Such ritual is not necessarily effective all the time. One afternoon, not long after, Daisuke's son, Fujio, slipped from the roof of the new building and fell to the riverbed 15 or 20 feet below.

"I thought he was dead," Daisuke told me when we met at Taka-yuki's *sake* shop. "I really did. Somehow the boy managed to stay upright as he was falling. I could see him flapping his arms in great circular movements as he tried to land in the stream itself. He hit the water feet first all right, but then he pitched forward and hit his head and chest on a rock."

Daisuke and Terukichi hurried down to where Fujio lay. There was a lot of blood, and the boy was rushed to the hospital.

"But he was all right. The doctors put a few stitches in his forehead. And his face was all swollen up, but there was no serious damage of any kind. We were lucky."

A few days after Fujio's fall, when the residents of Amagase were gathered together for the Kōshinsama celebration, somebody suggested that Terukichi ought to have a purification (*o-harai*) to "wash away" any bad spirits that might have invaded the building. Nobody wanted a second accident. Terukichi hemmed and hawed, but was finally prevailed upon to do as his neighbors wanted. But he couldn't have the ceremony performed the next day because he had to go into town, and Harimoto couldn't come up from town the day after that because he was busy. So it was arranged for the morning of the day after that. Then Terukichi put the ceremony off until the afternoon, saying that would be more sensible, seeing as how everybody would start drinking.

On the morning of the ceremony Terukichi cut the forefinger of his left hand to the bone while sawing up some wood for the building. The moral of the story is fairly clear. Not that people say anything directly to Terukichi himself. The fact that they gossip behind his back is enough to show their superstition.

"My mother-in-law always says that you shorten a person's life by taking his or her photograph, you know," Daisuke remarked, sipping his *sake* and tearing himself off a piece of a chicken's foot to chew with his drink. "And I was always told that if you took a photograph of three people together, one of them would soon meet with some bad luck. So you'd better be careful with that camera of yours. I also heard that if you pee on the road, it will rain on your wedding day. It snowed on mine."

One superstition, which Katsuhisa told me about one evening as we waited for our boys to come out of their *kendō* fencing class in the school gym, I have taken to heart. "You know that small plateau up in the hills I told you about? The place where I've built myself a little shack and planted some trees?" he reminded me. "Well, that used to belong to Haruzō. I'd always fancied the place, ever since I was a kid, and whenever I walked that way, I'd always make sure that I had a pee there. At the same time I prayed that the land would one day be mine." Pausing for a second to shift his toothpick from one side of his mouth to the other—and probably for effect as well—he continued, "After twenty years or so, Haruzō asked me if I wouldn't mind swapping land with him. He had only that silly bit up there, and most of the adjoining mountain land was mine. And anyway the bit he wanted was relatively new and didn't count as ancestral land, so I agreed. You should never sell land that belongs to the ancestors, you know. They are liable to get angry with you."

This I knew. I decided to start urinating on the land around our house from that day on—rather like a dog marking out its territory. In a way my act was one of expedience. Our cesspit is so small that if we all used the latrine, I would end up having to empty the pit at least once a week. But we are determined to buy this house, and the fact that the land was recently purchased by Takeshi and does not belong to his ancestors gives me hope that he will eventually accede to our request.

39   In the autumn most of the men of Yashiki village go off for a day on their annual outing. This is an affair organized by the *sōnenkai*, or "general-age group," to which all men from the mid-twenties to the mid-sixties officially belong. Age groups used to be important in a number of spheres of village life, but now people join them mostly for their entertainment value.

This year it has been decided that the group will go and watch the *sumō* wrestling competition being held in the prefectural capital. However, since the main bouts do not get started until well after three o'clock in the afternoon, there is plenty of time to fill in, and the older men have arranged for visits to be made to a rubber factory and a whisky distillery that are more or less en route.

A bus has been hired, and at about half past seven everyone gathers in festive mood down by the North Oni Primary School. After the usual greetings and expected delays, 40 men finally clamber on board, and we depart down the valley. People begin lighting their cigarettes, and the bus is soon mistier—and considerably less hygienic—than the swirling fog outside.

Terukichi is the man in charge for the day, and he soon stands up to address us all.

"Today, as you know, is the *sōnenkai* outing, and we're off to see the *sumō* competition. Last year we went to watch a baseball match. And the year before we visited the country's second-largest dam. The year before that was the very first year we had an outing of this sort, and that was when we all went off to Okinawa for the weekend."

It is always important in speeches of this sort to remind people of the past so as to set the present in a frame. This prevents deviation from an established norm and, like greetings, stifles creativity.

"Today, we're going to visit the Hoshitsuki Rubber Factory and after that the Nikka Whisky Distillery. We'll be at the factory at nine o'clock and the distillery at half past ten. Lunch has been fixed for noon at a roadside inn in the city. Then we'll go on to the *sumō* hall to arrive at three."

Michiya sucks in his teeth sharply. "We'll never make that factory by nine. It's already past eight, and there's more than an hour's drive ahead of us."

Terukichi sits down, and Haruzō begins to stand up. The bus swerves sharply and Haruzō sits back down rather more promptly than he had anticipated. Everyone laughs as he rises to his feet once more and gives a short speech welcoming us on the Yashiki village *sōnenkai*'s fourth annual outing. We should be grateful that we are being blessed by the weather (there is a ray of sunshine gleaming through the fog) and should thank Terukichi for making all the arrangements this year.

Haruzō sits down, and Tōsuke stands up to tell us who is present and who is absent and for what reasons. Daisuke and his father have been unable to come because of the death of Daisuke's mother-in-law. They have, however, kindly contributed 10,000 yen toward the cost of the trip. In their place, Būchan has been recruited as "pinch hitter." Unfortunately, no substitutes have been found for two or three other absentees—the most remiss of whom is clearly Takenori of Takao, who has apparently found it impossible to "get up" in time. This comment is greeted with a certain amount of derision by some of the younger men at the back of the bus. It is common knowledge that Takenori spends every night in town with one or other of his two bar-hostess mistresses and only comes back home at about ten in the morning.

Next it is the turn of Noda Moriyuki, who rises to encourage people to give more money than they already have toward the cost of the outing. Funds are a little short because of the absentees, and also because of one or two unanticipated extra expenditures. Moriyuki gives a full rundown on the day's costs: 72,000 yen for the bus; 26,000 yen for tickets to the *sumō* competition; 10,000 yen for tips for the bus driver and guide; and so on. All this means that they expect each passenger to pay 4,000 yen for the outing plus a 1,500-yen "membership" fee. Further donations would of course be welcome. In the meantime, certain kind people had contributed *sake* for the group's enjoyment. This, Moriyuki informs us, is now ready to be consumed. But first of all, the names of those who had contributed to the general good must be mentioned—Higuchi Daisuke, Sakakura Inoshige, Gotō Chitose, Sakakura Haruzō, and Būchan. This speech, like the others before it, is greeted with applause as Moriyuki resumes his seat in the center of the bus.

The clapping over, five bottles of *sake* suddenly appear—open and warm. Terukichi's son, Umao, has brought several lunch boxes packed with boiled foods, and these are distributed throughout the bus. Buntarō hands out plastic cups. By 8:43 in the morning everyone has taken the first of what is sure to be many sips of *sake* from a cup that can be placed snugly in a metal holder fixed to the back of the seat in front of him. The smoke gets thicker, voices louder. The amount of *sake* left in the bottles decreases in direct proportion to the increased volume of noise. Men's faces flush, and the whites of their eyes begin to be streaked with red. The outing has begun.

It is at this point that the bus guide makes her first public statement. With a brisk, clear "Good morning, everybody," she stands up and faces us—the only woman in a bus filled with slightly tipsy men. Her prim blue hat is pinned firmly to her cheek-length black hair; her lips are cherry red; the hands that clasp the microphone into which she speaks are sheathed in white cotton gloves. The microphone itself she holds as if she were some genteel lady sipping a cup of tea, keeping one little finger cocked up in the air all the while she speaks to us. We are welcomed on board this Ida Bus Company vehicle, with a flurry of phrases expressing her, and the company's, humility and gratitude at our patronage. Then we are given a rundown of the weather that would have done a radio announcer proud.

By this time we are slowing down to cross the red iron-girdered bridge that spans the Mekura River at Yūgure—the hamlet whose stationmaster recently acquired a certain transient fame when his photograph was used in a National Railways advertisement pasted on walls from Sapporo to Kagoshima during the summer vacation months. The guide continues to chat amiably about nothing in particular, before realizing that her passengers do not make a very sympathetic audience.

"The only things that make a noise in the morning," growls Michiya sleepily, "are birds and tour-bus guides."

But if talking is not on, some of the men on the bus are ready to sing. The guide passes the microphone to Terukichi who, as *sewanin*, gets the party going with a couple of off-pitch popular songs. It is then that I realize the cord running along one length of the roof of the bus, which I had taken to be a bell cord to stop the bus, is in fact strung up to allow the microphone to be passed back and forth among the passengers.

This is not the only facility the bus affords those who pride themselves on (or who are forced to participate in) song. The bus is also fitted with a *karaoke*, that marvelous hybrid phrase of *kara*, "empty," and *oke*, an abbreviation of the English "orchestra." We can sing along accompanied by fully orchestrated music, and this many of the men proceed to do for the rest of the morning. The guide shows her paces by singing a couple of songs most creditably; having a good voice obviously helps when applying for this kind of job. In between, we stop to be taken on a guided tour of the rubber factory, but some of the men are chagrined to discover that the only other people visiting the factory are four bus-loads of primary-school children. As Inoshige jovially remarks: "From *sōnen* to *shōnen*, middle age to childhood, again!"

Then we move on to the whisky distillery—except that it turns out not to be a distillery at all, but a bottling factory. Terukichi looks slightly embarrassed, but we are all led into a canteen-style room to be shown a short film of a real distillery and then we are allowed to sample liberal doses of what is made there. And that, after all, is what most people are interested in.

But worse is to come as the day goes on. At the roadside inn where we have lunch, beer is served to settle uneasily on the whisky, which is itself being digested hesitantly with the early morning *sake*. Several men decide that the only way to relieve themselves of all this unwanted liquid is to urinate from a balcony on the first floor of the restaurant. One innocent pedestrian puts up her parasol.

This discomfort turns into inebriated anger when we arrive at the *sumō* hall in the prefectural capital. Terukichi goes off with the tickets to arrange our mass entry into the building and finds to his horror that they have been issued not for the thirteenth day of the month, as he had supposed, but for the thirteenth day of the championships!

There is considerable confusion at this point as the back of Terukichi's neck turns bright pink, and he begins conferring with his committee members. Clearly, we are not going to take another annual outing in eight days' time. Having come so far, we have to get in somehow. Terukichi goes back to negotiate with the ticket office, and eventually we are allowed off the bus and into the hall, on condition that we watch from the aisles.

Inoshige takes me aside quietly and leads me off to the practice room to meet a wrestler whom he had got to know several years previously when he had come to buy one of Inoshige's pots. The silence of that packed room, so full of wrestlers that there is hardly room to move, is quite extraordinary. Almost the only recognizable sound comes from the whistling exhalation of breath as three wrestlers do their warming-up exercises in one corner of the long hut. It is all bare feet zigzagging in the white sand, hands jarring against a wooden pillar, muscles rippling along their oiled arms, sending lesser waves down the layers of skin around their stomachs.

Tired of standing in the aisles, I manage to join the press photographers. The fact that I am carrying a large telephoto lens and am a foreigner inhibits anyone from questioning me. I have learned to make use of my status as an "outsider."

40   In most societies, it would seem that those who use words fluently succeed to positions of power. Here in the Oni valley this fact is more apparent than it is—say—in the streets of London. Those in positions of authority manage to make speeches with great fluency. It is true that these may consist of nothing but platitudes; yet somehow their very delivery in formal situations prevents dissent. Noda Shōsuke, the headman of Yashiki village, has developed his public speaking to a fine art.

"Good morning, everybody. Thank you very much for gathering together when you are so busy. We are indeed extremely fortunate to be blessed by such fine weather as we have today. The reason for our gathering here is—." Here Shōsuke proceeds to name the event—a school sports day, a valley baseball competition, or the Pear Association's annual general meeting—and outline its history, before finishing off his speech. "And so that's why we are gathered here on a day in which we are indeed fortunate to be blessed by the weather. And considering how busy you all are, thank you very much for gathering. Thank you very much."

As Amagase hamlet chief, Haruzō prefers to say less at public gatherings and to confine his speeches to more practical matters. He is well versed in the art of misrepresentation, of gently shifting responsibility for his own actions to someone else, when it looks as if there might be some opposition to his plans. This is to be seen in the long-term project to have the valley road widened right up to his house at the top of Amagase. The moment that there is a hint of opposition among people living at the top end of Inekari near the school, Haruzō quickly pretends that the decision to widen the road there was taken by the school PTA.

Other men display less clearly motivated linguistic abilities, language for the sake of sheer entertainment, as when Inoshige gets talking over *sake*. He, too, is a man who will take over leadership of the valley's residents in due course. It is because someone like Inoshige is able to say not just the right thing, but a little bit more than the right word in the right place to the right person, that he moves slowly, but surely, toward a position of authority and power.

Yamaguchi Takeshi is not this type of man at all. He mumbles words out of the side of his mouth. Much of what he says is neither clearly articulated nor to the point. He has a habit of scratching his nose with the back of one hand as he speaks, and of turning his head sharply away from the person he is addressing and scratching his left ear with his right hand. He rarely looks you in the eye, unless it is to give you a rather mournful, doglike look—as though not sure whether he will be scolded or praised for what he says. As often as not, he then laughs—half-silently—his jaw dropping with a sudden burst of breath to reveal an irregular set of badly stained teeth. Takeshi is referred to by some as a *dombyakusho*, "country bumpkin" type of farmer. He is no fool, however.

Precisely because he does not use words well, precisely because he will never be able to attain any position of real authority in the valley, Takeshi will never *harm* anybody. He will never make real enemies. Certainly, he will have his drunken brawls and argue in-conclusively over the art of growing pears and how the cooperative should adopt his way of doing things. But such arguments will affect no more than a handful of other men in the valley and hence will not come to public attention.

The same can hardly be said for Haruzō, who seems prepared to trample all over other people in order to get what he wants. Haruzō is one man who certainly does have his enemies. At the moment he is struggling to get several square yards of Katsuhisa's rice field below the kindergarten so that the road in front of the school can be widened. Katsuhisa has already provided the land for the kinder-garten to be built on and is not prepared to cooperate further.

"Why should I give away my land for a road?" he asks, for once not quite his usual unflappable self. "Country roads, anyway, are made for people to be able to stop and say 'hello' to one another. There you are, driving along nice and quiet when you meet another car coming from the opposite direction. So you back along to a wider section of the road, so the other person can pass. You ex-change greetings and pass the time of day. And if it happens to be the evening and the person passing is a good friend, you may well end up drinking together. That's what country roads are for! If you widen the valley road, what happens? Cars will zoom past each other and all contact between people will be broken." He grins. "No. I actually think what Haruzō should do is campaign to make the road *narrower*."

Haruzō came away from one such meeting with Katsuhisa in a state of bewilderment. There are not many men who dare speak to him as Katsuhisa does. Half an hour later, he went back to his house with a couple of pounds of cooked chicken legs and half a dozen supporters, who tried to make Katsuhisa change his mind. They were not at all successful.

Haruzō was close to exasperation. "I expected a man like him to understand my point of view. After all, he is a teacher. But quite the contrary. He didn't give an inch. Katchan must be the stupidest person I've ever had to deal with, when it comes to roads."

But Katsuhisa has at least one supporter. A bridge below the Coordination Office is being widened, and the river downstream has been filled in to allow the bulldozer to maneuver more easily. My son Alyosha is furious. "They've filled in my favorite pool. That was the best place in the whole valley for fishing, and now they've ruined it."

41 The snake gourds (*karasu-uri*) come out in late autumn and hang from creeper-like branches during the winter months, brightening the gray days of December with flashes of orange-red in the otherwise dead undergrowth. Their juice is said to be exceptionally good for chapped skin and chilblains.

The children here say that the stones inside the *karasu-uri* are coins that belong to the crows (*karasu*). The gourd as a whole is the crows' bank, because you can't see the money inside. I surmise two things from the number of *karasu-uri* around our house. First, the crows are very rich. Second, what is true of the Japanese as a nation appears to hold true for crows as well: like the country as a whole, they are grossly over-supplied with banks.

Other remedies that people try here include putting Chinese cabbage leaves at the back of your neck when you have a temperature; placing pickled plums on your temples when you have a headache; and wrapping your throat in a muslin cloth filled with sliced onions when you have a cough or sore throat.

42 Alyosha is full of information now that he is growing up. "There are lots of words with 'robber' [*dorobō*] in them. We call it 'robber-sharpening' [*dorobō kezuri*], when we sharpen our pencils at both ends. And 'robber-wiping' [*dorobō fuki*] when we wipe across the floorboards instead of along them as we clean up after school."

Katsuhisa adds that whenever a thief broke into a house in the old days, the first thing he did was shit in the corridor. Apparently, this was designed to settle his nerves and enable him to proceed with his task. From this practice, Katsuhisa goes on to say, comes the term "*kusokurae*," meaning something like "go to hell!" Exactly what the connection is, he is too drunk to explain.

43 We have decided to ask Yamaguchi Takeshi formally whether he won't sell us our house.

"I don't see why he shouldn't," Inoshige says. "After all, he only bought that land fairly recently. It's not as if it belongs to his ancestors or anything. The question is, though, how much will you be asked to pay?"

Daisuke, who is with us, nods his head slowly as he stands by the workshop stove, one hand cupping his balls in a posture that men here frequently adopt.

"Well, Takeshi is a greedy fellow. Let's face it. And that means that he'll probably start out by asking for a million yen, even though there are only about fifty tsubo of land surrounding the house."

"I suppose he will," Inoshige concurs. "Although the land itself is worth hardly anything, is it? I mean, it isn't agricultural land or anything like that. As for the house, that's worth nothing at all."

"You might be able to get him down to half a million yen if you're lucky."

As usual with deals of this kind, each party has to have an intermediary. Inoshige volunteers to argue our case and arranges with Tatetarō again to act on behalf of Takeshi.

Inoshige comes up to the house to prepare our strategy.

"I've talked to Tatetarō, and it looks as if Takeshi will sell you the land. He's agreed in principle at least. The two of them will be here soon, so I'd better warn you about one thing. Don't mention a price first under any circumstances. Let Takeshi do that. Why? Because it is usually the first person to mention a sum of money who loses out in the haggling that follows. Keep a low profile. Smile nicely. And don't say things like 'Right! We're moving out!' if Takeshi at first refuses to sell you the house. I know you've only got three hundred and fifty thousand yen in cash, but I'll do my best."

Takeshi and Tatetarō arrive. It is dark, and the wild dogs bark at them as they come up the path to the house. The door is pulled open.

"*Gomen kudasai!*"

"*Ha-ai. Irasshai!*"

The two men come in and sit down at the *kotatsu* with the usual greetings. Kyōko serves tea. Inoshige and I had agreed to keep off the *sake*. Otherwise, nothing would get done.

Inoshige starts the proceedings.

"For some reason that none of us can understand much, Būchan here wants to live in this valley. I say 'can't understand' because it's difficult to work out why anybody should come from so far away and like such a remote place as this. Still, it's a bit of a compliment, I suppose, that he and Kyōko should feel the way they do, and I think we ought to return the compliment and try to help out the two of them and their children. And that's why we've got together this evening. To ask you, Takeshisan, to consider giving Būchan this house to live in, so that he can then say he has his own *furusato*, land of his birth."

"That's very well put, Inoshigesan," breaks in Tatetarō, nodding in agreement. "In fact, Takeshi here has already told me in private that he doesn't think it is right that you should go on paying rent. I'm glad to say that he's prepared to sell you the house."

I glance up with surprise, while Inoshige—clearly taken aback at the suddenness of this seeming turn for the better—nods and makes noises of agreement.

"He's prepared to sell you the house," continues Tatetarō, "but not the land. What do you say to that?"

Inoshige is obviously as astonished as I am. "Well? What do you say, Būchan?"

I think very hard, trying to formulate some kind of answer.

"Well," I begin, "I think it is extremely kind of Takeshisan to be so thoughtful. We've been pestering him for some time now to sell us this house, and we must have caused him and his family no end of trouble. I would be very glad, therefore, to accept this offer of the house. But there is one very small problem. Takeshi and I, we know each other really rather well after all these months. Any agreement that we made, we could be sure we would keep. If Takeshi sold me the house but kept the land for himself, I'd know that he was a man of his word. He'd keep his promise and not suddenly demand that I return him the house once I'd rebuilt it or something. No. That sort of problem would never occur between us."

I pause to sip my tea. Inoshige, Tatetarō, and Takeshi are all staring at me with some attention. It's too late now, I think, and plunge ahead.

"Nor would a problem like this occur with my elder boy, Alyosha, and Takeshi's son, Reisuke. Indeed, Alyosha has always been in Reisuke's debt. They've been out fishing together and camping together, and I'm sure Alyosha will continue to learn from Reisuke all his life. But supposing my grandson or great-grandson grows up and doesn't know about the agreement made between Takeshi and myself. Something might go wrong. There might be some silly sort of argument between him and your grandson, or great-grandson, Takeshisan. Then what would happen about the house? After all, it's just possible that my descendants would be thrown out. Obviously, such a thing is not likely to happen. But there is a chance. And for the sake of my descendants, I feel that I ought to give them the security of the land as well as the house. And that's why I ask you, Takeshisan, to sell us not just the house, but the land surrounding the house as well."

It is later agreed that this was a masterly speech. I had excelled myself. Tatetarō doesn't know what to do. First he sucks his breath in through his teeth. Next he hems and haws, looking first at Inoshige and then at Takeshi, who is staring down at the top of the *kotatsu* tabletop where we are seated. Then Tatetarō begins to chuckle.

"Well, I never could have believed it. Eh, Inoshige? Eh, Takeshi? Here we are sitting with a foreigner, an outsider, who has already started thinking like one of us. Būchan isn't interested in his own situation, but in posterity. He's thinking of the future of his family. That's really something, isn't it?" Turning to his cousin, he adds, "Takeshi! You have no choice but to sell Būchan the house and the land that it stands on. What do you say?"

Takeshi doesn't actually say anything. He sort of grunts and half-mumbles his assent. At least, what he mumbles is taken for assent because Tatetarō, now very clearly on our side rather than his cousin's, next tells Takeshi to name his price.

"Yes, that's what I ought to do. Name a price. The trouble is I've no idea how much the house is worth. Especially now that it's together with the land under it."

Sensing his cousin's hesitancy, Tatetarō neatly switches the conversation.

"Here's a nice story I heard the other day when I was down at the Agricultural Coop's main office in town. You know that stretch of mountain up above Takao? The bit they've decided to convert into pasture land? Well rumor has it that when Haruzō was younger than he is now . . ."

The negotiations are clearly going to take some time. Kyōko refills our cups with fresh tea. Tatetarō finishes his story. Inoshige makes some comment. Takeshi gives one of his silent laughs, and there is a pause.

"Well, Takeshi," Tatetarō inquires, "what do you think?"

Takeshi clears his throat and begins to speak in that strange, mumbling way of his. "Well, this house is useful to me, you know. I mean, the women come here in the spring to have tea on the veranda upstairs. I hire them, you know, from here and there to come along to the orchards. Six or seven of them. Reiko comes— that's Higuchi Daisuke's wife. And Moriyuki's wife. And they put little brown bags on each of the pears on the trees. It stops the birds. They eat the fruit when it's ripe, you know."

"Yes. There's a lot of hard work that has to be done, isn't there?" Inoshige says, encouraging Takeshi to go on. But Tatetarō interrupts.

"I suppose you do that sort of thing in England, too?" he says. "Covering apples and pears and things with paper bags?"

And off we go on another circular tour of conversational niceties. This is beginning to resemble a children's game. Still, we finally get back to the price of the land.

"Well, I thought I'd pull the whole place down," says Takeshi. "I mean, it's pretty shabby upstairs, and the walls are crumbling away in places. It doesn't look right. And it must annoy old Aso. And anyway Būchan says there are mice running all around the place."

"Ooh, mice!" exclaims Tatetarō. "You ought to borrow one of Inoshige's cats. That'd soon get rid of them all right. What sort of cat have you got, Inoshigesan?"

"A Siamese, I think it is."

"A Siamese cat. Some people go on special tours to Bangkok just so they can lay their hands on a nice little Siamese kitten."

Everybody laughs.

"They're supposed to be really hot and passionate. Talking of which, did you know that this house burned down once in a fire?" Tatetarō is clearly determined that Takeshi be given time to think about a suitable price for his land. "This part where we're sitting now, this is more than forty years old. But the bit upstairs is newer. That's only fifteen—no, sixteen years old. It burned down the year my elder daughter was born."

"Is it as long ago as that? How time flies!" exclaims Inoshige. "We never did learn how that fire started."

"No, we didn't. Of course, the whole place was originally a storehouse. It was part of the big residence owned by the landlord, Katō. The big house has gone now, of course. It used to stand just above this house, on the corner of what is now the pear orchard."

"That was before you converted all those rice fields to orchards, wasn't it, Takeshisan?"

Tatetarō is determined to get to the end of this story and will not be sidetracked.

"It was a pretty impressive place. Not that it was a main house [*honke*], or anything. Actually, Katō came from an even wealthier family of the same name who lived just above the school. These two, together with Kajiwara Buntarō and Tatetarō, Noda Shōsuke, and one other family in Takao, formed a group of six landlords. They all lived in fine residences, and that is why this part of the valley has been called *Yashiki mura*, the village of residences."

"Not many of them around now, though, are there?"

"No. The Katōs both upped and went. It's a funny thing about houses. Here is Būchan living here, and he's come all the way from a famous university. And the last person to live here, Katō Tamaki— no, not the man who was drunk at the funeral—a different Tamaki. Anyway, his son was so clever they say he went to Tokyo University. So this house has the distinction of having had two university students living in it."

With some manipulation of the conversation on my part, we get back to negotiating the price. Suddenly Takeshi asks, "How much are you going to pay me?"

I remember Inoshige's warning and decline to answer. "It's your house, Takeshisan. I think you should name a price for it."

"Well I've spent a lot of time building up the grass slopes below the house. I've put in lots of rocks, too, to make a wall. It took me and a neighbor two days to do that. And then there's the problem with your bath. I had to put a new one in recently because it kept leaking, even though your name is Moeran."

Takeshi drops his jaw and lets out his strange laugh. The rest of us laugh politely with him. Tatetarō even makes out as if he has never heard this joke before.

"The bath doesn't leak because it's Moeran who uses it. That's a good one."

We all laugh again. Takeshi is perhaps encouraged by this, for he finally gets to the point.

"Well, this is the way I see things. I've put in a lot of money and a lot of time and labor on this house. And if I sell it now, I'm going to lose a lot of rent. And rent comes to about a hundred and fifty thousand yen a year. And I figure that five or six years' worth of rent, plus the labor, would be a fair price to pay for this house." He pauses as he scratches his ear and gives me a quick, piercing look. "Say, one million yen. That's what I'll sell it to you for. One million yen."

There is silence, each of us nodding his head the way the Japanese do when they do not necessarily agree with what has been said but wish to maintain the appearance of at least not disagreeing. I try to do some mental arithmetic. One million yen, divided by the area of the land—say, 50 tsubo. That comes to 20,000 yen a tsubo, which is far too much. Good paddy land costs only 10,000 yen a tsubo in this valley. As for this land, it is more or less good for nothing. And we have already agreed that the house itself is worth nothing.

Still, I have time to marvel at Daisuke's prediction. He had said that Takeshi would start off at a million yen, and so he has. If this were a television quiz show, Daisuke would have won a trip to Hawaii.

Inoshige begins to talk. "Well, Takeshisan, that's a very interesting way of looking at it. I must say, I hadn't thought of working things out that way. But Būchan here has already paid a year's rent. What I suggest is that he buy the land for the cost of three more years' rent."

I'm tempted to butt in and say that there is no way I will continue paying rent, but I remember Inoshige's warning and keep quiet. Kyōko has at some point been quietly signaled by Inoshige to serve *sake*, and I grip my cup tightly in desperation. Inoshige is already offering a hundred thousand over our limit, and negotiations have hardly begun. At this rate, the bargaining will end up around the six- or seven-hundred-thousand mark, and that is twice as much as we can afford to pay.

To my surprise, however, Tatetarō nods his head, thinks for a moment, and says, "I think Inoshige's proposal is very good. Takeshisan, you should accept their offer."

Takeshi really has little alternative but to do as he is told. After all, his own intermediary has agreed to Inoshige's terms. So Tatetarō quickly tells Inoshige to write the whole thing down so nobody will go back on his word.

So we have bought our house and land for a little less than $2,000. And I even manage to talk Takeshi into letting us have a piece of the adjoining land as well. He agrees to let us pay him in two installments, which means that we will have until next April to find the remaining 100,000 yen. It is all too good to be true.

Takeshi is looking less and less happy with each new agreement. "What about the two plum trees on the land I've given you?" he asks.

"Write it down in the contract," Inoshige quickly tells Tatetarō. "Fruit from the trees on Būchan's land should be shared between both parties."

"Does that include the gingko tree?" asks Takeshi. He is referring to a tree that he had planted less than two years ago.

"Yes, yes. I'll write that down, too," Tatetarō answers impatiently. But there is no room on the sheet of paper, and it seems silly to draw up a new sheet, just for this, so we end up getting all the gingko nuts too.

In due course, after we have put away several bottles of *sake*, the others leave. They will come back to look at the house during the day sometime, so that they can fix the boundaries precisely. No, there is no need to tell the Town Council about the deal. It would be too much of a hassle. There isn't enough land to be taxed or anything. I can give Takeshi a couple of bottles of *sake* or something every year to make up for the few hundred yen that he might be charged by the tax collector for his orchards.

And so they go out into the night, leaving Kyōko and me hugging each other with joy and marveling at the way the country farmer is determined to lose his hold on nothing. Fancy trying to anticipate a gingko-nut harvest when the tree has only just been planted. The really funny thing is that Takeshi has no idea whether it is a male or female tree. He just wanted to be sure. Just in case.

44 That last paragraph about a farmer's not "losing out" needs to be emphasized. Inoshige tells me that he met Takeshi down at the Valley Coordination Office the evening after we had made our deal. "He was muttering something about a renegotiation, so I quickly escaped to where Tatetarō was drinking. He told me it was out of the question. Anyway, pay him your first installment as soon as possible. There's a rule here in the valley that if a land deal falls through, the seller has to pay back twice the sum received before any renegotiation takes place."

So we go down to the bank and withdraw the last of our savings. Then we put the money in an envelope and take it to Takeshi's house. As luck would have it, it is lunchtime when we arrive, and Takeshi is sitting by the back door, taking off his boots. Entering the earthen floored area, we thank him for his kindness the other evening. Hanako comes out when she hears our voices, and we apologize for keeping Takeshi up so late over such a selfish matter.

"Not at all, not at all. I'm glad things went well," she smiles.

We produce our envelope full of money and hand it to Takeshi. Not too readily or happily, he accepts it. We leave before he changes his mind.

But the next day Takeshi comes up to the house and tries to return us our money. We politely refuse it, saying that if he isn't satisfied, he ought to give the money back to us in front of Inoshige and Tatetarō. After all, they are the ones who witnessed the deal.

I telephone Inoshige, who tells me not to worry and to leave things up to him. He must have phoned Tatetarō, and Tatetarō must have talked directly to Takeshi, because the following morning Takeshi comes up to the house again. This time he has a receipt for the money and flashes us something more like his usual toothy smile.

It is a fine day but cold, and Takeshi appears in no hurry to start work in the orchards. Do we want that old stone grinder below the veranda upstairs? No, I say. That is Takeshi's, to do with as he pleases. All we have bought is the house and land; not the contents of the house.

"What about that stone mortar? You know? The one you use for pounding rice in your kitchen."

Takeshi remembers everything when it comes to property. Yet we know that he doesn't really want stone grinders or mortars, because he has plenty of both in his own home. This much he has admitted. He neither wants nor needs such things for himself. All he wants to do is make sure that nobody else can make use of them. Then we discuss the land. Takeshi points out that we agreed only on the land around the house, and not on an irregular triangular section leading down the path to the road at the side of the house. I am confused. This is the piece of land on which the famous gingko tree and one of the plum trees are growing. It was for this piece of land that I had fought so hard a few nights previously. I reassure Takeshi that we will give him the fruit from the plum tree. It is clear that that is all he wants. Learn the tactics of the Japanese bazaar, young man, and keep your wits about you at all times!

45   Yesterday we had the first snow of the year. The boys raid Takeshi's store for the tough plastic bags in which his fertilizer comes. Then, with their classmates, they tread down the snow along the slope of Buntarō's orchard and build themselves a sled run. One by one, they queue up at the top, sitting themselves down on the slippery bags, grasping one end between their fingers, and, paddling their way with their feet, begin to zoom down the hillside. So much more effective than the old wooden sleds. Except that nowadays, of course, the children frequently tack split bicycle tires onto the runners. In this way, sleds can still match the plastic bags— especially when the snow is not too deep, as now.

Today there is sun. Just a little, but enough for beggars like ourselves to hang out the washing.

46   The end of the year.

We have eaten seaweed, because now is the time to enjoy ourselves. We have eaten black beans, so that we will work next year until we are black with dirt and sweat. We have eaten "passover" noodles (*toshikoshi*), which Kyōko went to make at Misako's this morning, because they are long and thin, and we are supposed to live long and "thinly" (in other words, not extravagantly). These are indeed country foods.

I have had my plum wine and shoveled away hunks of ice to clear the road. I have gazed at the stars under which the road is now freezing. I have listened to the haunting sounds of Kyōko's koto echoing in the night. How good it is, indeed, to have as friends

music and the sights of nature. Mountains and fields, all smothered in snow—nothing remains.
Yukutoshi . . . Ah, the end of a year . . .

47 . . . And *kurutoshi*, the coming year.
The cold *omiki* is the best *sake* of the year. Who can doubt that? We walk through the night, guided by the snow and the sound of the temple bells. Inekari's deep booms; Takao's slightly tinny clang. At the Tenmangū shrine above the school, we throw in our coins, clap our hands, and bow our heads. Michiya offers us cold rice wine, and we exchange New Year greetings.

"*Akemashite, omedetō gozaimasu . . . Kotoshi mo yoroshiku onegai itashimasu.*"

Michiya leads us over to where our fellow villagers are standing around a fire blazing in the yard of the shrine. Katsuhisa is warming *sake* in four-foot lengths of green bamboo. These are propped up against the fire and burned brown by the flames. The *sake* that is poured for us into freshly cut bamboo cups is permeated with the scent and the taste of bamboo. There is no better way to drink *sake*.

The year begins then, warm and friendly. This is our valley . . .

48 At 11:00 A.M. the New Year's celebrating begins in earnest. All the children in Yashiki village have been asked to attend a prize-giving ceremony for the calligraphy that they did at school at the end of the term. Michiya, who teaches calligraphy in his spare time and whose work has won prizes in prefectural competitions, does the judging, and the son of the temple priest is deemed to be the right person to give out certificates and prizes of exercise books. The children stand shivering in the cold, while the adults assemble slowly and exchange greetings once more in the yard of the Tenmangū shrine. The early arrivals have resurrected the embers of last night's fire, and there is one place at least where we can warm ourselves. Once again the men warm *sake* in the bamboo lengths; once again we drink from bamboo cups. Ash flies in the wind, alighting on people's hair. For once, men have discarded their caps and walk around bare-headed under the lowering sky.

By half past eleven the prize-giving ceremony is over and people start preparing for the big event—the *uso* lottery. *Uso* is the name given to wooden birds that are carved from soft wood at the end of the year by all the men living in Yashiki village who are members of the Tenmangū shrine. The birds are roughly painted red and sky-blue and have a number brushed on their bases. These range from one to 99 and are prefixed by one of the five syllabary letters—*i*, *ro*, *ha*, *ni*, or *ho*. Right at the end of the year, when the residents of Ōkubo met to pay their dues, we had been encouraged to purchase lottery tickets at 350 yen apiece. Most households bought half a dozen or more tickets—a lot of money to spend in some cases, but it is here that social values take over from purely monetary ones. By supporting the lottery, people support the Tenmangū shrine's ac-tivities. Just as individual interests give way to those of the house-hold, so household interests give way to those of the community and village as a whole.

"Have you changed your tickets?" Shichirō asks. "You should give them to Tōsuke there, and he'll give you an *uso* for each ticket."

The lottery is a novel one. The winning numbers are determined by two people firing arrows alternatively at a revolving target, di-vided and numbered in ten sections. This year Katsuhisa's eldest daughter, Naomi, and Inoshige's youngest, Rumiko, have been asked to act as archers. They both wear brightly colored kimonos for the event. Michiya, Takayuki, and Umao are in charge, and to-gether they cordon off the target with rope, using firewood as poles. The children, who have swarmed around the table to exam-ine Inoshige's bow and arrows, are ushered back out of danger. Michiya and Umao make sure that the table is set firmly in the ground. Then they lay the bow flat on the table and each holds one end firmly, so that the arrow points directly at the target a few feet away. This way neither of the two girls will be able to miss the target or accidentally hit bystanders.

Finally all is ready. There are five kinds of prizes awarded: special, first, second, third, and fourth. We start with the lowest category and work upward. Inoshige calls for silence.

"Good morning, everybody. The lottery is about to begin, and so I hope you have all exchanged your tickets for the birds. I have been asked to spin the target while the two young ladies here shoot their arrows in turn. If everybody is ready, we'll begin."

He spins the target, and Rumiko fires her first arrow. Inoshige stops the target and withdraws the arrow.

"Zero!" he calls and spins the target once more. Naomi shoots. "Seven!" We check the numbers on our half-dozen birds. "Anybody with the number zero-seven on the bottom of their bird is entitled to a fourth prize. Regardless of the *i*, *ro*, *ha* letters," Inoshige explains in a loud voice. "We will do the same nineteen more times."

The girls start firing arrows once more. 72 . . . 31 . . . 16 . . . and so on, until 20 numbers have been selected. One hundred people in all have won fourth prize of a bamboo rake.

We then move on to the third prize. "This time, only five numbers will be selected. Once again the letters don't count." Rumiko aims and lets go her arrow, followed by Naomi. 85 . . . 36 . . . 72 —

"Stop! Seventy-two doesn't count. It's already come up as fourth prize. No number can count twice. Naomichan, fire a second arrow!"

This she does. The arrow strikes the zone for seven: 77 is all right. And so it goes on. Twenty-five people win plastic bowls.

For the second prize, only three numbers need to be selected. One of them is 97, which has already come up as third prize. Rumiko reshoots, and 96 is the magic number for five people, each of whom receives an aluminum bucket.

Only one number counts for first prize, and there is an air of tension now. 45. Five people win mattocks.

Finally we move to the special prize. It is here that the *i-ro-ha* letters become significant, for there is only one prize of 10,000 yen. The first arrow marks the group—*i*. The second selects the first digit—9. The third establishes the last digit—7. 97 has reared its head again.

"Not ninety-seven again!" exclaims Munetoshi in some disgust as he shows me his bird with *i*97 painted on it. "I could have won ten thousand yen, but all I got was a plastic bowl. Oh, well, it can't be helped, can it?"

But if Munetoshi is airing his disappointment, others become tense with expectation once more. Katsuhisa's son, Norihisa, can hardly contain himself. He has *i*90.

"Come on, Naomi! Get a zero. Please!"

Naomi takes aim. Inoshige spins the target. She lets the arrow fly. There is a dull thud as the arrow hits the target. Inoshige slows it down and calls out, "Nine! *i*-ninety-nine is the winner!"

People are checking their birds when Jirō, the mushroom grower, raises his arms in delight.

"I've won! I've won!"

One or two of his neighbors look eagerly at his bird.

"No, you haven't," Munetoshi tells him sternly. "You're holding your bird upside down. That's sixty-six, not ninety-nine. The *i* should come before the number. Not after it."

"Is that so?" Jirō doesn't look terribly disappointed. "I haven't won. I haven't won!" he shouts out with a laugh, and everybody joins in his laughter. His mistake was a simple one, since the *i* syllabary letter looks similar whichever way you look at it.

As for the winner, nobody knows who it is. He or she will have to be found at a later date.

49 The Oni valley's New Year "opening ceremony" begins with what is known as a *seigen* marathon, time race. People of both sexes and of all ages are invited to estimate the time they think it will take them to walk, trot, run, or canter from the Agricultural Coop down to the South Oni Primary School and back, a distance of about a mile and a half. Enthusiastic people can go down to Takeshi's waterwheel and back—two miles in all. Anyway, speed is not the criterion by which this event is judged.

"Let's face it, Būchan," says Munetoshi, who has turned up in a T-shirt and shorts. "Nobody is in training at this time of the year. We've been eating too much to run around very much. No. The idea is to get people participating. So we thought a race where you had to estimate how long it would take you to run a certain distance would be a good idea." He trots off, raising his knees high toward his chest, just to show that if others are not in training, he at least is.

Still, Munetoshi has a valid point. The weather has been awful, and very few of us have been able to take any exercise since the end of the year. But now, finally, the snow has melted, and the road is clear. A motley group of schoolchildren, young boys, and middle-aged men and women gather in the great courtyard between the

Coop and the Pear Sorting Station. But they are only there to watch. The turnout of racers is slow, and by midday—the proclaimed deadline for the race—there are hardly enough people to make it all worthwhile.

But it seems that latecomers are wise to the experience of past years, and one after another, men roll up in their vans, wearing track suits and caps, which they doff to one another as they set about their usual greetings. Local officials come in their suits and brown leather shoes: the man in charge of the Valley Coordination Office; Noda Shōsuke; Sakakura Haruzō; Hageyama, the headmaster of the North Oni Primary School; the Pear Growers Cooperative chief; and the chairman of the Oni Valley Youth Association (whose members, incidentally, are already out with stopwatches timing preliminary runs).

Eventually Haruzō calls everybody to order over a microphone and loudspeaker—the inevitable gadgetry that is as much a part of life here as in the city. The opening ceremony begins, and Noda Shōsuke steps forward. The new year is greeted, the weather praised, our gathering when so busy duly thanked. The purpose of the *seigen* marathon is explained by the vice-chairman of the Oni Valley Physical Training Association. Haruzō stands up in front of the neatly ordered lines of participants and says more or less the same thing. The Valley Coordination Office chief explains the rules of the race. And then it is time for the Youth Association's chairman to instruct us all in how to do loosening-up exercises.

"Right!" calls Haruzō. "Numbers one to twenty-three line up for the one-and-a-half-mile course. One, two, three, four—where's four?"

"Here I am!" It is Munetoshi, now wearing a white headband to add to his athletic look.

"In line then. Five, six, seven, eight. Good. Nine—where's nine!" Haruzō calls again through his microphone.

"Gone to have a pee," comes a voice from the crowd.

Eventually, all are accounted for and lined up across the road below the Coop. A policeman gets on his motor scooter and drives off to the halfway mark.

"That's not a policeman. Just an imitation one. You can always tell by the boots," Takayuki informs me.

Noda Shōsuke, as headman of Yashiki village, has the honor of firing the starting gun. One member of the Youth Association, Daisuke's son, Fujio (now happily recovered from his fall), is given responsibility for timing the race; another member, Mikiko—Takeshi's youngest daughter, who works down at the town police headquarters—has the task of recording the times.

"*Yo-oi . . . Don!*" Shōsuke gives the traditional "on your mark, get set, go!" and pulls the trigger. The gun goes off with a loud bang, and everyone who is not in this race starts clapping, as the "runners" start off down the road at their various speeds.

The participants at this distance are mainly primary-school children, accompanied by fathers or mothers who frantically count out the seconds that they feel are ticking by. As we go down the valley road, we are occasionally met with bursts of applause from residents of houses lining our course—old grannies with children strapped to their backs and granddads resting on their sticks. The last of us are met well before the halfway mark by keener boys in a hurry to finish. The imitation policeman is standing at the turning point and hands each participant a card as proof that he or she arrived.

As we approach the finish line, some people suddenly break into a sprint, convinced that they are behind their stated time. Others slow down to a walk for precisely the opposite reason. As we cross the finish line, our numbers are called out and our times recorded by Mikiko, and then fingers get busy with the abacus.

The second group of runners is started—this time by Haruzō, who stands at attention and pulls the trigger. The pistol fails to go off the first time, but eventually the group is away. More desultory clapping, while those who have completed their race gather to check their times. It seems that most were in better training than they had anticipated, and there is much face-pulling as they hear how well, or badly, they have done. The men light cigarettes to while away the time.

Soon, the first runners of the second group come back, but one toddler had had a tantrum until his mother agreed to let him participate, and now she is breathlessly carrying him on her back, a good five minutes behind everyone else. Everyone, that is, except for Kyōko who, having been prevailed upon to take part, has made ample allowance for her long skirt and boots. As the two of them come unhurriedly up the long curve of the valley road, Kyōko suddenly disappears from view.

"I was bursting to go to the bathroom," she explains later, having been last but one across the finish line. "So I dropped into the Coordination Office. My call of nature went on twenty-nine seconds too long!"

Mother and child also reach the end of their walk—the mother, embarrassed at keeping everyone waiting, breaks into a trot for the last 50 yards and comes in nine seconds too soon as a result.

Finally the "long-distance" runners are started. And run they do. The smart ones, like Munetoshi, are wearing T-shirts and shorts, headbands, even white working gloves, and they do a few jumping-jacks to impress the opposition, before sprinting off down the road. They come back a good deal faster than the mile-and-a-half groups, and the applause this time is sincere. Red faces, first sweat of the year, as the young men race home with impressive times that are also impressively close to their official estimates. The practice beforehand was obviously worthwhile, because Munetoshi comes in third, five seconds too slow. A young boy who lives near Takeshi is second, having reached the finish line four seconds too fast. The winner is the recently married Eisuke, who is seventh home but only one second off his estimate.

"His bride's been timing him when they do their nightly gymnastics," Buntarō says knowingly. "That's one sport we older men do faster than the young. You can count on that!"

Results in the shorter race are not so good. The winner is four seconds too slow; second place ten seconds too slow; and third something like a minute too fast. The closing ceremony takes place. Shōsuke gives his "Blessed by the weather" speech yet again. More speeches arc given—the same phrases uttered in a different order—and then prize certificates are awarded. These have been hastily penned by the Coordination Office chief and are handed out in a somewhat perfunctory manner by Haruzō.

Finally we are dismissed from our ranks, and it is time to start drinking.

50   From far away in the morning silence comes the sound of a flute. It is Maya piping his way home from school. Kuro and Roku, the two dogs, immediately get up from where they have been lying by the front door and go to meet him. I notice that one plum flower has blossomed on the tree beside the house.

All of a sudden, the sun comes out on the mountain path.

51 Seijin no hi, the coming-of-age day. As Masaki's twins come to greet us in their ornate kimonos, we breathe in not the scent of perfume, but the pungent smell of mothballs.

52 The past three days I have spent driving to and fro in Katsuhisa's battered pickup truck, between the house and the mountains above Amagase. I have loaded it with rocks dragged from the riverbed, and these I then used to make a stone wall below the bathroom. It was a jigsaw puzzle, trying to fit together uneven, jagged shapes, and I now appreciate how well constructed are the stepped rice paddies in the Oni valley—marvels of patience and strength.

I now realize that I have built a European wall, selecting shapes that were square or rectangular, laying them end to end in overlapping layers like bricks. Yet here the walls are made with round or rhomboid-shaped stones, which are dropped into one another in a manner totally different from my brick-laying style. No doubt one day in the distant future, some archaeologist will try to puzzle out why one short wall in the Oni valley is so different in its construction from all the rest.

I realize, too, how well adapted the Japanese physique is to certain forms of labor. It is so much easier to push a heavily loaded wheelbarrow if you have short legs. As for myself, I ease myself into the warmth of our iron bathtub and lie there for an hour until the pain in my back eases.

53 These days it is the widening of the road through Yashiki village and the creation of a "green slow-driving safety zone" above Inekari that seem to be uppermost in people's minds.

Last weekend there was a parents-children marathon race. First of all we had lunch, which was prepared by each of the five hamlets making up the village. Last year the whole of Inekari and Ōkubo turned up at Katsuhisa's house to help get food ready, but the place was so crowded that a lot of people ended up talking in the background and did little by way of food preparation. This year, for the sake of efficiency, Misako took it upon herself to split up the work among those women who had children at school. She, Hideko, and Kyōko baked 300 (!) rolls. Munetoshi's wife and a few other working mothers prepared rice-balls before they left for work in the morning. Other hamlets were assigned different foods—Hirao had to prepare some fried chicken wings, Amagase boiled vegetables, and Takao various salads. Then all of the village's PTA members ate in one room together—unlike the families of Kago village at the top of the valley, each of whom saw to their own needs.

"They say the hamlets up there are too isolated for people to get together and prepare things the way we do," explained Munetoshi. "At least, that is their excuse. If you ask me, they just can't be bothered."

After the race there was the usual celebrating by the men. Everyone was called upon to contribute 500 yen toward drinking expenses, regardless of whether he was able to attend or not. Those who worked in town were detailed to bring back the usual delicacies to go with the *sake*—raw fish, raw horse meat, and more pieces of fried chicken dipped in soya sauce.

But before the drinking began—and the women were there, of course, to warm the *sake* and serve it—there was a discussion. The PTA chairman, Iguma Katsunori, got up and said that the PTA was going to support a plan to widen the road in front of the school. He presumed that nobody had any objections. Put that way, nobody seemed prepared to say very much. Perhaps nobody cared. But then Michiya put up his hand and suggested that the chairman should not make any final decisions until everyone had had a chance to discuss what was, in his humble opinion, an important matter.

"That's all well and good," retorted one of Iguma's relatives in a loud voice, "but what we have to realize is that it is very rare for the Town Council to offer us people of the Oni valley anything at all. Yet, here they are, suggesting that they can pay for a new road. What I think is that we should not refuse this offer of free money. After all, it's going to be one of the few occasions when people are going to be allowed to spend our tax contributions on something that is for our own good. The chance is too good to overlook and"—

"But is building a road good for us all?" Katsuhisa interrupted.

Nobody said much in answer to that gentle question—least of all Hageyama and his colleagues from the school, all of whom sat silently throughout the discussion. The matter was left undecided when somebody pointed out that the *sake* was getting cold. The drinking began.

The subject comes up again today when I go to mail some letters at the local post office. Michiya corners me, obviously bent on passing a little bit more than the mere time of the day.

"Let's face it," he begins after the usual pleasantries, "the Town Council somewhere in that building it occupies probably has a plan drawn up to build a two-lane highway all the way from Fujioka to Kamayama. Anything to bring in the tourists. But at the moment, anyway, the plan is virtually impossible to put into effect. Certainly not in its entirety. But the authorities have to start the ball rolling somewhere, and so they air the idea of a green safety zone, which they know is bound to please someone like Iguma Katsunori. If they manage to get that through, then they'll begin to work at widening other sections of the road up and down the valley."

Michiya runs his hand through his thick crop of hair before continuing. "What we have to do here is decide whether we really need the sort of road being planned for us. As I see it, the problem is twofold. In the first place, there is the matter of what people say, as opposed to what they mean. Second, there is the matter of land.

"To take the first problem first. You can safely assume that what people in the valley say is not particularly trustworthy. Everyone is playing a game. What they say in public and what they say and do in private are two different things entirely. We know that all too well. Remember, we've been born and brought up here. We've been to school together, or with one another's brothers and sisters, and there's not very much we don't know about people's backgrounds, their families and motives. We can tell the difference between *tate-mae* [the public 'front story'] and *honshiki* [the 'real thing' that comes from the heart]. It's very difficult for someone like you,

Būchan, who has come in from the outside to be able to discern the truth. So don't jump to too many conclusions too quickly.

"In this way, perhaps, farming villages are rather different from fishing villages. At least, that's what I sometimes think, although you, of course, are the expert on things like that. People living in fishing villages say exactly what they think, and if their opinion is accepted by the rest of the community, then that's the end of the matter. If everybody disagrees, well then that's the end of the matter, as well. Things are more open and shut with fishermen.

"What I'm getting at is tied up with my second problem. That of land. My own feeling is that people in fishing villages are able—or have learned—to be so frank with one another because they don't live off the land. Instead, they work in small boats, far out at sea where their lives are often at stake. They can't afford to mess about with words in a crisis. They have to be direct in their dealings with one another in order to survive in heavy seas.

"But that's hardly the case with people like us who live in farming communities. For centuries we've clung to the land. We've worked it to make a living. We've struggled to protect it against the ravages of nature and man. What's worse, we've had this wretched system of land tenure that has forced the poor farmer to sweat and toil away for year after year, only to see almost the whole of his harvest go to some rich landlord or other. As I see it, these things account for two of our characteristics. First, we're delighted to see somebody else lose a piece of his land; and second, we're real stickers. Nothing will make us give an inch of the land that we do own. Mark you, you didn't do so badly yourself when it came to bargaining with Takeshi, but there are always exceptions to prove the rule," he grins.

"Still, there comes a time when somebody has to give an inch. Concerted pressure can do the trick. We may not want the road widened, but the thought of someone losing a bit of land as a result—especially if that someone happens to be a once-rich landlord like Katsuhisa—is enough to get us all urging him to yield to the Town Council's plan. It's a bit like the story of the spear and the shield. You know, the paradox that cannot be answered. What happens when the strongest spear in the world strikes the strongest shield? When the spear that smashes all shields strikes against the shield that resists all spears? Does the desire to see someone else lose his land come out victorious? Or will that desire be worn away by the tenacity of the landowner?"

Michiya leans back in his chair, clasping his hands behind his head, his eyes twinkling. Then he adds gratuitously, "Actually, the problem of land also affects labor relations. You'll find that a completely different attitude is taken toward campaigns for wage increases by those unions whose members still own or farm some land. Those unions that are totally free of rural influences are really able to band together and force through their demands. But those that are not always end up with a certain amount of individualistic or factional maneuvering. That's because the members of those unions figure that if the worst comes to the worst, they can always go back to making a living off the land.

"Of course, management takes advantage of these farmer-mentality unions. Precisely because their members are not totally dedicated to the group image, the managing director of a company can approach each worker individually, take him aside, and say, 'Look! Don't tell anyone else, but I've decided to give you a little bit extra in the way of wages. You've served me well and worked hard. Okay?' But then the managing director says the same thing to each of his workers, offering them a bit more than they have, but not as much as the unions want. None of them can then stand up in public and demand a proper increase in wages, because they are afraid to admit what they believe is true—that each is earning a little bit more than his mates. There's Japanese business for you!"

54   Today is the first Day of the Horse of the year and also Fox's Day (*o-inari-san*). Takeshi places some festival red rice in front of the fox-deity shrine at the end of his pear orchard next to the driveway to our house. In the evening the hamlet meets to celebrate its first Kōshinsama gathering, and again conversation centers on the widening of the valley road. Masaki starts things rolling.

"Well, I'm the hamlet chief this year, and in my opinion it would be bad for everyone in Ōkubo if all of us don't get together properly before Yashiki's annual general meeting in two weeks' time. Something has to be done about the road. We've got to come to some decision or other this month because otherwise we'll be too late for the town budget, and we'll miss the boat this fiscal year. That's why I think all of us households in Ōkubo should get together and come to a group decision before the village meeting."

Masaki's point is taken. The conversation is immediately monopolized by two or three men, who begin talking all at once to their immediate neighbors. I find myself the target of Munetoshi's thoughts about what would be best for one and all.

"It's all very well widening the road, but look what is going to happen to the kindergarten," he says. "At least half the playground there would be lost if the road were straightened out past the school. And that would mean that the preschool children, like my Shinchan and Sachiko, won't be able to have their sports day any longer. Not unless they use the primary school's grounds."

Munetoshi's last sentence has been heard by others.

"That would be tricky, Munechan. The Town Council would never buy that. What if an accident occurred? Who would take responsibility then?" Buntarō asks.

"Perhaps the primary school and the kindergarten could merge then?" Masaki suggests, without much thought about the bureaucracy involved.

"Impossible!" retorts Tōsuke. "It would never work out. Too many problems would have to be solved."

"Anyway," puts in Katsuhisa, "if that happened, I'd have given away my land for nothing." He reminds them of who had permitted the kindergarten to be built in the first place.

Tōsuke turns the conversation to the paddy fields that would be lost if the road is straightened out.

"Let's face it, a couple of people stand to lose a lot of land, and that is not necessarily a good thing at all. As Katchan says, he has already given up some land for us all, and he provided us with the Village Hall. It would be unfair of us to ask him to give away more land. On the other hand," he continues as everybody nods, "if the road were widened and straightened out, the school would gain quite a bit of land. It could then extend its playground. Of course, the fire station gets in the way a bit. But I'm chief fireman this year, and I might be able to arrange something."

This is a totally new idea that clearly nobody had thought about, and there is silence. But then Shichirō seems to echo everyone's feelings when he quietly says, "If the authorities want to widen the road, they should start from the bottom of the valley at Fujioka, not in the middle."

Later I meet Inoshige and tell him what was said.

"There is a man called Inoue living in the big house immediately below the Valley Coordination Office. I don't think you know him. But his father managed to do precisely what Shichirō was hinting at—widen the road from the bottom of the valley as far as his front door. And no farther. He was a town councilman and used all his power to get the road straightened out and put through where once there were only fields. You remember I told you how the old road used to wind all over the place. With the new road, people were persuaded to give up their best land right in the middle of the valley. If you ask me, old Haruzō up the road is trying to do the same thing. Let's face it, we all like to leave some memento behind us when we retire or die. Haruzō is aiming to become village headman when Noda Shōsuke stands for election to the Town Council. One thing he wants to remind people of is that it was he who managed to get the road widened from the Valley Coordination Office up to his front door at the top of Amagase here. That's the sort of mentality [*konjō*] people like Katsuhisa, Michiya, and I are up against."

55   Today is a national holiday, and Katsuhisa decides to work off the hangover he got from drinking in Amagase till four in the morning by taking me off into the mountains. We get into his rusty old truck, drive down the valley to Fujioka, and then take the old road up round the back of Mount Toyama. After a mile or two, the road takes a turn for the worse, and we start bumping our way up hill through the forests. We pass through a vast smoky dell, where workhorses are hauling down great cedar trunks, while men burn tree stumps and the debris left over from the felling of a whole plantation.

Farther up the road we come across two lumberyard trucks.

"Hello, that one belongs to Haruzō. I bet he's up to no good again," Katsuhisa grunts as he swerves to avoid a pothole. "Old Harusan is in collusion with someone, using that winch on his truck to haul up large rocks from the riverbed. He'll sell them to city people, who use them in their ornamental gardens, you know. And at what a price! More than one hundred thousand yen apiece,

I'm told. And here's Haruzō getting them all for free. It's illegal, of course, but in a deserted place like this, who's to catch him in the act?"

We jolt on, past jeeps parked at the side of the road by those doing their last day's hunting of the year.

"The season ends on the fifteenth of February. After that, nobody is allowed to shoot any wild boar again until the autumn."

The road winds on up and up, until we get to some frozen snow. Katsuhisa brings the truck to a halt.

"We'll need chains from here on," he says and, clambering out into the snow, slings the chains out from the back of the truck. In his accomplished hands, the job of putting on the chains takes no more than a couple of minutes, and soon we get going again.

After another quarter of an hour we pass a large wooden building set above the roadside. "That's the lodge belonging to the Forestry School where I used to teach," Katsuhisa informs me. "Many a weekend I've had to spend there with my students."

Soon after, the road comes to an end. We get out of the truck and start walking up through the cedar trees, across frozen snow to the mountain ridge and the firebreak that separates this valley from the Oni valley beyond.

We walk along the ridge. Far below us we can see Serabōzu, Katsuhisa's "haven," set on a plateau way above the valley. It is to Serabōzu that he climbs when he wants to escape the tirades of his mother or the grievances of his fellow villagers. I can just make out his little hut among the trees that he has planted there. And then, way down below the plateau, there is Michiya's house, with its steep thatched roof, and beyond that the hamlet of Hirao, with its stepped rice fields.

Katsuhisa is holding a sickle with which he snips away twigs that are in the way or adeptly slashes through a creeper that is twined around one of his trees. This is his mountain, and he is particularly proud of the fact that he has not planted any cedar here.

"Everyone has been planting cedar trees in this valley—ever since the prefectural authorities tried to encourage forestry as a local industry soon after the war. Everybody plants cedar because it grows so fast. Just thirty years and trees are full grown, ready to be cut down and sold for a fortune. At least that was what people thought at the time. But there's a glut of cedar now. Too many people grew them. Too many farmers out to make a quick profit as usual. It's the same with the pear orchards, you know."

As we walk on, he points things out with his sickle. "This is all maple, you know. The best time for us to come again would be autumn. We could bring up some *sake* and enjoy the view. And that down there is beech." He uses English words for the names of trees and plants, sometimes writing them down in the snow with the tip of his sickle when he is not sure of them.

"Here we have gingko trees. Very small ones. But they'll get bigger in due course. G-I-N-K-Y-O is how I saw it spelled in a book. Is that right? Shouldn't it be K-G-O? or is it G-K-O?"

Put like this, neither of us is very certain. Somehow, none of these ways of spelling looks right in the snow. We walk on and come to some yew trees. I tell him about the English longbow. Then I get onto the subject of Christmas trees and mistletoe.

"Kiss under it?" Katsuhisa looks pleasantly surprised. "Well, fancy that. The strange things people do with plants."

As we walk across the frozen snow, putting our feet down carefully so as not to break the crust and fall through some 10 or 12 inches, Katsuhisa touches—almost caresses—the trunk of each tree he passes. It is obvious that this mountain retreat of his is where he is most at ease. In spite of his wealth, he is not a political man, ready to use people to his own ends. Perhaps because of his wealth, he has been able to learn to enjoy nature, rather than struggle with it like most other people in the valley.

Suddenly he stops.

"You see here, where the bark has been torn off this tree trunk? That's a deer sharpening its antlers. Look! Here too. And here. And over there."

Later on he points to tracks in the snow. "A dog. Probably a hunter's. And here are a wild boar's prints. Made not long ago, by the look of it. The snow has been freshly turned."

Finally, we come to the crest of the highest mountain around, and here we crouch down to eat Misako's buns and drink tea from a flask. We can see the central massif over to our left toward the prefectural capital. Behind us is the sacred mountain with its cluster of shrines visited by pilgrims from all over Japan. Way below us are the pear orchards of Ōkubo, and beyond them, over the ridge, the broad sweep of the plain and the town.

"You see that village across there?" Katsuhisa points out a huddle of houses with his newly carved toothpick. "That's Miyo. The word means Three Tails, but it's written with the Chinese characters '1 *shaku* 8 *sun*'—about twenty inches—because that is supposed to be the total length of three rabbits' tails put together."

As he cautiously peels an apple with his sickle, Katsuhisa decides to discuss the matter of the road. "There's not really very much chance of anything being done this year. The two Gotōs on the kindergarten committee are in favor of a school zone, but I'm not, and neither is Katō Tamaki, that funny old man who runs the chicken farm at the bottom of our road. You know, the one who got drunk at Akihito's funeral. So the committee is split two-two. Not that you can ever be quite sure what Tamaki will do. He's such a contrary man. But I think that this time, for a change, we are on the same side.

"And then there's the problem of widening and straightening the road. All the parents of the kindergarten children are against losing part of the playground. The primary school on the other side of the road stands to gain extra space, but it would mean cutting down that nice row of old cherry trees, and with luck people will be against that. After all, we don't have that many cherry trees around here. Plum, yes, but not cherry."

He pauses to take a bite from his apple and then munches noisily as he continues.

"No. The real problem lies with the rice fields on the far side of the Village Hall. Two farmers are renting them from the Tenmangū shrine up the road from the school. Now that shrine—as you know— is kept by more than seventy households. That means all of them are going to have to get together to discuss whether it is or is not a good thing to give away land that ultimately belongs to the agricultural deities, just so a road can be built over it. Now, it so happens that Tamaki is in charge of shrine affairs this year, which means that everything should be all right. The fact that the shrine is registered as a charitable trust means that any business involving the registration or disposition of land or property has to be signed and sealed with a special stamp. And that all takes time. But time is precisely what Haruzō hasn't got. He's trying to rush things through before the end of this fiscal year and is probably hoping to get a nice big job for his own contracting firm into the bargain."

He throws away the core of his apple and smiles.

"So it looks as if we can survive for the moment. Actually, the Tenmangū was involved in the building of that road up the far mountainside behind Takao. Inekari Hiroshi and I resisted right to the very end, refusing to let the Town Council have the land for their experimental cow pasture. But finally we just had to give in. There was too much pressure from everyone else. Anyway, it was rather nice to watch some other hamlet having its environment destroyed while we lived on in peace. The foundations of every single house in the community must have been ruined by all the heavy trucks rolling by. Also by the dynamite they used to blast the road around the hillside.

"No. This time, we've really got to stick it out. I'm not going to let old Haruzō have my rice paddy, not for anything in the world. If he wants to widen the road, let him start right outside his own house at the top of Amagase and set a good example by giving away his garden and the south wing of his house. And then he can work downard until he gets to the school. If he does get that far, I might reconsider, but I'm not promising anything."

56   Michiya has more to say about widening the road.

"That road isn't something that is going to get the go-ahead in a hurry. Certainly not this February or March. What people don't realize—particularly those running the PTA—is that a number of different problems are involved. How much should the road be widened? Is a sidewalk necessary? Does the road have to be straightened as well? And so on and so forth. And, before we even get to that stage, there is the matter of land. Katsuhisa owns the rice paddy on one side of the kindergarten, Inekari Tetsurō the fields on the other side. Now, as far as Katsuhisa is concerned, the problem is not, Do I want to sell the land, or not? It is, Does a country valley need a wide road along which cars can speed as fast as they please? Thus, it is no use the PTA's coming along en masse and trying to get Katchan to sell them the few feet of land required.

"But with Tetsurō the problem is entirely different. Here we have a farming man's best rice paddy threatened. The one thing Tetsurō doesn't want is to lose that particular piece of land because it provides him with the bulk of his rice every year. Still, it is just possible that he will part with the land if everybody comes to ask him to do so. Obviously, they would have to offer him another piece of land of comparable size and quality in exchange, and not just money. And where they are going to find that sort of land I have no idea. Nobody seems to have thought that far ahead. So it's pretty unlikely that anything drastic will happen for quite a while. It's no easily solved matter, this road-widening business."

57   Gossip in this valley (as in most small communities, I suppose) seems to be aimed at maintaining, perhaps even creating, a moral order here. When the women get together, they are quick to point out that Kuroda Takayuki gives you only five yen for every *sake* bottle returned to his shop, whereas Inekari, his neighbor, gives eight yen. Kyōko is really astonished at the things that are said about people living close to us. The term she uses to describe this is "bad mouth" (*warukuchi*), but I myself am not convinced that the gossip is truly malicious. It stems rather from the fact that people are very closely acquainted with those around them. Nothing is secret. Nothing is sacred. Kyōko in her way is the same. She tells me about how Misako has made a private arrangement to sell homemade bread to the local supermarket. No doubt I will pass on this information when drunk or in a fit of absent-mindedness (old Yuki does not know about her daughter-in-law's income). Gossip is information, and we all need to be informed if we are to maintain cohesion in this valley.

Katsuhisa probably wouldn't agree with this remark. "I don't know why people bother with gossip. If somebody says something like, 'That young wife down the hill, she's no good at all,' everybody will immediately chorus their agreement. Yet nobody would dare say anything like that directly to the woman's face. That's bad. I wish people would be more frank, more direct." Katsuhisa's wish was shared by Yoshida Kenkō, incidentally, more than six centuries ago. Japan doesn't seem to change all that much sometimes.

A lot of smaller companies in Japan seem to rely on personal networks to keep up their sales. Tupperware is a good example of this sort of sales approach in the West, along with certain cosmetic firms. Here, too, Tupperware is just as active. Kyōko teaches cooking to one of the company's representatives and will be expected to buy something in due course. She also teaches a girl whose uncle is sole agent for a company selling an extract of prunes, and this too she is invited to order. Then she buys bottles of liquid cleaners from two girls who are promoting the use of nonabrasive "natural" cleansers and who also attend her classes. Here there is a clash of interests, for the sister-in-law of another of Kyōko's students sells soap powder and liquid cleaners too. These are said to be "pure" and are made in Hong Kong. The problem of which people in her network she should favor is solved when it is discovered that the Hong Kong products are not all that they are made out to be. Gossip and information once again.

Of course, to a large extent Kyōko buys things through this personal network (*tsukiai*) because she needs—or is made to feel that she needs—them. Other products that are not directly connected with cooking or housework are trickier to make up one's mind about. Katsuhisa's mother, Yuki, for example, has obviously let her own brother's wife know about our existence, for we are now being bombarded with leaflets about life insurance policies. This *tsukiai* is a complicated business. Kyōko is thinking of borrowing a small patch of land from Katsuhisa so she can plant her own vegetables this year. The question is, is it really necessary to buy life insurance just so we can get permission to use some land?

All these group pressures are hard to withstand, especially when there is the threat of gossip acting as a kind of social sanction. To some extent, then, gossip forces the people being gossiped about to conform very rapidly to what everyone wants or to suffer the consequences: ostracism by the group he has stood up to. In the sense that such a person is then forced to be adopted by another group, gossip helps to realign people in different cliques, although it can of course lead to total isolation, assuming that no other group is willing to accept a newcomer into its folds. Not that any of the hamlets in Yashiki have ever gone to such extremes.

Still, it is no easy thing to make your way into a new group, as Katsuhisa is quick to point out.

"It is strange, this business of the outsider and group membership. Look at Masaki, our next-door neighbor, for example. He came down from Ichinotsuru, way up in the hills, when his house was burned down. When was it now? Twenty? Thirty years ago?" Katsuhisa pauses to try to work out a span of time that I know to be 34 years. "And yet old Tamaki at the bottom of our road still refers to Masaki as 'that man who recently came to live here.' After all these years, poor Aso is still not really one of us."

58 Michiya sees gossip as a further example of the distinction between what people say and what they mean, between, in his terms, *tatemae* and *honshiki*.

"Look at it like this," he says, taking a scrap of paper from his post office desk on which to draw. "Here we have—say—ten households, all living together in a community. Suppose somebody dies in one of these houses. Then all the rest go along to offer their condolences and make all the noises appropriate to the bereaved. But in actual fact most of these people couldn't care less whether the old granny next door drops dead or not. All the same, they put on the appearance of caring, because when it is their turn to die they hope others will care about them.

"So here we have *tatemae*. If you look at things the other way around, you could say that gossip reveals people's *honshiki*. Here they are," he points with his pencil to his doodle on the scrap of paper, "here they are, all living under group rules in the community, in the something-or-other association, or whatever, and yet they aren't interested in the welfare of that group at all. That they seem to be so is merely superficial appearance. In actual fact, people put themselves right at the center of their lives and proceed from there. The individual's personal interests are first and foremost. This is where gossip comes in handy. You can use it to your own advantage to get at those who pose a threat to your own interests."

Michiya takes a second sheet of offwhite paper from the ink blotter on his desk. "If you don't believe all this, then think about what used to happen here when the trees were harvested for timber. In the old days, after somebody had had some trees chopped down on his mountain land, people would come and ask him for permission to grow root vegetables, beans, and so on in the area until the seedling trees he had planted had grown to good size. Now, supposing several households were interested in doing this, because they were part of a hamlet situated close to the mountain land in question, for example. If they were really group-oriented, they would have joined together and partitioned the land among themselves before planting their crops. Better still, they would have all cooperated to farm the land together.

"But is that what they did?" Michiya asks with his freckled grin. "Is it? No, of course not. Instead, each household head went along privately to see the landowner and tried to get special permission to work the cleared area on his own. And of course, to secure that permission, somehow one had to show that one's own household was 'better' than any of the other households concerned. Plenty of backbiting and innuendo were necessary there, I can assure you.

"Still, there is gossip and there is gossip, if you know what I mean. Some of it is passed along with a definite aim in mind. A lot more is really quite harmless. I don't want to sound too superior, but you will have noticed, I think, that women are particularly fond of spreading rumors—mainly of the harmless variety. The trouble with women living in the country is that they have no social authority. It is men who make the decisions about agriculture, household expenses, and so on. Consequently it is the men who are in overall command of social affairs. If they gossip, then they do so with a particular purpose in mind—like trying to get mountain land to cultivate.

"But women have no social position, so their gossip is likewise of little social value. It is in fact just a kind of entertainment. In the old days there was very little in the way of entertainment in mountain villages like ours. Nowadays, perhaps, things have changed a bit. We've got television sets, for a start. But there still isn't much to do here, and nothing very exciting ever happens. That's why the arrival of somebody like yourself, Būchan, causes such a stir. So the men, they drink *sake*, and the women, they gossip. That is our form of entertainment.

"The trouble is, of course, that although things are said about other people in a fairly lighthearted manner, when the person gossiped about hears what has been said, he is likely to get pretty annoyed. All that *he* hears are the words used out of context, and on their own like that they can sound pretty harsh. Yet when they were actually spoken—in the middle of a party, for example, when men were rolling on the floor drunk, or at a gathering of women to make bean curd—these same words might have sounded really quite harmless. Not completely harmless, of course. Otherwise, there'd be no point in saying them in the first place. People like gossiping. It's fun to see what sort of reaction one gets!"

59   Kajiwara Tōsuke's mother has died. She had a stroke a few years ago, and this left her a bit mad—always forgetting when she had last eaten and demanding food at all times of the day and night.

There was plenty of gossip when the wives of Ōkubo got together to prepare the funeral feast last Sunday, and all of it was aimed at Yasuko. She had neglected her mother-in-law, refusing even to feed her. The older women didn't know what the world was coming to these days. Young people had no respect at all for their elders.

That evening Misako had to listen to her mother-in-law holding forth to relatives and friends about the young. Yuki is one of the more self-centered people in the valley and rarely does anything for anyone unless it is going to reflect to her credit. Misako fumed quietly before making some excuse and coming to let off steam at our place.

Maya didn't seem particularly surprised that the old lady had died. "Ah, yes," he said, "I heard Naruhisa saying that there was no point in giving old people anything to eat. It's a waste."

Children can be terrifyingly frank. At the same time, one can see the dangers of gossip and the prejudices that it creates even in the young. Naruhisa is Tōsuke's eldest son and presumably passed on what he had heard being said in the family. Did it come directly from his mother, or not?

60   Inoshige's mother, Den, is getting weaker. She spends more and more time in bed and talks now of wanting to die. Today I find her sitting in her chair on the veranda overlooking the drying yard.

"I'd like to die while you're still around, Būchan. Then you can see me off to the next world." *But one year short of a hundred, the lady with the thinning hair . . .*

61   Women are not divorced around here. Rather, they are chucked out (*dasareru*) of their husbands' homes. Yashiki appears to have its fair share of involuntary dropouts. There is a house upstream from the *sake* shop in Inekari, behind the sheds where Takayuki stores his beer and wines. The family there "lost" the young

wife fairly early on. Then the husband went off with another woman, leaving the two children by his first wife to be brought up by their grandmother. She is old and not at all well off, so she gets some assistance from the Town Council. When the first wife died recently back at her home on the southern tip of the island, the old woman held a token funeral for her in Inekari.

More recently, two wives have been chucked out for little more than their failure to satisfy members of their husbands' households. Kuroda Eisuke's elder brother, who lives this side of the valley going down toward the Agricultural Cooperative, has just got rid of his wife and is left with two primary-school children to bring up. Just below the school, Inekari Tetsurō's main house has just chucked out the wife for what was termed "general incompetence."

"She just couldn't do a thing right," complained the mother-in-law and suggested that the girl was an idiot. Presumably she has preferred to ignore the fact that it was she herself who thought the girl suitable for her son and arranged their marriage.

But old women are like that. There are tales of grandmothers that reveal once again the difference between the toothless smiling old lady who bobs her head when you pass the time of day with her outside the house and the whining hag who gets at you day in, day out inside the house, where nobody can see what is going on. Tamaki's wife, Mihoko, used to have to carry her mother-in-law to the lavatory countless times a day for five years because the old lady absolutely refused to wear nappies and endure the indignity of being changed in some "inappropriate" room of the house. Haruo's mother used to fling away the food brought to her by her son's young bride. "Do you expect me to eat muck like that?" she would exclaim. "Bring me something that tastes decent!"

No wonder that in the distant past, when there was not enough food to go around, people used to leave the old women alone in the mountains to die.

62 Rumor has it that a woman committed suicide by drowning herself in the Oni River a month or two after my arrival. She is said to have been a wife in her early forties, with children of primary- and secondary-school-age, who was having an affair with a younger man. Unable to stand the secrecy that her love demanded of her, she threw herself into the river when it was in full flood after the summer rains. Her body floated downstream for some way before it was found and dragged out of the water.

"Got it all wrong again, have you, Būchan?," Inoshige grins as he settles down to a morning's work making dinner plates at the wheel. "I don't know who told you that story, but it's not what happened at all. Either somebody is trying to confuse you, or else he or she has got things muddled up. There were three incidents that occurred in fairly quick succession the summer you arrived in Kamayama. First of all a classmate of mine—he wasn't a classmate in the literal sense of the term, but we were of the same age. That's why I call him my *dōkyūsei*. Anyway, this classmate of mine had a fight with his wife and decided to commit suicide. He'd always been a bit strange in the head, from early childhood."

"You can say that again," puts in Ayako from the middle of the workshop, where she is sitting on a stool decorating teacups. "Do you remember the time he came up here drunk one night and kicked all the glass out of our front door. It took all of us, and Terukichi and Umao, to hold him down while we called the police."

"Anyway, this classmate of mine was called Kawazu. He went off to the post office and handed over his savings book to Michiya. 'I'm going to commit suicide,' he said, 'so I'd be grateful if you would let my wife have all the money that's left in my savings account.'"

"Did he really? That was thoughtful of him," Ayako observes.

"Old Mitchan took this statement with a pinch of salt. 'That's fine,' he said, 'but before you do it, do you think you could be so kind as to let me have your signature stamp. Then I can make out the withdrawal slip for you.' Kawazu did as he was asked and Michiya said jocularly, 'Right! Off you go and die then!' and Kawazu turned to leave.

"'By the way,' Michiya said casually, always ready to pass the time of day, 'how are you going to commit suicide?'

"'With this rope,' replied Kawazu, pointing to a piece of rope knotted about his neck. He then went out of the post office, jumped down in the rice paddy, and crossed over to where a bridge spanned the river."

"Well, I never. He was carrying a rope with him all the time," Ayako exclaims as she takes down a new tray of teacups to decorate. "How do you know all this anyway?"

"Michiya told me. And anyway, people had gathered by then to watch the event. You know how it is. One moment there's nobody in the valley at all, and the next everybody is crowding around trying to see what you're up to. Apparently, what happened next was Kawazu tied one end of the rope around his neck to a concrete railing, then lowered himself carefully down the stone retaining wall. Nobody knows to this day what he intended to do, but when he was halfway down the wall, he suddenly slipped and fell into the river."

"What? With the rope still tied to his neck? How awful!"

"Yes. Michiya and the others rushed toward the bridge. Seeing Kawazu lying motionless in the raging torrent, Michiya decided to cut the rope. He felt that this would be safer than trying to pull up the injured man. Anyway, he looked as if he was already dead. So he cut the rope from the railing, and Kawazu's body was carried downstream. It finally surfaced at the small dam just above the South Oni Primary School."

"It's incredible how far bodies are carried in rivers, isn't it?"

Inoshige decides to ignore Ayako's comment and finish his story. "The police came, of course, and the first thing they asked Michiya was why he cut Kawazu loose. They made it plain that they suspected him of murder. After all, he knew that Kawazu wanted to kill himself, and yet he had made no attempt to stop him. Poor Michiya. He got little help from any of the others who had witnessed the accident. To some extent that is because he has long been a member of the Communist Party, and that doesn't make him the most popular man in a conservative valley like this. I mean, being a Communist is almost a crime in itself here."

"What happened to Michiya?"

"Oh, he spent several uncomfortable hours being questioned—extremely hard—by the police down in town. Then the autopsy report came. It showed that there was no water in Kawazu's lungs. He had died of a broken neck. Not of drowning. So Michiya was let go. He was pretty shocked, though."

"I'll bet he was. What about the other incidents you mentioned, then?"

"Well, one of them concerned a woman living well down the valley in Suzuka village. She was quite friendly with Munetoshi's wife, Sumiko, and worked in a bar in town that was run by a 'madam' who was divorced. One night, the madam's husband came back, brought out a machine gun, and shot all three hostesses, together with his wife and daughter."

"What? Right there in the bar?" Ayako is shocked.

"Yes. Don't you remember? It was in the papers. Murdered the lot of them right in front of some customers. They were a bit shaken up, I can tell you. The man then drove off and committed suicide in a love hotel in the prefectural capital. That was where his body was found several days later. I don't mind about him dying, but I feel sorry for the girls. I knew one of them. She was an attractive girl, who once asked me to make love to her." Inoshige's eyes twinkle as he finishes both his story and a tray of plates, and stands up to light a cigarette.

"Inoshigesan!" Ayako exclaims, looking at him with mock seriousness. "How many times do I have to tell you not to mention things like that in public!" Then she adds more soberly, "You should be careful about the places you choose to drink downtown."

"Yes, I should. You're quite right." He blows a lungful of smoke up toward the ceiling. "Anyway," he says to me, "I imagine your informant got those two stories mixed up. What's more, there was another case of drowning last year, and that doesn't help. Some old man in Hirao got a bit drunk and fell into the river. His body was eventually washed up in Teruyama."

"Yes. And that's more than nine miles away," says Ayako. "The other side of town. Incredible, isn't it?" she says, turning to me.

It certainly was. Judging by Ayako's reaction, people around here were far less concerned about the death of an old man than with the fact that a corpse could be carried such a distance by what's really no more than a stream.

Ayako gets up and stretches. "Rivers are pretty frightening things, aren't they?" she says and shuffles off out of the workshop to get some tea.

63 Michiya is right, of course—member of the Communist Party or not. What people say should be done and what they actually do are frequently poles apart. Tonight, for instance, Kyōko was supposed to be teaching the women of Ōkubo and Inekari how to do a few yoga exercises. Kajiwara Yuki, who is chairwoman of the Valley Housewives' Association, had expressly asked her to do this.

By 8:00 P.M., a quarter of an hour after the meeting was to have begun, nobody had turned up at the village hall. Kyōko eventually went back up the hill to Yuki's house and asked her what was going on. It was clear that the older woman was not herself in the mood to attend.

"It's pouring, and tomorrow we're holding the thirty-third- and seventeenth-year remembrance services for my two deceased husbands," she explained. "And anyway, in weather like this what can you expect? Nobody wants to come out in the rain." And she proceeded to telephone each of the wives and cancel the yoga session.

Since Yuki is chairwoman of the Housewives' Association, nobody says anything that can be interpreted as contradicting her orders. If you are old and have some recognized position of authority here in the valley, you can do what you like. This is precisely what those who are old rely on—the inability of people to speak up and argue their own opinions coherently. That is why Sakakura Haruzō has been able to get so far with the road-widening project. Not that he has been able to establish a school safety zone. Katsuhisa categorically refuses to sell his land, and the project has had to be shelved—temporarily, at least. Now Katsuhisa is trying to stop the Town Council's planning department from dynamiting an enormous boulder that stands by the narrow road between Noda and Ichinotsuru.

"The land is owned by Noda Shōsuke," Katsuhisa explains. "I've suggested that either he move the rock or refuse to allow the road to be widened up there. He owes me one, but I don't think he's going to pay any attention. Shōchan and Harusan are great ones for scheming together. You remember when we passed Haruzō's truck up in the mountains a while back? I hear that the rocks they hauled up out of the riverbed were for a town councilman. There's government for you. Making laws with the right hand, breaking them with the left."

As we stay in the valley longer and longer, we come up against more and more frustrating incidents of this sort. While some people, like Katsuhisa and Inoshige, can be so generous and broadminded, others can be so very petty. One of Maya's former teachers stopped work in the middle of last year to have a baby. She was

replaced by a temporary teacher who is very popular with the children, but has to leave in the middle of the school year so that the
former teacher can come back. Some parents were unhappy when
they heard about this arrangement. It would be better to change
teachers at the end of the school year, rather than in the middle. So
they began making inquiries about whether it would be possible to
keep the temporary teacher on until next spring. Of the thirteen
families involved, nine wanted the present teacher to remain, three
were against, and one was undecided. Of the parents against, the
most outspoken was the class's PTA representative. He was asked
to call a meeting of all those concerned to discuss the matter but has
absolutely refused to do so. *He* is against the move to keep on the
temporary teacher, so what is there to discuss?

It appears that the reason for his pique is simple. Parents should
have approached him first and allowed him to be seen to take the
initiative. *Tatemae* again! Form before content . . .

64 We have decided to rebuild our house—not all of it, but the
older section, which is virtually uninhabitable. For the past few
weeks we have been discussing plans with Daisuke and have asked
him to do the work for us.

We had originally planned to have the house rebuilt after the
rainy season was over, but Daisuke has now suggested that we pull
down the old part of the house in the next day or two. This means
that we will have no kitchen, no bathroom, and no water until the
new part is completed. So Kyōko talked things over with Misako,
who in turn talked things over with Katsuhisa about our renting
two spare rooms they have in a wing of their house above some
storage space. There is a lavatory attached, and Kyōko and Misako
have agreed that they could do the cooking together. These upstairs
rooms used to be lived in by Katsuhisa's younger brother, Kōichi,
just after he got married, and they had been especially prepared for
the newlyweds.

Even though the whole matter has been arranged informally, we
still have to make a formal request of Katsuhisa. He will then relay
the request to his mother. So we go down to Mon, explain that we
have asked Daisuke to rebuild our house, and ask whether it might
be possible for us to rent the rooms above the store room.

Katsuhisa agrees, of course, and apologizes, as he takes us up to see the rooms, that there are a few bits and pieces stacked away, and the place needs some cleaning up. That's true enough. There is a mass of furniture and belongings piled in one of the rooms, but clearly something can be done about the mess.

"I can always help you out," says Katsuhisa, "but now I'd better go and talk to my mother. She's locked away in her room behind the kitchen as usual."

We go downstairs and hang around the garden in front of the house, while Katsuhisa goes to tell Yuki what is happening. They are a long time talking. Finally, we hear the sound of a door opening and voices as the two of them go out by the back door and straight up to the spare rooms. We continue to wait by the main entrance to the house, sitting on the trestle table set up under its deep eaves and facing out onto the pebble-fronted garden with its close-clipped azaleas, maples, and miniature pine trees.

After what seems an eternity, Katsuhisa comes halfway down the stairs and beckons to us to join them. We follow him up and find Yuki kneeling in the middle of the *tatami*-covered floor. We, too, kneel, apologize for being a nuisance, and ask whether we can make a *muri na o-negai*, a "quite unreasonable request." Yuki begins by saying what a cramped and dirty place this is—not a fit place for people like us to inhabit. We assure her that we don't mind at all.

"But there's no kitchen," she protests. "There's nowhere to cook."

"Perhaps if you could allow us to use a little of the storage space downstairs to set up a stove in?"

"But what about a bath? We would all have to share a tub."

"Yes. That is true. But we are used to camping out," I say somewhat unconvincingly.

"And what are you going to do about these rooms?" Yuki asks, with a disdainful wave of one hand. "All this furniture. And this bedding. These books. What a mess! Kōichi always says he's going to take them away, but he never does. I suppose he has no space, really, in that flat of his above where he works."

We assure Yuki that we will clear up everything by ourselves. We will no doubt be a considerable nuisance to Misako, but we beg her forgiveness in advance.

Yuki opens the windows to let some air in.

"You really do get such a nice breeze coming through here in the summer, you know. It comes down the ravine from behind the temple, and it's nice and cool. But the sun is so hot in July. And there are no eaves here. You'll need blinds for these windows. How long do you intend to stay?"

We assure her yet again that all we need is a roof over our heads. A bit of discomfort is nothing.

Eventually, without actually saying so, Yuki gives us her permission to stay. We gather this more from the tone of her questions than anything else.

"When do you want to come?" she asks.

"Well, it depends on Daisuke's schedule. We'll have to ask him first and then let you know, if that is all right. But it might well be before the end of the month."

"It's not a very good idea to build a house during the rainy season, you know," she warns us. "Anyway, I must phone Kōichi at once and get him to come up and remove his things. I suppose we can stow the rest away somewhere."

It is then that I make a mistake. I always seem to make an error in every negotiation—mainly because I am so conscious of the need to be diplomatic and reveal nothing.

"Quite a lot of things could be stored away in the cubbyhole at the back of the other room, provided they were stacked properly."

"Oh? So you've been up here before, have you?" Yuki asks ever so casually, immediately aware of the fact that Misako and Kyōko have been arranging things behind her back.

But then she carries on, as though my suggestion is of no significance. "It's nice here, isn't it? I often come up in summer and sleep here in this room." And having gently hinted that we will be putting her out in more ways than one, she sits down in a rocking chair in one corner and gazes distantly out of the window. Katsuhisa mutters something about how he must do the same; the main house is so unbearably hot in summer. And the view here is really nice.

Yuki gets us to move a big chest of drawers in which she has stored away her formal clothing for funerals, weddings, and so on. May she put some of her things in one of the two wall cupboards

and leave the other one free for us? Of course, she may. We intend
to bring just a few things with us from the house. The rest we will
leave in the second-floor rooms and take as we need.

So we leave—once again thanking Yuki for her cooperation and
apologizing for the inconvenience. We will let her know when we
want to move in, the moment Daisuke tells us his schedule.

A couple of days later Kyōko hears from Misako that she and Yuki
had gone ahead and cleaned up the two rooms on their own. After
that, her mother-in-law had phoned Kōichi and told him that we
were moving in, and that his things were in the way. He'd better
come and remove them at once.

This annoyed Kōichi no end. His immediate reaction was to demand of his mother whom she valued more—him or us? It was
clear to us that Yuki had only agreed to let us stay in her rooms
because we were there at the time the request was made. Having
realized that the whole matter had been arranged behind her back
by Katsuhisa and Misako, she had decided to take out her pique on
Kōichi.

"You shouldn't have spoken to Kōchan like that, Mother." Even
Katsuhisa felt moved to reprimand her. "You should have explained
things properly. And there was no need for you to speak to him as
abruptly as you did."

By way of a reply, Yuki began talking about other houses in the
neighborhood that were empty and would be ideal for us to borrow. There was one in front of Takayuki's *sake* shop. And another
next door to Gotō Jirō's. They were not her houses, of course, but
she was full of ideas about how other people could help us. Anything to save herself the trouble.

Kyōko hears all this from Misako. It is obvious that Yuki does not
want us to stay. So we change our plans. We will, after all, camp in
the second-floor rooms of our house during the six weeks it will
take for the rest of the house to be pulled down and rebuilt. If we
have Daisuke put up a temporary extension by the upstairs entrance, we will have somewhere to cook.

But how to relay our change of plan to Yuki? That's the next
problem. She mustn't know that we know that she doesn't want us
to stay, because then she would guess that Misako has told us what
was going on and would really take it out on her daughter-in-law.

So Kyōko tactfully asks Yuki whether we may use the upstairs rooms for storing our things. Upon reflection, she tells her, we have decided it was a bit much to ask for all of us to be allowed to live in such a cramped space. We would be causing the whole household too much trouble.

Yuki denies that it is any trouble at all; we are welcome to stay. But Kyōko declines and repeats her request that we be allowed to leave some of our belongings there instead. This is readily accepted by Yuki.

"What a pity we're not all going to be living together," she lies. "I'd been looking forward to it so much."

65 People must never lose face. Yuki is a good example of that. In the old days the people of Mon were landlords and always had plenty of money. As a result, they could never sell things for money. Instead, they were expected to give things away to the local farmers. Now Yuki grows vast quantities of rice, vegetables, and beans— much of which she allows to rot. And yet she will rarely—if ever— give food away. Now that the landlord-tenant system has ended, it would be beneath her dignity to patronize the local people any more.

Misako, on the other hand, has no compunctions about selling rice on the quiet—probably about 450 pounds a year, at 135 yen per pound. Cheap at the price. Fortunately, Yuki doesn't inquire about this side of household affairs, and so Misako is able to make enough pocket money to pay for personal items. Not that she can buy expensive clothes or anything. Yuki would be the first to notice.

66 Our next-door neighbor, Masaki, has had two bees in his bonnet. One concerns how he can get rid of the wild dogs. The other is how to stop the grass bank below our house from crumbling away.

"You ought to plant some azaleas there," he said some time ago. "They would make that area where we turn our cars around look nice in the spring. And they would stop the bank from falling away when the summer rains come."

Katsuhisa heard about this and volunteered to help.

"This is the sort of thing I should be really good at," he said with a shy grin. "I am, after all, supposed to be a botany and forestry teacher."

But all that was more than a month ago, and somehow neither of us managed to find the time to get the job done. When he was free, I was tied up with research, and when I found myself with a day or two to spare, he was up to his toothpick in school business.

But then Daisuke suddenly phones to say that he is ready to start work on rebuilding the house. He'll put the old part down next Wednesday, then re-lay the foundations and do the raising-of-the-roof-ridge ceremony in early June.

This means that we have to act fast. An extension is to be put in upstairs, and there are a couple of large rocks next to the entrance that will have to be moved, together with three azalea bushes. Katsuhisa decides that Sunday will be the best day to do our transplanting and hence ingratiate ourselves with Aso Masaki.

So far as I know, all three azalea bushes lie within the boundaries of the land that Takeshi had agreed to sell us at the end of last year. They are growing approximately three feet from the side of the house and lie on the house side of the path, which I presume forms the land boundary. Although Wada Tatetarō has not yet drawn up the final contract, I figure that I'm entitled to move the azaleas if I wish.

At the same time, there are several other azalea bushes on a plot of untended scrubland next to the orchard at the back of the house. For several months now, both Takeshi and his wife Hanako have said on various occasions that they must get around to clearing up this piece of land so they can grow vegetables there. Anytime we want to transplant the azaleas to the area around our house, they tell us, we are welcome to do so.

Since Katsuhisa has all day free, and since it is clear that Masaki would just as soon see the whole bank lined with azaleas, we decide to put in three or four of the bushes growing on Takeshi's plot of land. Just to make sure that this will be all right with him, Kyōko telephones him to let him know what we are up to. He is out, but we leave a message with his mother, asking her to get him to call us back as soon as he gets home.

Then we begin digging up the three enormous bushes next to our main entrance upstairs. Katsuhisa is never one to do things in too much of a hurry, so by the time we are finished it is lunch time, and we take a break. We phone Takeshi again, but he is still not home, so we explain what we are about to do. Takeshi's mother sounds quite happy with our plans.

And so we move four bushes from Takeshi's land. Masaki comes out of his house and watches us do the work. He stands in the middle of the parking area, cursing the dogs, telling us where to put the bushes, and making a number of pleasantries, while ensuring that he does not actually give us a hand.

We have just filled in the earth around the seventh, and smallest, azalea and are stamping it in around the roots when the telephone rings. It is Takeshi.

"What on earth's going on up there?" he shouts in Kyōko's ear. "What's all this about my azaleas?"

Kyōko explains what we are doing and tells him that we have taken the liberty of transplanting some bushes from his plot of land behind the house. This, she thought, had been agreed to some weeks before.

"Yes, yes," Takeshi snaps back impatiently. "It's not that I'm concerned about. What do you think you're doing moving the azaleas from in front of the entrance to the house when that is my land. I haven't given you permission to touch those."

At this point, Kyōko calls me to the phone. Takeshi is extremely worked up.

"Yes. I've sold you the house. That's true, but the land boundaries still haven't been fixed. You've no right to touch anything on the land around that house without my permission."

This I dispute. The boundaries were drawn on paper at the time of the sale. True, we had never—the four of us—got together and gone over the land in broad daylight, but Takeshi had put his seal to that original agreement. He had accepted that the land with the fruit trees on it was ours, and he knew that we were going to extend our house by three feet toward the path, because I had discussed that with him only ten days ago. He hadn't objected then. Why was he worrying about azalea bushes that were between our house and the path. This land was ours. It had to be. Otherwise we had no access to the house.

"That's where you're wrong. Quite wrong," retorts Takeshi. "Nothing's been fixed. Nothing's yours."

It is now my turn to get angry. If nothing is mine, how come I have paid him 450,000 yen? If that's the way he is going to behave, we'd better call the whole deal off. I then add—imprudently—that so far as I know, the custom in the Oni valley is that the seller has to return twice the sum originally paid in the event of a *nagashi* ("whitewash") in a land deal of this sort. What kind of man is Takeshi, taking all my money quite happily and now saying that he is only going to give us the land on which the house stands? Anyway his mother had given us permission to dig the azaleas.

"My mother!" snorts Takeshi. "My mother's useless. She's a woman and knows nothing about such things. This is a man's affair."

"In that case," I counter, "why did you have to get your mother's permission to sell us the house and land in the first place?"

There is a stifled gasp, and then silence. I suggest in a more conciliatory tone that Takeshi phone Tatetarō, his intermediary, and that the two of them come up to fix the boundary as soon as possible. After all, we have arranged to pull the house down in three days' time.

Takeshi then begins shouting something at the other end of the line. He is very angry, and his speech, which is never clear at the best of times, is so slurred as to be incomprehensible. I hang up on him.

I realize at once that this is another in a long line of mistakes. So I phone Tatetarō, but he is out and all I can do is leave a message with his wife asking that he phone me the moment he gets home. Then I go outside and talk the matter over with Katsuhisa and Masaki.

"Yes, you ought to go down and apologize to Takeshi, Būchan," Katsuhisa advises. "Then you can arrange to meet up here when your tempers have cooled a bit."

But before I can even start my motorbike, Takeshi himself appears in his 600-cc truck. He strides toward me in fury.

"What do you mean by cutting me off just now? Eh? There I was talking to you and you hang up on me. What do you mean by it? And what do you mean by telling me to phone Tatetarō and bring him along to discuss the matter? Eh? Who are you to tell me what to do? So you want a whitewash, do you? Well, you've got it. How much do you want? Eh? Twice the original sum? You've got it. I'll bring it up tomorrow morning."

I point out that any whitewash would have to take account of the fact that Daisuke, the carpenter, has started to cut the timber for the new house. That work would also have to be accounted for. But Takeshi is too angry to pay attention.

"I may be a farmer, and you may be a university teacher, but all you ever want is your own way. All you do is cause people trouble. I've put up with an awful lot on your behalf, you know. I don't complain, do I, when your kids leave their bikes under the roof of my store? Or when you hang your washing out to dry there, even though it does get in my way? I'm an *ippon nashiya*, a plain old farmer who's interested only in his pear orchards. But you! You're something different."

Katsuhisa listens to this tirade with head bowed, scudding the ground with one boot and nodding, now and then interjecting a "Yes, that's so" and making other noises of agreement. As he explained much later, it wasn't that he did agree with everything that Takeshi was saying, but in situations such as this, it is better to back down and do as people want you to do. It gave Takeshi a chance to let off steam and made him feel better. Anyway, he wasn't in any frame of mind to be objectively rational. There were all sorts of petty things that had been piling up in Takeshi's head over the past few months, and this was a good opportunity for him to get them all out now. Let him do so. He'd feel better for it afterward.

But without the benefit of this sage advice at the time, I press the argument, trying to explain why I had moved the azaleas and why I had suggested calling in Tatetarō. He is, after all, Takeshi's go-between.

"So what?" Takeshi retorts. "This is a problem between the two of us. It's got nothing to do with my go-between."

"In which case, why did you insist on having go-betweens in the first place, when I asked you to sell me the land? I thought the idea was to prevent arguments like this from happening."

"Anyway, I'll bring you your money tomorrow."

"I wonder where we're going to live now," I sigh.

"What do you mean, wonder where you're going to live?" Takeshi looks surprised. "You can live here in this house. You can rebuild the house, if you want. But the land's mine."

He strides off and begins fiddling around with the tank in which he puts his insecticides. Katsuhisa wanders along with him, to act as a sponge for his anger. Masaki has long since beaten a quiet retreat into his house, determined clearly not to get involved. Kyōko and I begin scything the grass in front of the house. We agree that perhaps it is time for us to leave the valley. We are never going to be accepted here, after all. Both of us feel curiously relieved.

A little later, Takeshi goes around the back of Masaki's house, and we hear him saying something about continuing to live together as good neighbors. Then we see him down on the road, examining the azaleas we've transplanted. It is time for another monologue, a staccato of broken phrases.

"So this is where you've planted them. Well, you've really made a mess of it. Look how cramped the parking space is! And look at this branch! The way it's sticking out. It'll take the paint off my car if I turn it around here. This used to be a rice field in the old days. There was only a path down here by these houses. And then Aso came to live here. And it was a bit inconvenient, so I made a road here. But then Aso left his cars here and made it difficult for me to turn my truck around. That's when I gave Aso some land to build his garage on. Didn't I, Asosan?"

Masaki prefers not to question this falsification of recent local history and mumbles some agreement from the front of his house. Kyōko continues tidying up some of the scythed grass around the edge of the parking space where Takeshi is standing.

"And this here," he points to the slope just below our house, "this was a path for Aso to go up to his house. Along there. It was a path, generally speaking. And now there's an azalea bush in the way."

"But that's because the earth falls away when people walk up and down. It endangers the foundations of our house. Isn't that right, Masakisan?" As usual, I have to say something. I have not yet learned the art of total withdrawal, of suffering people's irrationalities in silence.

"Generally speaking, there should be a path," Takeshi insists. "And the idea of my making a parking space for cars was to make the area wider. But you've gone and planted azaleas there. It's cramped."

Kyōko straightens up and says, in that matter-of-fact, calm voice she uses when she is angry, "Let's put them all back, then, where they originally were."

Takeshi makes noises of agreement. "Yes, parking places should be big, not cramped. Generally speaking."

It is time for Katsuhisa to comment. "But you yourself have planted trees along the edge of the parking space behind you. That's hasn't helped."

"That's true. There are one or two trees here. But generally speaking . . ." Takeshi has run out of steam. "I'll bring the money up tomorrow," he says and walks off up the road to where his van is parked.

"Būchan, go and apologize to him," Masaki advises.

"Yes," says Katsuhisa, "it'll keep him happy."

So I take their advice and rush off to intercept Takeshi, who is assuring Kyōko that this quarrel is between him and me and has nothing to do with her. He is about to get into the truck when I draw myself up stiffly and then bow very formally.

"I'm sorry to have caused you so much trouble and to have made you so angry."

His reaction to my bow is instinctive. He too stands up straight, takes off his cap, and returns my bow.

"Not at all," he replies, making one or two apologetic noises. It is always the form that matters most.

Katsuhisa and Masaki stand around chatting for a while after Takeshi has driven off. They tell us not to worry. Takeshi is just letting off steam. Now that he's got everything off his chest, he'll feel better. Tatetarō and Inoshige will soon persuade him that he's in the wrong. Things will return to normal.

But we are not convinced. Today's argument is not one that is going to be patched up permanently, like a piece of invisible mending. Is this to be the end of our stay here in this valley? *Why should the cherry petals flutter to the earth so restlessly?*

67   In the evening I go across to Amagase to see Daisuke and tell him what has happened. We'll have to ask him to stop work on the house until the argument with Takeshi is cleared up.

But if I thought our quarrel was to be the major event of the day, it was as nothing compared with what took place in Amagase. For a long time Terukichi had been trying to marry off his youngest daughter, Michiko, a cheerful girl who looks after her brother Umao's three daughters. After several attempts at finding her a suitable husband had fallen through for one reason or another, Terukichi asked Haruzō whether he could help. Haruzō soon found a suitable partner and, after the usual negotiations, the marriage was arranged for the 20th of the month—the same day we were to pull down our house. Michiko's husband-to-be came from the local town, but worked on the mainland in Hiroshima, so the young couple were going to live there.

Today had been fixed as the day Michiko would take her leave of the villagers of Amagase. All the women were invited to Terukichi's, along with those involved in the arrangement of the marriage. Daisuke was there as chief party maker (*shōban*) and *sake* pourer.

All went well until the women had left and only the men remained behind in Terukichi's new extension to his noodle shop. Apparently, one of the women came in from the kitchen and began clearing away the empty cups, plates, dishes, and so on, but Haruzō told her to stop doing that while guests were still present.

"I'm not really sure what happened next," Daisuke says, almost apologetically, "because I was a bit drunk and half asleep in the *kotatsu* across the way."

"He always gets like that," Reiko laughs. "Have you noticed?"

"Anyway, I suddenly became aware of the fact that there was a lot of noise and shouting. I got up and found Haruzō and Terukichi locked together in fury. So I separated the two of them and took Haruzō to one side. He's got a bad habit sometimes of shooting off his mouth after he's drunk too much. I figured that that was what had happened now. So I told him to calm down and behave himself. This was a time for celebration, not for argument."

"Quite right, too." Reiko is suitably impressed with her husband's common sense.

"Haruzō saw sense and apologized to Terukichi for what had happened. They had more or less patched things up when in came Terusan's wife and said that if that was the way Haruzō was going to behave, she—Akemi—wasn't going to let her daughter be married." Daisuke laughs, but with some embarrassment.

"So Terukichi suddenly found himself torn between two choices. Either he supported his wife or he kept his peace with Haruzō. In the end, he opted to side with Akemi, and a free-for-all broke out. Eventually, I said it was a matter for relatives to sort out and left."

After telling me all this, Daisuke comes back to my argument with Takeshi.

"That really annoys me, you know. That bit about the land. Why, only a few weeks ago we were drinking together at some party or other and actually discussed the matter of land boundaries. I told him you had asked me to rebuild the house. And I knew you had no record of the sale and not much in the way of documents, either, to show that the land was yours. I pointed out that that was not really legal and made Takeshi realize that there mustn't be any problem in the future. For all our sakes. I was going to have to do a bit of fibbing when it came to registering the plans for the new house down at the Town Council's offices.

"Takeshi responded then really positively. Of course he understood, he said. He even thanked me for my concern and told me to go ahead as I pleased. And that means," Daisuke taps the tabletop to emphasize his point, "that means he didn't object to our building out that little bit toward the path. Well, if there's going to be another meeting between you two and Inoshige and Tatetarō, I want to be in on it. I'm going to give Takeshi a piece of my mind, I can tell you."

At least I have one ally. Next I walk down to Inoshige's, to find only Ayako at home. As I settle down to wait for Inoshige, she tells me more about the wedding row. Apparently, things had never really gone smoothly between Terukichi and Haruzō from the start. After all, the two households haven't been the best of friends in the past. Why should things change so miraculously now? Things began to get bad when it came to the collection of the dowry. Normally, the bridegroom's side bears the cost of the transportation of the furniture, bedding, and other things. But in this case, because the couple were going to move all the way to Hiroshima, Haruzō arranged with a relative of his, who was acting as go-between on the groom's side, to get in touch with another relative of theirs, who ran a furniture sales outlet, to transport the goods by ferry to Hiroshima. For some reason or other, Terukichi had ended up paying all the costs, when they should have been borne by the other party. Ayako is convinced that it was this that had sparked the row. At the same time, everybody knows how Haruzō has a habit of blowing his top occasionally when he's had too much to drink.

At this point, Inoshige comes staggering home from town, where he had spent the evening with friends, since he had not been invited to Terukichi's. But he is sober enough to remark on the irony of so many quarrels breaking out on Daian, the day of great peace and safety according to the lunar calendar.

Then he telephones Wada Tatetarō, who has already heard something from Takeshi about "having a tiff with Būchan." Takeshi was apparently smiling when he mentioned it and told Tatetarō he was going to return me twice the amount of money I had paid him for the house and land. Inoshige quickly points out to Tatetarō that that wouldn't be enough. There are Daisuke's carpentry expenses to be taken into account as well. It is arranged very politely ("If you could possibly spare the time . . .") for the five of us to meet the following evening at Inoshige's.

Inoshige then telephones Daisuke, even though it is already past midnight, makes Reiko get him out of bed, and invites the two of them down for a drink. A few minutes later, they arrive. Ayako gets out some bottles of beer, and we all sit in the *kotatsu* discussing the day's events. Inoshige's son, Shigeki, is there, and is astonished to hear the sort of thing that goes on in village life. He finds it hard to believe that people fight over a few feet of land or ruin the lives of their grown children just to save their own face.

Shigeki's reaction in turn astonishes me. I find it altogether remarkable that children should be so sheltered from the adults' world. Children here have their own lives. They play together. They are frank and open with one another. They very rarely quarrel. And yet once they have grown up, they have to learn to hide their feelings, to behave completely differently. Adults and children live in worlds that are perhaps even more separated than those of men and women.

68   This morning, Takeshi came up to fumigate his pear trees at 5:45 A.M. and the thump-thump-thump of the two-stroke pump engine soon woke us all up. This is one way to get one's revenge!

Inoshige has already told me the tale of a famous potter who started up business by borrowing a workshop from a farmer in Bizen. This farmer had himself tried pottery-making once, but failed. When he saw how successful this potter was, the farmer grew jealous and built three very large chicken coops, each backing onto one wall of the workshop. The potter was soon driven out by the noise of hens clucking, not to mention the smell. Am I to lose out in a similar manner?

Takeshi at first refused to attend this evening's meeting and told Inoshige over the phone that he was going to return me my money. There was no need for him to get involved as well. Inoshige demurred. He had been expressly requested by me to intervene. Reluctantly, Takeshi agreed to attend the meeting.

Then we went up to see Daisuke. We needed to plan our strategy. How much had Daisuke spent on the house—materials, labor, and so on? It was agreed that he would state a figure considerably greater than the true expenditure. Reiko looked worried and warned her husband not to overdo things. Tatetarō might come up and check what work had been done.

Inoshige then went back to wait for Takeshi and Tatetarō to arrive. He would hear what they had to say first and then call us down. We wait . . . and we wait . . . half watching television, half discussing the marriage argument. There is little to add to what we already knew except for the fact that Michiko's wedding has been canceled. But then, as the saying goes, "A household's shame must always be concealed." We are not expected to know anything, although Misae had heard the bridegroom's go-between and parents arrive in Amagase at four o'clock in the morning and had seen them leave just before breakfast. They had come back in the middle of the day.

Terukichi's house was like a morgue. A notice had been put up on the door of the noodle shop saying that it was closed. Inside people were locked up, presumably negotiating. Occasionally someone would go in or come out, looking grave and serious. The only person who didn't know that the marriage had fallen through was the bridegroom himself. He lived in an apartment without a telephone and had not yet been contacted. As for Terukichi, he was really going to have to pay for his row with Haruzō. He would have to hand back twice the dowry payment for failing to hand over the bride. That meant something like 1.5 million yen, or more than $6,000.

At last the telephone rings. It is Inoshige summoning us down to his house. There we find Takeshi sitting in the *kotatsu* with Misae, waiting for Tatetarō to get off the phone, where he is trying to clear up some Agricultural Coop business. Finally he finishes and the discussion begins.

It is a long and involved discussion in which at times we conduct ever-diminishing circles of repetition. Takeshi starts by saying he doesn't want to give us the land, just the house. I repeat my point about the possibility of a row in the future if we have no security over the land. Tatetarō points out that Takeshi had agreed to sell me the land. I then add that we are prepared to return Takeshi the house and land, since he is not happy with the arrangement. All he has to do is return the money I've paid and give Daisuke back what he has spent preparing to rebuild the house. Inoshige, who has already warned me that he doesn't want to appear to be lending me his shoulder to lean on, suggests that Daisuke's expenses be split 50–50. Tatetarō accepts my counterargument that I don't deserve to pay half for something that had not been half my fault.

As we get more and more involved in the question of how much Takeshi should pay me and how much he should pay Daisuke, frequent consultations take place in the room adjoining the *kotatsu* room. First Inoshige, Tatetarō, and Takeshi get in a huddle there, trying to thrash out an agreement. Then Inoshige and myself. Then Takeshi and Tatetarō. And each time we come back into the *kotatsu* room, we make a new offer.

Inoshige suggests that I phone Kyōko to let her know what is going on, and Takeshi decides to phone his wife—in spite of the fact that he always calls women "idiots" and had told Kyōko only yesterday that this was a man's affair. *Tatemae* and *honshiki* again?

Then Takeshi and Tatetarō go off into the next room. Inoshige has time to tell me in a low voice what has gone on.

"He has nine hundred thousand yen in his pocket. I saw it. He actually showed it to me earlier this evening. That's the amount of money he was prepared to pay you back if he had to. But then he began to quibble about lowering Daisuke's expenses from three hundred thousand to two hundred and fifty thousand yen. I told him, 'Fine. I'm sure Būchan will agree, but think of what the people of this valley are going to say when they find out what's happened.'"

We are interrupted by Tatetarō, who slides open the door and announces that Hanako is coming up to the house. She is angry with Takeshi and wants to know what is going on. Inoshige is itching for a drink and asks—for the second time—whether we might not have a bit of alcohol. It is almost midnight, and we are all too tired to object.

Just then, Hanako arrives, together with their son Reisuke, who looks as black as thunder and mutters at his father to stop complaining. Hanako is ushered straight into the guest room by Tatetarō, who later calls in Takeshi for another conference. Then Inoshige is asked to join them, and Daisuke and I are left to chat with Ayako and Misae. It is all a bit like a game of musical chairs.

Inoshige comes back with a new proposal. We are to return to our original agreement. The land will be mine. The boundaries will be properly drawn up, and the sale registered with the Town Council. We can park our car in the parking area, and Takeshi promises never to complain again.

This is fine, I respond, except I am convinced that Takeshi is, as usual, doing what he has been told to do and not what he wants to do. Something is going to happen some day in the future, and we will be back to square one. I am very grateful to Hanako for taking the trouble to come up and speak to her husband, but . . . There is something eminently satisfying sometimes in the way that Japanese allows you to end a sentence with the word but. It implies so much.

Tatetarō nods. "You're right, Būchan. Takeshi is never clear about anything, and there is no guarantee, as you say, about the way he'll behave. All I can say is that Inoshige and I will be around to make sure there are no more problems over land boundaries."

"The thing is, I don't want to keep on having to rely on you and Inoshige, Tatechan. You are my friends, and it strikes me that the quickest way to lose friends is to ask for their help every time you're in trouble. You'll have to give us time to talk the matter over. That's all I can say."

This is accepted, and we begin drinking. And suddenly, Takeshi decides to apologize.

"I'm lacking cultivation. I've only been to primary school, and I've got a lot of faults. You, Būchan, have in the past called me a '*daitai* man,' a 'generally speaking man,' because I tend not to be precise about things. Well, generally speaking, that's correct. But then, generally speaking, that's the way we behave here in the country."

"Yes, generally speaking, you're right there, Takeshisan," Tatetarō agrees. "But then Būchan is a foreigner who's been brought up in a city, and that makes it difficult for him to fully understand the generally speaking feeling of the country."

By this time, we're all having a good laugh. *Sake* cups are being exchanged with some briskness to show that there are no really hard feelings. After a little more chat about dialects and the country, Hanako makes a move to leave. Takeshi immediately adopts a formal kneeling posture and, to my surprise, gives a short speech:

"I am a man of little education, unlike you, and I have caused you a lot of trouble. I apologize for this. I have in the past mentioned that you shouldn't, generally speaking, park your car in the parking area, but please forget all that. I promise to keep to the proposal put forward this evening, so please go home and discuss it with Kyōko, Alyosha, and Maya. I hope that you'll be able to agree to the proposal, and that everything will proceed amicably."

He bows, and I reply that we will do our best to reach a decision the next day. Everybody gets out of the *kotatsu* and kneels on the *tatami*, exchanging bows and thanking Misae and Ayako for their hospitality. We apologize for keeping everyone up so late, and then Tatetarō, Takeshi, and Hanako leave. Daisuke and I stay on for a while, discussing the outcome of the meeting. It is all up to me now. Hanako is much admired for telling her husband to behave himself. That is the sort of thing Haruzō's wife ought to do. It is because of her weakness that other people's marriages are ruined.

Women get the blame for everything in the end!

69 Having publicly refused to give their daughter away in marriage, Terukichi and Akemi, together with some of their neighbors and relatives, have now all got together and urged Michiko to get married after all. But this time, Michiko has refused. She never really liked her future husband, it seems, and anyway she couldn't possibly marry him after all that has happened. Apparently, the prospective bridegroom is to come and see Michiko tomorrow. I shudder to think what his parents must be thinking of the whole affair.

The enthusiasm with which people in Yashiki village relate what bits of gossip they have heard merely confirms the truth of the saying, "One man's sorrow is another's joy." Households will secretly revel at the misfortunes of their neighbors. But that is only on the inside, of course. Outside, they make sure to look suitably concerned as the occasion demands. I would hate something unpleasant like this to happen to us.

In a way the argument between Haruzō and Terukichi has deeply affected Kyōko and me. We have been made to realize how difficult it would be to live here in this valley. After a long discussion, we conclude that the best thing would be for us to return Takeshi his land and forget all about our dreams of living here. Neither of us wants to go through the same kind of argument again; nor do we fully trust Takeshi.

"You're right, Būchan," says Daisuke as, together with Inoshige, we sit having a few drinks together a couple of evenings later. "Takeshi isn't one to be trusted. You know, he phoned me last night. Yes, he did. Trying to find out what was going on with you and Kyōko. And from the way he spoke, I had a sneaking suspicion that, if ever you decided to leave the valley and sell Takeshi back his land, he wouldn't give you anything at all for the house. Just the land and no more. He's that sort of person."

"I think Takeshi is having second thoughts about parting with so much money," says Inoshige, "and now he's trying to wriggle out of it. What we have to do is scare him off a bit. What I think is that if Takeshi starts quibbling about how much to return you and Daichan here, I ought to intervene. 'If you're not going to buy back the land at the proper price,' I'll tell him, 'then I'll buy it. I'll buy it from you, Takeshi, and lend it to Būchan.' What do you think of that?"

Having by now put down quite a lot of *sake*, we all think Inoshige's suggestion is pretty hilarious. It is definitely time we made a night of it down in the town. So we get up to go and bathe and eat. As we leave Daisuke's house, I ask about Michiko and the wedding.

Daisuke's face brightens. "It's all been arranged. Michiko's agreed to get married, and the wedding has been fixed for the twenty-third."

"Yes. It'd be nice if your problem could be solved as satisfactorily," chimes in Inoshige, turning to me.

"Michiko's a good girl. She obviously decided to put her parents' interests first," says Daisuke.

"Yes," Inoshige nods, "that way she stops further unpleasantness."

"Poor thing," I comment sadly.

Inoshige laughs. "You should be saying, 'How wonderful! I'm glad everything worked out so well.' Still, I can understand how you feel."

When I get home, I find Hanako talking to Kyōko. I have seen the Yamaguchi truck parked at the end of the track by the fox-deity shrine and feel apprehensive about meeting Takeshi on my own. Hanako looks worn out. We exchange greetings, and then she asks me whether we won't stay on at the house. She's been so upset that she hasn't been able to eat for two whole days. Their daughters are threatening to leave home. "If Būchan and his family go, then so do we! That's what they told me."

Yet it is clear from what Hanako says that she has little idea of how the argument started or of what Takeshi has said and done. He has never discussed the land transaction with her; nor has he mentioned his quibbling over land boundaries and trees and, later, money. He obviously firmly believes in his statement made the other evening to the effect that women are idiots—fools who should be kept out of men's business.

Hanako asks us to reconsider our position. For the sake of form more than anything else, we agree to talk it over again, but also explain that neither of us feels that Takeshi is very reliable by nature. It isn't that we have anything against him personally. We feel sorry for Hanako and her children. It is just that we don't want to go through this sort of unpleasantness again.

So there we are. Do we stick to what *we* think and have decided is the right course of action? Or do we do what any Japanese would do in such a situation and yield to the emotional arguments of those involved? We find ourselves caught between those dichotomous poles of "rationality" and "feeling," of "principles" and "adaptability," that seem to characterize English (and to a large extent Western) thought, on the one hand, and Japanese thought on the other. Do we want to live here in this valley, creating a network of obligation and debt, *giri* and *ninjō*, of "unrequited passive love" and "presumption upon" others, *amae* and *meiwaku*, which will last until we die? *Avoid contention with others, bend yourself to their views, put yourself last and other people first—that is the best course.*

Together we decide that if we are to create such a network of give-and-take, we would prefer to do so in a less stifling atmosphere, where people are more prepared to accept that an individ-

ual is entitled to his own opinions. So we adhere to our principles
. . . regretfully.
Only violets remain, mingled with the reeds.

70 But to explain everything in terms of abstract principles is
not going to be sufficient to convince those involved. Publicly, at
least, Takeshi has backed down and agreed to sell us the land. Our
refusal to accept this proposal cannot but be seen as stubbornness.
Somehow we have to strengthen our position, and our Būchan,
who has never in his life been bothered with political strategy, now
finds himself having to tell lies in order to survive.

The story that Kyōko and I relay to Inoshige is this. In order to
rebuild the house, we have had to borrow money from a friend.
This much is true. The rest is a slight travesty of truth, but will
suffice: this evening our friend telephoned to ask what was happening about the house; we had to tell her all about the land argument,
as a result of which she has advised us not to rebuild. In other
words, she is withdrawing her financial support. Even if we keep
the land, we cannot now rebuild the house. We also add that Kyōko's parents and brother have told us that we should hand back the
land. By framing a personal decision as a family decision, we will
strengthen our position.

Inoshige accepts this fabrication of half-truths. He will call me
back in due course. Why do I have to lie like this to my best friend?
Is this what living in the country does to people? Or is it living in
Japan?

At 11:00 P.M. I am called down to Tatetarō's house, where I find
Takeshi, Daisuke, Inoshige, and Tatetarō himself all fairly drunk
and bleary-eyed.

They look at one another, before Tatetarō begins.

"So, where do we start? Are we going to do what Daichan suggested?"

"Yes, but we don't have to say all that."

"We can leave out the bit about . . . you know."

"Yes, okay."

This is like some spy thriller, with me trying to tie up all these
threads of speech and weave them into something that makes sense.
Eventually, Inoshige puts me out of my misery. The proposal is,

return the land, Takeshi will pay 250,000 yen to Daisuke, and I will pay Daisuke 300,000 yen. Everybody loses out. It is a sad affair and somewhat embarrassing. If the proposal is passed, Daisuke is paid at once, and I get my money back when I leave, if I leave, the house in Ōkubo.

I am slightly confused. "Whose land is it now, then?"

"Your land."

"But we have to decide how long it's going to be your land," puts in Tatetarō, "because, after that, you'll have to leave."

"No. He doesn't have to leave," Daisuke corrects him.

"But if he doesn't leave, then he ought to pay rent or something."

"Yes, and he ought to pay a higher rent than before," adds Inoshige.

"No, no!" (Takeshi)

"Yes, yes!" (Inoshige)

"Well, we can decide about that later," says Tatetarō.

"But if I have to leave, when do I have to leave?" I am confused by what is rapidly becoming a Mad Hatter's *sake* party. "And if I don't leave, when will we decide the rent? And when will I start paying rent? I have to know because if the rent's too high, I may have to find somewhere else to live. And that could be difficult."

Inoshige shakes his head in slight bewilderment that somebody is still sober enough to think straight.

"You've got a really good head on your shoulders, Būchan. I hadn't thought of all that. How about *o-bon*? Or the end of August?"

"That's silly," says Tatetarō firmly. "Financial affairs go in half-yearly sections and the lower half of the year doesn't start until October first."

"Right. So Būchan has the land till the end of September."

"Never mind about that," mutters Takeshi.

"No," insists Inoshige, "we've got to fix it while we're here."

"No, let's not. Because Būchan might not be here in October, and then we'll have wasted our time fixing rent."

"But I do intend to be here in October."

"Oh, do you?" Tatetarō's face lights up as he offers me his *sake* cup. "That's good. I must say, it's really nice, isn't it, having a foreigner come and live here in this valley. Oni has its good points, don't you think?"

"Yes, it's got a tradition," says Takeshi, looking at Inoshige. "Pottery."

"And pears," Daisuke adds to keep Takeshi happy.

"And carpentry," says Tatetarō quickly, but not very convincingly.

"You ought to sell your pears to the tourists," Inoshige tells Takeshi.

"That's a good idea," says Tatetarō. "They're nice and sweet."

"But not too sweet. There's nothing worse than a pear that's too sweet," Daisuke observes.

"You're right there, Daichan. But crispy pears are all right, aren't they?"

"Ah! Crispy pears. Now, they're another matter entirely."

Tatetarō is warming more *sake* in a kettle on the stove beside him. Inoshige suggests that we clap hands to signify that an agreement has been reached. Does Takeshi agree?

"Well, I agree," he answers, "but there are just one or two things I want to say. There was that problem with the land boundary and the azaleas, and that arose really because Būchan thought the boundary was in one place and I thought it was in another."

"Quite so, quite so," murmurs Daisuke sleepily.

"And there's something else," Takeshi continues, oblivious of the fact that all of us seem to find his sudden speeches wholly out of place. "When Būchan here went back to England for a holiday, I told him I couldn't give him a farewell gift [*senbetsu*] of money, but that he could keep his things in my house rent-free while he was away. I also gave his children two thousand yen each at New Year."

I decide not to mention that I had brought back Takeshi and his family gifts that more than equaled in value what I may have saved in a couple of months' rent.

"And even though Būchan has been paying me rent all these months, I've spent half of it repairing the stone wall where it had crumbled away below his house. And then the bath leaked, and I had to spend the other half putting in a new bath and chimney. So you can see that I have done a lot for Būchan, out of goodwill."

"Yes, yes." Daisuke is nodding off.

"Well, if Takeshi accepts the proposal, let's clap hands on it. Do you agree, Takeshisan?"

"I suppose so."

"Right, then." Tatetarō is being his usual brisk, business-like self. "Takeshi pays two hundred and fifty thousand yen to Būchan to pass on to Daichan."

"Shouldn't he give it straight to Daichan?"

"Straight to Daichan?"

"Yes. It's got nothing to do with Būchan."

"Right." Tatetarō tries again. "Two hundred and fifty thousand yen to Daichan, and Daichan will give back what's left of the half million yen that he received in advance from Būchan as soon as he's worked out all his expenses. Būchan stays where he is until the end of September, when the land is returned, and Takeshi here pays back four hundred and fifty thousand yen to Būchan. And if Būchan wants to stay on, he will have to rent the house for—" Tatetarō pauses, "for . . . how much?"

"Eighteen thousand a month," says Inoshige quickly.

"Right. Eighteen thousand. But that sum is subject to negotiation and confirmation. Okay?"

"Okay."

"Right then. Clap hands."

We all kneel formally around the *kotatsu*. Just then the door slides open, and Tatetarō's son comes in, on his way back to his room from the bath.

"Ah, Tatehiko, you're just in time. Come and witness this. We're going to clap hands," says Tatetarō. "You don't know what we're clapping hands for, of course, but witness it, all the same."

"Right!"

"Ready?"

"Ready."

"O-o-o-o-o-o-h!" We clap our hands rhythmically together twice: *clap-clap*.

"O-o-o-h!" And twice more: *clap-clap*.

Then we bow to one another.

"I'm indebted to you for your help."

"Not at all, thank you very much."

Tatetarō warms more *sake*.

"It's been a sad affair, really. And rather embarrassing for us all, too. It's a pity things didn't work out the way they seem to have up in Amagase with that wedding row. But there you are. Būchan is a foreigner. He sees things differently."

"It's not a bad thing being a foreigner," says Inoshige, coming to my rescue.

"No, of course not. I didn't mean that. Foreigner isn't a word we use disparagingly. Not at all. Westerners are people we Japanese look up to. Not like the Koreans, whom we have made fools of for ages."

"No, not like Koreans at all."

"For some reason or other, we've always despised the Koreans. And that's really bad. After all, we're all human beings, aren't we, Būchan?"

The conversation jumps from one topic to the next for another half hour or so, and then Takeshi suddenly begins to sing a ballad:

> I'm sorry, my darling—
> Let's go back to the way things were.
> It's not that I don't love you,
> But my wounded heart cries out in pain.
> You are too beautiful for me,
> So please forget this foolish man that I am.

This pleases everybody a lot—and the more so because Takeshi substitutes "man" for the "woman" of the original song. Tatetarō decides to write down everything that we've agreed on before complete inebriation makes him forget. Then we get up to leave.

"Let's go down to drink in town," Inoshige suggests impulsively.

"It's a bit late."

"All the bars will be shut."

"Why not spend the night here, then?" suggests Tatetarō.

"No, no. It's time we went home."

"And report what has happened to our wives," I add mischievously.

"You shouldn't do that," says Tatetarō quickly, swallowing the bait. "This is a matter for men."

"Yes. A matter among the five of us," adds Inoshige.

"We don't want the whole valley to know about this."

"No, keep it to ourselves. Much better that way."

And so we take our leave and go outside to the chorusing of frogs in the rice paddies. Takeshi shakes my hand.

"I'll probably be up in the orchards tomorrow." He grins, and one of his silver-capped teeth glints in the light outside Tatetarō's yard. "See you then."

"Yes," I reply.

Then I drive home. I feel empty, hollow, worn out. I don't want to do anything at all.

71 These mountain silhouettes that I know so well, these sounds of birds calling, of the wind in the pear trees, of the bamboo swaying. They will never be mine. Perhaps they never, after all, were mine. I who am caught in this bridge of dreams.

III Voice of the Cicada

The cicada's voice
Gives no sign it knows
That death is near.

—*Bashō*

72 It is said that the most precious thing in life is its uncertainty.

Yesterday, I came back from a trip to Tokyo in order to be in time for Alyosha's birthday. I phoned Kyōko from the airport and arranged for her to meet me at the bus station. When I arrived, she was looking pale. Alyosha had had an accident. His teacher had phoned about an hour before, saying something about the boy having hit his head while diving into the school swimming pool. There was nothing to worry about, but—just as a precaution (*nen no tame*)—Alyosha had better be seen by a doctor.

We drove to a small private clinic on the edge of town nearest the school. The place seemed deserted. But a nurse heard us arrive and came out to meet us. We were shown into the surgery. Baba, the teacher in charge of swimming, was hovering nervously nearby. The moment he saw us, he began to apologize.

"I'm sorry," he kept on repeating. "I'm so sorry."

Before we had time to ask what had happened, the doctor—a man named Harada—came in. He was a fairly elderly man with a deeply tanned face and a bristly gray pencil-line mustache. Nodding to us, he walked across the surgery to where Alyosha was lying and slipped his fingers under the boy's neck.

An early cicada began chirping outside the window.

"Unless I'm much mistaken," Harada began, "your son has fractured the third and fourth bones in his neck. I think that the fifth is all right. I'm afraid this means that the boy has only a sixty percent chance of survival. And if he does survive, he will almost certainly be paralyzed. From the waist down."

It is strange how people react so differently to the same information. Faced with the appalling bluntness—an almost brutal honesty—of Harada's diagnosis, Kyōko fainted and I laughed.

"We haven't brought this boy up the past twelve years just so that he can die on his birthday," I replied. How the unexpected makes one say the even less expected! Is it that stupidity is defined by a person's inability to deal with the unanticipated phrase, or event?

"Are you sure that the bones in his neck are broken?" I asked.

Harada pursed his lips momentarily. His mustache bristled even more. "Pretty sure. The trouble is that I have no way of checking. My X-ray assistant is away at the moment. We'll have to wait until he comes back."

"And when will that be?"

There was a brief consultation between doctor and nurse.

"I don't know. Apparently he has gone for a driving lesson. Nurse here has tried to contact him, but he had already left when she got through to the driving school. It may be eight o'clock before he gets back. Maybe later."

"Isn't there anything we can do in the meantime?"

Harada sucked in through his teeth, the way Japanese frequently do when weighing up whether to be honest and say what they think, or not.

"Not really," he said.

I looked at Baba, who was standing to one side, eyes fixed firmly on the floor in front of him. He was obviously in no state to make any suggestions. I asked Harada whether there was any way we could get Alyosha X-rayed promptly.

This was what the doctor had been waiting for. The town's Central Hospital had emergency facilities. They had an ambulance and a specialist. And besides, their director had just come back from a long stay in the States. He could speak good English.

This piece of information came as a considerable relief to me. There is nothing more difficult than having to deal with illness—especially serious illness—in a foreign language. It was not that my Japanese was not good enough to understand what had happened. Rather, it was a matter of learning how to cope with a totally new situation. Even in English, terms like cervical column and spinal paralysis were outside my own experience. I needed to be led gently through this new field of knowledge. One way to feel reassured would be to hear about everything in English, as well as Japanese. Language became the blind man's stick.

And so we arranged to have Alyosha moved to Central Hospital by an ambulance whose siren wailed mournfully in the thick and heavy dusk. Alyosha was X-rayed as soon as we arrived and then brought back to the casualty area. We waited outside in the corridor with Baba, who was still apologizing for what had happened. He seemed to be in more need of treatment than any of us. We tried to console him by telling him not to worry; it probably wasn't his fault.

The hospital director called us in. Harada had been right. Alyosha had fractured the third and fourth bones in his neck. He had also severely compressed the second bone. His cervical column looked a bit like a winding mountain track.

"At this stage, there isn't very much we can do." The director pointed to the X-rays clipped to a well-lit viewing screen. "We'll use traction to try and straighten his neck out, but the main thing at the moment is to keep the swelling down. You can see here how close the bones are to his windpipe. If that swelling gets any worse, I'm afraid that his windpipe will get blocked. That's what we've got to watch, because he might suffocate. But," he was kind enough to add very quickly, "I've never known that to happen yet. Not in my experience, at least. It's just a possibility that we have to be aware of."

He walked over to where Alyosha was lying, deathly white, terrifyingly still.

"As for paralysis," he continued, "we'll have to wait and see. At the moment, Alyosha is fully conscious of all his senses. He can feel it when I touch his toes and that's good. Considering the force with which he must have hit his head, that in itself is quite remarkable."

And so began a long night when I refused to believe that Alyosha might not survive. Kyōko went home to look after Maya. Separately we spent a sleepless night. The director had told us that the first 24 hours would be the most dangerous.

And then the next 24 hours.

And then, perhaps, we could begin to relax.

73   And survive he has. It has been a long three weeks, longer for Kyōko perhaps than for myself, since she is the one who has been with him almost all the time, looking after his needs. In Japanese hospitals relatives have to look after patients who are immobile. It is difficult to grasp fully how precarious Alyosha's situation

is. Predictions for the future are quite terrifying. The slightest accident—a fall, perhaps, or a bump on the head—may well kill him.
Yet he walks around and feels no pain. He has to wear a collar, of
course. But he looks all right. And because he looks all right, and
because somehow I have to comfort Kyōko and not allow her to get
too worried or depressed, I myself adopt an optimistic attitude that
he *will* be all right.

This optimism is shared by people in the valley, who are convinced that he has recovered. "Oh! He's out of the hospital. He
must be okay" is what Kumao said one day. "I saw him walking
down to Takayuki's *sake* shop. He'll soon be back to normal" is the
way Jirō put it. People cannot—or, is it, will not?—understand that
he might be killed tomorrow, and that this is what we, as parents,
have to live with.

I find myself caught up in a paradox of selves. Within the closed
circle of my family, I have to put a brave face on what is an inexpres-
sibly awful situation. Alyosha himself must be made to feel that
there is hope. And yet at the same time, in my relations with the
outside world, I do not want to let people gloss over and forget
what has happened. My optimism is in fact their unconcern.

This can be seen particularly in the way the school authorities
appear to have suppressed news of the accident. One night, about a
week ago, I met Michiya.

"What?" he exclaimed. "Broke his neck? I'd heard he'd had an
accident, but nobody said anything to me about its being a serious
one. I'll talk to the PTA about this."

He was true to his word. Apparently, the PTA has now told the
school to get a move on and find out whether Alyosha's accident is
covered by the usual insurance plan for children. It seems that it is,
and that we are entitled to a 40 percent rebate on our hospital bills.
While Alyosha was in the hospital, every member of Ōkubo—except for our next-door neighbor Masaki—came to visit him. Each
family left 1,500 yen in an envelope as a get-well present. Alyosha's
classmates have given 100 yen each, and all the school teachers 300
yen. All this has to be returned in equivalent value.

Who is responsible for the accident? This is going to be the crux
of the matter, once we get beyond our present struggle for survival.
As far as I can judge, everyone seems intent on avoiding responsi-

bility. In a way, it would be easy to blame the teacher in charge, Baba. That is what the headmaster, Hageyama, obviously antici- pated, for three days after the accident he came to visit Alyosha in the hospital, accompanied by his deputy. Almost the first words they said then were that they intended to have Baba stop teaching. Both Kyōko and I were astounded at this and immediately told Hageyama to do nothing of the sort. After all, no inquiry had been made into how the accident had occurred. It was quite possible that Baba had not been at fault. For a start, the pool was only three feet deep, and that is hardly the safest depth at which to practice diving. The headmaster seems indirectly to have accepted this argument because, since Alyosha's accident, the eleven- and twelve-year-olds have been taken to a larger and slightly deeper pool for swimming practice.

But what frustrates me most of all is trying to make other people realize that this sort of accident could have happened to any one of their children, and indeed might still do so as long as they are made to dive into such shallow water. Alyosha is lucky to have survived, and without any apparent physical impairment. The doctors shake their heads in disbelief. Tell that to the local people, however, at a meeting of the PTA in Yashiki—as I did last night—and the imme- diate reply from Buntarō is that the depth of the pool has got noth- ing to do with the accident. The teacher in charge is to blame. He could be right, of course, but I also know that Buntarō has been having a running battle with Baba because softball practice is being interfered with by the very fact that the older children are being taken down to town for swimming practice after school. Buntarō is in charge of the school softball team this year. At least, he has taken it upon himself to run the practice sessions that are held every after- noon and evening in the great buildup toward the annual match with the South Oni Primary School, and he objects to anybody who meddles with his authority. Every night until dark, he makes the children bat, field, run, throw, and shout until they can hardly stand up, let alone walk home, from exhaustion. This is all part of the spiritual training (*seishin*) that accompanies the teaching and learning of all sporting activities in Japan. In this case, the children become sacrificial victims of a few fathers who want to make up for other social deficiencies and show other valley adults what sort of mettle they are made of. To be seen to be administering exercises in "spiritual training" does wonders for a man's status in the local opinion poll of gossip.

Yet a number of mothers are patently fed up with their children coming home exhausted after half past eight in the evening. The schoolteachers are fed up because the children have neither time nor energy to do their homework. But nobody says anything by way of complaint—except, of course, when gossiping among themselves. But then again women's gossip is women's gossip, and teachers' gossip is outsiders' gossip. The men in the valley don't bother with either.

"Mark you, Būchan," Katsuhisa tells me one night. "Buntarō's attitude is typical of people living in this part of the island. People get themselves elected to positions of authority by default mainly. I mean, people like me are too lazy to do things ourselves. So we let others take over. The trouble is, once somebody does get into a position of authority, he can order everyone else around and nobody will question his authority. It's easy to govern from the top."

What surprises me is that Katsuhisa sees this only in terms of a local trait. To my mind, what he says holds true of most other parts of Japan.

74   It's a busy time of year for school activities. The next thing on the calendar is the *tezukuriten*, or "handmade exhibition." It is strange how people are unable to take a fresh approach to a recurring situation. The whole program has to be arranged with reference to last year's affair: who contributed the beans last year? what time did we start last year? what food and drink did we provide last year? It doesn't matter if the teachers would prefer to finish earlier, or if some people feel that it is unnecessary to provide food and drink. Last year it was . . . ; this year it will be . . .

The main idea of the *tezukuriten* is to raise funds to buy books and other equipment. It includes everything, from homegrown vegetables to homemade bread and pottery. Some 400 items or more are auctioned off to the highest bidder. Parents stand around the assembly hall chatting to one another, occasionally authorizing their children to bid for them, and there is plenty of laughter and competitive bidding. My two pots, for example, are put on the block at 200 yen each. The first goes under the hammer for 800, the second for over 1,000, bought by Inoshige, who outbids one of the schoolteachers. Of course, the last thing Inoshige wants or needs is a pot made by an amateur like me. But his bidding reveals one aspect of the Japanese economic system that, as far as I know, is not all that frequently commented upon. One buys things out of *tsukiai*—a personal relationship with someone—and not just because one wants them. This means that goods have not just a market value, but also a social value. So today's "handmade exhibition" is in its way a miniature replica of Japan's "economism"—people buying things to help out the school, as thanks for past help and as an investment for future relations. The cash paid can be quite inconsistent with the actual value of the goods purchased. One puts personal relations before all else.

75   People in the "outside" world are worried that nothing much is happening about Alyosha's accident. I have been given an introduction to a Mr. Hirose, secretary to a government cabinet minister in Tokyo. I make the long trip to the capital and visit Hirose in the Diet Members' Building. He hears me out and then agrees with me about the depth of the school pool.

"We Japanese are always that much behind the West," he says. "These school pools were built primarily in response to the boom in swimming brought on by the Olympic Games held here in 1964. I know because I used to work in the Ministry of Education. But swimming and diving are two different matters. You're probably right. Three to four feet seems a bit shallow for children to dive in."

He proceeds to telephone the Ministry of Education and speaks to someone in charge of swimming activities. He explains what has happened to Alyosha and suggests that those concerned look into the matter of water depths and diving.

"It's a bit shallow, you know. A bit shallow."

All this took place late on Friday afternoon. On Sunday afternoon, Baba comes up to see Alyosha at the house.

"Headmaster Hageyama and his deputy headmistress, Kaku, were pretty angry with me today," he begins in his disarmingly naïve manner. "Yes, they phoned me up before eight this morning and told me to report to the school at once. I spent the best part of two hours writing up a report on your accident."

Why this sudden activity? It transpires that the Ministry of Education, goaded by Hirose's telephone call, got in touch with the prefectural Education Authority the following morning. Somewhere the ministry people had got their lines crossed, because they demanded to know why someone had been killed in a diving accident and the ministry had not been informed. The prefectural people, in total shock, phoned through to the town's local Education Authority. What was going on? Why hadn't they been told about the accident? The local people replied that, as far as they knew, nobody had been killed. There had been a slight accident with a foreign boy. That was all. Still, to make sure, they called up the headmaster and demanded an immediate account of what had happened to Alyosha. That was why Baba had been summoned to the school. He and the two administrators sat down and wrote a report. It took them until well after midday to finish it.

In the meantime, the specialist at Central Hospital has told us that he can do no more for Alyosha. He should see a spinal surgeon as soon as possible. Although he arranges an appointment for us to see a doctor in the prefectural capital, we both of us wonder why he didn't let us know before that he felt he was not fully competent to deal with Alyosha's injuries.

The deputy headmistress, Kaku, insists on accompanying us on the long drive to the city. We eventually find the hospital and join those queuing in the waiting room. X-rays are taken. Then much later we are shown into where the surgeon, Urayama, has been seeing patients for the past four and a half hours nonstop. The X-rays are up on the screen in front of him. He looks at them and then at Alyosha. Then he shakes his head.

"You're lucky to be alive. If only you'd been brought to me immediately after the accident, perhaps I could have straightened your neck out. Drill a hole in each temple, thread a steel bar inside the cranium, and use traction that way. Still, it's too late now. We'll have to operate on you." He motions to Alyosha to lie down and begins checking his reflexes—feet, hands, knees, elbows. He shakes his head again and sits down.

"Still, it's a bit of a waste to operate. I mean, apparently there's nothing wrong with him. If only his neck could somehow heal on its own."

Urayama suggests that a proper corset be made for Alyosha, with a special support for his neck, and that he wear it for the next three to six months. With luck, the muscles around his neck bones will heal and strengthen enough to hold the cervical column in place.

The deputy headmistress stands in the background, listening to everything. All she can say afterwards is, "That's all right, isn't it? Isn't it?" We can only make noncommittal noises. Urayama has merely confirmed that Alyosha is lucky to be alive, and that his life is very much in danger still. The deputy headmistress is more optimistic. The fact that an operation is not, for the moment at least, necessary means that—as far as she is concerned—Alyosha is on the mend. I am less optimistic. Urayama makes it clear that even though Alyosha's neck may get better now, there could well be complications when he gets older. Somehow I have to ensure that Alyosha will be protected against the future—which means that I am going to have to pinpoint responsibility for the accident.

76 Kyōko has her own network of friends and acquaintances among the women of the valley. Some of them I know from my own social network. Others are completely new to me. Aso Harumi is one of those I have never come across. But perhaps that is not so surprising after all, for her husband works in the furniture company situated right at the bottom of the valley in Fujioka, and her father-in-law is usually away doing temporary construction work in places like the prefectural capital. They live way up at the top of Ichinotsuru and don't mix much with people lower down the valley where we are.

Harumi herself comes from Osaka. It is strange to hear a broad Kansai dialect being spoken here—reminding us of our years in Kobe, where the children were born. This does not mean, though, that Harumi cannot be fitted into our scheme of the valley. Her husband's household is the main house from which our neighbor Masaki's family branched two or three generations ago. That was well before his house burned down, and he came down the valley to Ōkubo.

Harumi's husband used to work in a pharmaceutical company in

Takatsuki, and that was where they had met. They decided to get married, even though Harumi was his elder by several years, and planned to settle down there. But then Aso fell ill, and they came back to the Oni valley with their son, Yoshio, who is in Maya's class at school. It is this, together with the fact that we used to live in the Kansai area, that sparks off a friendship between Harumi and Kyōko.

Harumi is worried about my being away so often. "Don't let it be known around the valley that Būchan is away so much," she warned Kyōko, "or else you'll find someone knocking on your door late at night and trying to do a bit of night crawling [*yobai*]."

Kyōko began to laugh this off as another male put-on, but Harumi cut her short. She had been awakened one night a few weeks back by a terrible din. Her in-laws were yelling at each other, and she could hear the sound of another man's voice, too. As she roused herself from her sleep, she suddenly realized what it was that had struck her as strange. Her father-in-law wasn't supposed to have been in the house. He had been away doing construction work in the prefectural capital. But it seemed that he had come back unannounced and caught his wife in bed with another man who lived "as close as your nose is to your eyes."

So it looks as if the golden rule of *yobai*—the one that I am always quoted about its not being done within the community—is a case of do as I say, not as I do; another example of *tatemae*. Harumi's mother-in-law spends her whole time in the company of men, working in the mountains lopping the lower branches off the cedar trees. And it may be that she has always carried on with them, although she apparently denied it to her husband that night and swore that this was the first time she had ever been unfaithful. Anyway, the three of them sat down then and there in the *kotatsu* and hammered out an agreement. Harumi had served them tea and listened to the argument going on from behind the sliding screen. The lover was given a choice: pay a fine for his behavior, or the injured husband would let the other man's wife and the whole community of Ichinotsuru know what had happened. The lover chose the fine and found himself the next day withdrawing half a million yen from his savings account with the Agricultural Cooperative— the price of Aso's silence and of maintaining his own social status.

And the fact that this man is both prepared and able to pay so

much can only mean that he is a rich landlord. There are only two
such wealthy households in Ichinotsuru. Only one of these fits Harumi's description of living cheek by jowl with them. Perhaps, after
all, it is true that *an elephant can be securely tied with a rope plaited
from the strands of a woman's hair*.

77   I have been in touch with the local Education Authority in
town. The person in charge of everyday affairs is Wada Hiromi,
uncle of both Takeshi and Tatetarō.

"We both of us live in the same valley, Mr. Moeran, and you're
renting a house, I gather, from one of my nephews, so I can assure
you that I will do all I can to help. I think at the moment what we
have to consider is the school insurance scheme. This will, of
course, provide you with compensation for your son's medical
costs. But at the moment the coverage only lasts for two years, and
what I want to ensure is that the plan will pay for treatment for
Alyosha after he returns to England. Leave things to me. I'll check
with the Ministry of Education in Tokyo."

I am impressed with Hiromi's concern. Friends in the outside
world are less so and insist on my getting written confirmation that
the local Education Authority accepts responsibility for Alyosha's
accident. After all, he was doing as he was told when the accident
occurred: diving under instruction during school hours in an institution he was compelled by law to attend.

The quickest and most efficient method of obtaining an admit-
tance of responsibility is to start at the top. So I make an appointment to see the town mayor. Out of politeness, I then inform the
school headmaster of what is going on. Hageyama looks perturbed
and asks me to cancel my appointment. After all, he, his deputy
headmistress, and Wada Hiromi are doing all in their power to
help. If I go and see the mayor, they are going to be roundly told
off, because the mayor doesn't in fact know about the accident. In
other words, the town's Education Authority has been keeping this
matter entirely to itself.

As Hageyama talks away, trying to justify everyone's behavior, he
lets slip the fact that the reason for Hiromi's insisting on getting
the school insurance program to pay for Alyosha's medical expenses
after we return to England is that, if this is not done, responsibility

for the accident will be seen to rest entirely on Baba, the teacher in charge, together with Hageyama, the school headmaster, and the local Education Authority. By getting a guarantee from the insurance program on our behalf, those concerned are hoping to evade the central issue. If Baba were to be accused of incompetence, the whole system would come under fire.

What I have hitherto thought was goodwill on the part of all concerned, I now realize is nothing more than the evasion of responsibility. Every coin has its second side, and the reverse does not necessarily imply a strict opposite to the obverse. I wonder, though, just how logically those concerned have worked out the implications of their actions. Is it a conscious evasion of responsibility? Or is everyone just trying to do his, or her, best to help and by this very willingness creating paradoxical situations? This is where it becomes really difficult to distinguish between *honshin* and *tatemae*.

As a result of my visit to the mayor's office, Kyōko and I are called down to the school for a meeting. It is a weekend, and nobody is in the teachers' common room apart from Hageyama and Wada Hiromi. After a few pleasantries, Hiromi begins.

"Mr. Moeran, the first thing to make clear is that the town, in others words the local Education Authority and the school, is not prepared to accept responsibility for the accident to your son. Not until responsibility is proved. The school obeyed regulations laid down by the Japan Swimming Federation and endorsed by the Ministry of Education. The pool was filled to a depth varying between eighty-five centimeters in its shallow end and one meter ten centimeters in its deepest part. Where Alyosha dived in, it was ninety-three centimeters deep. Activities conducted in the pool at the time of the accident were in accordance with the Ministry of Education's regulations. You, of course, may question the content of these regulations, but as set out they were obeyed by the headmaster here, and there is nothing illegal about that. All of which means that the only one who can be blamed for what happened is the teacher, Baba. But so far as can be ascertained, Baba did everything according to instructions laid down in the teaching manuals. There is, therefore, no reason for the town to accept responsibility for Alyosha's accident."

Hiromi is quick to admit that this is the "cold, official" view of things. However, as someone personally involved in the case and acquainted with us all socially, thanks to his kinship ties with Ya-maguchi Takeshi and Wada Tatetarō, Hiromi wants to make sure that everything turns out well.

"What I would like to suggest, therefore, is that we consider the school insurance program. There are various paths open to you, although none of them can be taken until Alyosha has been exam-ined again by the surgeon, Urayama. What I want to avoid, though, is any idea that Alyosha is completely cured. Why? Because if that happens, there is going to be no way that I can prevail upon the people in charge of the insurance program to guarantee Alyosha's medical expenses in the future. The idea is to leave the future open to doubt."

This completely confuses me, for I fail to see the logic of Hiro-mi's argument. From what the doctors have said so far, it seems highly unlikely that Alyosha will ever be completely cured. I can only insist, therefore, on a written document admitting the local Education Authority's responsibility. As a parent, I owe Alyosha that much at least. Somehow his future must be guaranteed.

"Yes, I agree with you entirely about this matter of guarantee," answers Hiromi quickly. "That's why I want the school insurance people to guarantee Alyosha medical care for life. Then the ques-tion of responsibility will not occur, will it?"

It takes us the best part of a week to get over that!

78   Katsuhisa lazes at home on the last day of the summer hol-idays. "Bathing," he begins, apropos of very little, "is a fairly new custom, you know, in this part of the world. At least, it is in the summer. In the old days people used to dowse themselves with water outside in their yards. We only had proper baths in winter. Even then, we had to carry the wooden bathtub outside and place it where we wanted. In the garden or somewhere. Things have changed, though. On a day like this I wouldn't mind sitting in a bathtub outside in the garden here." He grins and scratches the stubble of his unshaven chin. "I can quite happily sit in the water of the stream above Amagase and spend a day there now and then."

We fall silent, our voices almost drowned by the barrage of cica-das' voices. Katsuhisa whittles away at a block of wood, which he gradually shapes into four straight figurines.

"In the old days, you know, the 'honor the man, despise the woman' complex was so strong that women used to have to wash their clothes in separate buckets from men's clothes. Yes, and they even had to dry them on separate bamboo poles. Things are much better nowadays."

He carves little indentations in the figurines, shaping a mouth here, a neck there, before using a special knife to peel thin slivers from the bottom of the figurines right up to the heads. The wood curls up with the knife to rest about the head in a perfect set of ringlets.

"People somehow seemed to enjoy themselves so much more in the past, didn't they? Perhaps it was because they worked harder. Now life is so much easier, although there will always be people trying to impress you with how difficult their work is. But let's face it, anyone can grow rice. It's the easiest thing in the world. All you do is plant it and it grows. It's hardly surprising the government pays us not to grow rice. Nobody wants to grow anything else, though. There's too much hard work involved."

Misako is redoing the old kitchen. Since she has learned from Kyōko how to make bread and is now selling it to one of the bigger supermarkets in town, she has been visited by the health authorities and been given all sorts of instructions about what she must and must not do. Yuki has been so astonished at her daughter-in-law's success that she now occasionally helps pack up the bread and rolls in plastic bags. In a rare moment of goodwill, she then agreed to changes being made in the kitchen.

"Misako called in Daisuke the carpenter the very next morning, just in case my mother changed her mind. It was just as well." Katsuhisa holds his figurines at arm's length and critically studies them. "Three days have passed, and she is already showing signs of going back on her word. But it's too late." He makes a minor adjustment to a head of "hair" and proceeds to glue his figurines to the wooden bases he has ready and waiting. "Now, my mother is busy clearing out those two rooms above the storage space over there. You know, the ones you nearly rented from us. Perhaps my mother is going to move out of the main house. What a lovely idea!"

Because Misako is now earning a fair amount of money, her position is much stronger in the Kajiwara household. It is always possible, of course, that Yuki's selfish dominance will come to an end, but somehow I doubt whether this will happen for a while yet. The older woman seems to have a mesmerizing effect on her daughter-in-law. For example, when Misako had the plumber in recently to put in a new bath, the whole family had to go down to the public bath this side of town. As they left the house, Yuki asked Misako whether she'd remembered the soap. She said she had and got in the car. But as they neared town, she suddenly realized that she only had one bar of soap, and that they would need two—one for her husband and son, another for the women. Terrified at what Yuki would say when she found out, Misako began surreptitiously biting the cake of soap in two. Her seven-year-old son noticed her doing this and exclaimed in a penetrating voice that he thought his mother must be going bananas. Misako stopped gnawing away at once and bought some soap at the nearest drugstore. Apparently she had the taste of soap in her mouth all evening. So Yuki wasn't the only one foaming at the mouth!

A story like this can only strike one as bordering on the absurd. How could anyone do anything so irrational—especially when every public bathhouse in Japan sells soap at the door? Accepted rationality, then, suggests that to chew soap when soap can be bought is beyond one's powers of reason. And yet Misako's act was entirely rational in the context of her relationship with her mother-in-law. There is no such thing, then, as Rationality—with a capital R and in the singular form. There are merely rationalities—as many rationalities, perhaps, as there are relationships between people.

As for the figurines, Katsuhisa gives them to me later that evening. "The long thin one's you," he explains. "And that's Kyōko. And those are the two children. In a few years' time, I expect Kyōko will be the smallest of the four, the way Alyosha and Maya are growing. But I'll make you another set then, so don't worry."

79 Today, that magnificent event to beat all other events—the children's sports day at the primary school. The flags that bedeck the playground are the same as those that are hung in the rice fields to frighten the birds. The entrance gate, through which the children file before each race, has castle towers that make it look rather like one of those love hotels you see along the main road to the prefectural capital. A panoply of caps, track suits, cameras; of headbands, grubby knees, and faces plastered white—first with makeup, then much later in the afternoon with cornstarch after a "candy-eating race." And the lunch boxes! Each household tries to outdo its neighbor in preparing magnificent repasts—sea bream, plain and seaweed-wrapped rice-balls, shrimp, ham, bamboo shoots, lotus roots, fried chicken, broccoli, cherries, tea, and juice. That was the meal Munetoshi's family brought along. Those who have little money tend to spend more on such meals. Conspicuous consumption is occasionally acceptable here in the valley.

Sports days are being held at every primary school in the district, and the local supermarkets in town were mobbed yesterday with people buying up food for today's packed lunches. It is said that the biggest supermarket makes as much money in the few days leading up to this occasion as it does on the last day of the year.

80   At the very end of August and in the first week or two of September, speechless visitors suddenly make their appearance in the valley. Quietly, one by one, they take up their positions in the rice fields and, as if frozen by the sun's glare, gaze in still delight at a mountain's ridge, an irrigation ditch, or the steep-thatched roof of a nearby farmhouse. The scarecrows are here once more.

As I wander around taking photographs of these strange images, I gradually become aware of the variety of shapes and sizes used by the valley's farmers to frighten away the birds. Some scarecrows are simple stick figures, with an old colored sweater strung across the crossbar and a hat or bonnet placed on top. Others have straw tied around the sticks to give body to the form. Yet others have a white cotton cloth drawn tightly over a ball of straw—a little like the *teru teru bōzu* hung from the eaves by children to ward off the rain. Is it that scarecrows are also guardians of the weather, helping the rice to ripen in the early autumn sun?

Scarecrows pointing to the sky, scarecrows with flags in their hands, scarecrows crucified in the rice fields. Farmers' straw hats, women's bonnets, mannequins' wigs, laborers' helmets, fishermen's hats, or even kettles upside down.

These images are not limited, of course, to the rice fields. Plastic bags, cut and hanging from posts like streamers in the wind, are not all that different from the flags that fly from the tops of medieval castles in Kurosawa films, or from those flown by protestors at Narita airport. Tin cans, with bells inside that rattle and clatter in the wind, these are the sounds used to frighten away devils. The cacophony of festivals. "Scarecrows" can include squares of tinfoil and car mirrors, which, like many religious objects, gleam to attract attention.

Some farmers place triangular red-and-white flags along the perimeters of their fields. You can see these bedecking garages, or arranged between trees when people set up temporary stalls and sell fruit there in the late summer. What is designed to frighten in the first instance is meant to attract in the second. Scarecrow is, of course, the wrong word, for scarecrows in the end draw attention to themselves. Their very immobility makes us consider them longer, perhaps, than they deserve.

"Those sparrows aren't as stupid as they used to be, you know," Katsuhisa tells me, gently prodding a sleepy frog with his shoe-sock (*jikatabi*). "It's only the first five or six days that the scarecrows have any effect. After that, the birds pay little attention to them. They come and go as they please. It's probably compulsory education that's responsible. Or maybe it's the fact that scarecrows are always painted with smiling faces. I mean, you never come across a farmer smiling as he wades through the rice paddies, looking for weeds and insect-damaged plants. No. Those sparrows aren't stupid at all."

81   Inoshige, Ayako, and I sit under the eaves of their house, listening to the sound of the rain. Two slowworms (*mimizu*) inch their way across the concrete yard, and there is talk of picking them up and frying them in the embers of the bonfire.

"Somewhere, I can't remember where, they eat slowworms, you know," Inoshige says. "But you've got to be careful. They explode and eject a nasty blue liquid all over you."

"Yes," adds Ayako, "you should keep your eyes open when you relieve yourself outside. If you urinate on a slowworm, it'll squirt its juice all over you, and your penis will swell up—this big." She holds out her hands to indicate the diameter of a small football. "Slowworms don't like urine."

"Slowworms remind me of the local bus," Inoshige contributes. "When it first started coming up here to Amagase, there was no bus stop, of course, and people often used to get on and off where they pleased. On a wet day like this, the driver would stop at almost every house, as Haruzō, Daisuke, Terukichi, Michiya, and the rest came out one by one to climb on board. We used to call it the Mimizu because of the way it crawled down the hill."

Later on in the evening, Michiya drops by, and more anecdotes are told over *sake*.

"I was at one of those smart Western-style restaurants the other evening," Michiya relates. "They had napkins on the table. You know the way they fold them up like hats and leave them between the knife and fork? Well, old Jirō was with me. He'd never been to a restaurant like that before, and do you know what he did? He picked up the napkin and solemnly placed it on his head. Then he began to eat his meal."

"The strange things that happen in restaurants," laughs Misae. "I suppose it's because we're not used to them that we do such silly things. Do you remember Reiko and the tea?"

Now, it is Ayako's turn to laugh. "Yes, I do. We were at some restaurant after a Housewives' Association meeting down in town. Reiko was served tea in a cup with a lid on it. I don't know why, but she thought it was a cup of boiled fern tips [*zenmai*], and she began to stir it with her chopsticks, before absentmindedly licking them."

"And Akemi from across the road," Misae continues, eager to get in the punch line, "then asked Reiko whether it tasted good and sweet. Reichan nodded, and so Akemi began stirring her tea as well."

This is a good excuse for Inoshige to tell us again his favorite drinking story.

"Do you remember when we decided to pluck a chicken while it was still alive?"

Michiya's face immediately creases with a smile. "You mean, when we wanted to find out if it could run around without its feathers?"

"And of course it couldn't."

"Wandering all over the place—a bit like Haruzō when he's really drunk. What a place to fall into, though. Right into the cesspit."

"What a time for the tax inspectors to arrive! You know, Būchan, it was a pretty rare thing in those days to see people from outside the hamlet. Even when somebody from somewhere like Ichinotsuru passed through, we'd all stop whatever it was we were doing and stare."

"That's true, Inoshige. So when somebody came especially to see us, we'd use the occasion to get together and have a party."

"With the tax inspectors, of course, we were pretty scared, and so we did our utmost to please them."

"Nobody liked them. They came to find out how much rice we were growing and how much money we were making. They also used to search each of the houses really thoroughly, to make sure we weren't hiding anything illegal."

"Which, of course, we were. We used to grow our own tobacco and make our own cigarettes. And we distilled our own *shōchū*."

"Sometimes, though, we bought some really cheap stuff from some Koreans who made it in town and then peddled it up here in the mountains."

"So when the tax men came, we had to hide things under the floorboards, or anywhere else safe that we could think of. The night we served them the raw chicken in ginger, soy sauce, and shit, one of the inspectors got really drunk. He kept asking for more *sake*. And we didn't have any. None of the legal stuff, anyway."

"Do you know what he did?" Michiya asks rhetorically. "The tax inspector sent me and Haruzō down to Fujioka to buy three bottles of *sake* from the brewery there. He wrote it out on a sheet of paper, telling the brewers to charge it to the local tax bureau. And off we went. But old Haruzō was really cunning. We stopped by my place on the way down, and Haruzō got a brush and some ink and changed the figure three with two deft strokes into five. We got two bottles of *sake* free at the government's expense and hid them away for the next party."

"But still that inspector wanted more to drink. Eventually he said, 'Look! We won't tell on you. Just give us some of your home-made stuff. You must have some somewhere.' So Haruzō took him at his word and went and got a bottle of the *shōchū* made by the

Koreans. Where did he keep it? Why, in the back of his ancestral altar. The inspectors never thought of looking there!"

82   The Oni valley has been designated a "model area" by the local police office. This designation is not an honor, as one might suppose. Oni is a "model" only because of the number of traffic violations that occur here. The valley has the highest rates for speeding and for drunken driving in the whole district.

83   Some people seem to be dogged by bad luck. Our next-door neighbor, Masaki, is one of these. He himself lost a leg in a forestry accident. His second son, Akihito, who was due to take over the family property, was killed in that fall soon after we moved to Ōkubo. Now Mihoko, his wife, has broken her neck.

Masaki himself seemed almost to have a premonition that something would happen. Several days ago, I gave him a lift to town and, by way of small talk, commented on the fact that I hadn't seen Mihoko for a day or two.

"She's out working," he grunted in his usual critical manner. "There's some construction job going on along the river, just below the Coordination Office. We passed it awhile back. I didn't want her to go, but it was Haruo who lives up at the top of Ōkubo who insisted, and I could hardly turn a neighbor down, could I? Still," he said, shifting his artificial leg into a more comfortable position, "it's not the sort of weather for that kind of job. It's too cold. Anything could happen."

And it did. On the third day on the job, Mihoko slipped from the roadside and fell about six feet down into the river. She hit her head on a concrete ledge that had just been completed, and broke her neck.

"It's the fifth bone," Masaki explains in that angry but matter-of-fact tone that he has learned to adopt in the face of adversity. "The main nerve running down her spine has been severed. Yes, completely. Doctors have tried to repair the damage, but it's no use. My wife is paralyzed from the neck down. She'll never walk again."

I just don't know what to say and wonder whether, perhaps, like my fellow inhabitants in this valley, I am not becoming too preoc-

cupied with my own troubles to care about those of others. I hope
that this isn't so. Still, the fact that three people living next door to
each other should suffer the same sort of accident is frightening. Is
there a jinx about this place?

Misae thinks it is the steep hill behind our houses that is responsible for our misfortunes.

"And there's something else," she adds quietly. "You've got several household gods in your downstairs room, haven't you? Well,
check them out. If one of them is split down the back, get rid of it.
Take it to the old priest at the temple and ask him to look after it for
you."

Yuki is not impressed when she hears this.

"No, it's not that at all. Generally speaking, I think you could say
it's the fox-deity shrine that's the cause of all the trouble you've
been having up there. You know, the one at the end of Yamaguchi's
orchard, near where the road branches off to your place. That
shrine didn't used to be there at all, you know. It was located farther
up the hillside above where you and Masaki live. But then they built
the road up to Buntarō's place some five or six years ago, and they
had to move the shrine. Now the direction is all wrong. That part
of Ōkubo is not a good place to live. You'd be wiser to move."

We are back to different rationalities here. I suppose that I myself
would classify all the accidents under the general rubric of "carelessness." Tamaki's son slipped and fell into the river above Amagase
while under the influence of *sake*. Alyosha was made to dive into
water that was ridiculously shallow. Mihoko slipped early on a
frosty morning when there was ice on the road. This of course
forces me to assume that it was a lack of care that led to Tamaki's
losing a leg and to his house burning down. Yet some people do not
find pure carelessness a satisfactory explanation; hence they resort
to the supernatural to explain what is perhaps natural, but seems
somehow unnatural.

If this sounds confused, I may perhaps be excused, for coinci-
dences abound. When I took down the household gods from their
shelf in our *kotatsu* room downstairs, I discovered that two of them
were indeed split right down the middle of the back. Kyōko took
them immediately down to the temple. The old priest was extremely reluctant to take them, but was eventually prevailed upon
to do so. It is little things like this that make us feel more at ease.

84   Some plants are named by their functions. There is one type of wood that is said to be particularly suitable for making slingshots. It is known as a *gomujū no ki*, an "elastic gun" or "slingshot" tree. Another tree around here is known as a "bird-holding" tree (*torimochi no ki*). You can make use of its bark to catch small birds. First pound the bark, then knead it into a paste. Add water and it becomes really sticky. This goo you then paste onto a tree branch so that, when a small bird alights, it cannot fly away. A lot of children catch and keep birds this way.

Dillweed does not grow naturally wild in this climate. And yet a number of people use the herb. This struck me as strange, because nobody has ever even heard of rosemary or basil, let alone use those herbs. Apparently, dill was brought to the valley by men who, like Tamaki, were imprisoned in Siberia and learned about dill's uses from the Russians. They refer to the herb as *roshiagusa*, or "Russian grass." One woman has been making dill pickles out of cucumbers for more than 30 years now.

Kyōko's legacy to the valley will undoubtedly be bread—in particular *yomogi* ("mugwort") bread. Until now, *yomogi* has been used only in rice-cakes. "Culture" is indeed a strange affair.

85   At about nine o'clock yesterday morning, the fire alarm was sounded. The siren seemed to come from down the valley first of all, before being taken up by the Yashiki siren a few minutes later. I thought that maybe the fire brigade was having a full-scale practice. It is near the end of the year, and the voluntary fire brigades all over the prefecture have just started the first of their all-night vigils.

But the sirens went on and on. I looked outside from the veranda of the house and saw a column—and it really was a column—of black smoke rising from behind the ridge beyond Noda Shōsuke's house. Being tired and not fully awake, I thought it must be a forest fire.

As I stood there, Buntarō came racing down the road above the pear orchards in his little van. Well, at least one of the local firemen had heard the alarm. No doubt the others would congregate in due course. They would find out where the fire was, scuttle around trying to decide what to do, and end up drinking a lot of *sake* later on in the day.

I went back inside for a cup of coffee. Eventually the siren stopped its relentless wail, and the stillness returned to the valley, inching stealthily through the cedar forests. One of the wild dogs scratched its fleas. A crow balanced precariously on the top of a tall tree. There was the snipping of shears as Takeshi pruned his pear trees on the hillside.

About an hour later, I looked outside again and noticed that the black pall of smoke had thinned to a grayish haze. There was hardly any wind. The firemen must have been doing their job well and have got the fire under control. This was just as well, because we have had no rain for two or three weeks now.

Later I dropped by Mon to find Misako looking excited.

"There's been a fire, you know."

"Yes, so I noticed. A forest fire?" I asked casually.

"Not at all. It was the top house in Hirao. It's burned down completely. By the time the fire was discovered, it was too late for the family to salvage anything. What's more, the road doesn't go up as far as the house, so the fire engines couldn't get up there. They couldn't find a source of water near enough for their hoses to have any effect. Everything went up in flames. The family of three escaped all right, but they've lost everything. They haven't a single belonging."

It is at moments like this that one marvels at the efficiency of country life in Japan. The family was immediately given shelter by relatives and neighbors in the same community. It was also arranged that each house in Yashiki village would prepare one meal for the refugees. Every hamlet got together to decide how much condolence money to give. Ōkubo fixed on 2,000 yen a household. Those living closer at hand, together with relatives, will be paying between 5,000 and 10,000 each. Every house in the valley, from Fujioka at the bottom to Ichinotsuru at the top, will make some sort of contribution to the homeless family. Unlike the condolence money given to the sick or bereaved, this money does not have to be paid back in equivalent kind.

The closest relatives of the family concerned, together with the head of Hirao hamlet, spent the whole day walking around every house in Yashiki, apologizing for the inconvenience people had been caused and thanking them for their condolence money (which had not at the time been handed over). Here we have the acceptable face of responsibility.

It is not clear how the fire started. At first I was told that it was a result of a stove catching fire when the young wife was preparing rice for the rice-cakes that everyone makes for New Year. Later on, we heard that it was because the wife was drying her bedding with an electric dryer. People have said that the storehouse was ablaze when they arrived. Only after that did the main house catch fire.

Do people air eiderdowns or cook rice in a storehouse?

86   It's no use. Alyosha's neck has not improved, and he has to go through surgery. What's more, there are complications. Further X-rays have shown that the ligaments holding the pin joining Alyosha's neck to his head have been torn. Somehow his head must be secured, and a second operation will be necessary a few months after the first. Needless to say, we tell Alyosha nothing and pretend that Dr. Urayama wanted to see us about something else. This is the first time I have consciously had to lie to either of the boys.

One of us has to be with Alyosha now for the next four weeks. Maya is going to stay with one of his school friends for the next few days. We leave the house in Ōkubo empty and frozen around with snow.

Alyosha is taken down to the operating room at one o'clock in the afternoon. I hold his hand all the way and, as we watch him being wheeled through those great swinging doors, neither Kyōko nor I can hold back our tears. I wish I were not the father of that child.

The operation goes on . . . and on . . . and on. We try to pass the time by having something to drink in a cafe across the road from the hospital. The hours drag by. We soon run out of things to say and can only hold each other's hands. Tightly.

Eventually we go back to the hospital and wait nervously outside the operating room. The red light is still on; the surgeons are still at work. What is happening in there? What was supposed to be a two-hour operation has now been going on for four hours.

At a quarter past five, somebody comes out of the operating

room and walks hurriedly down the corridor. It is hard to tell who it is behind the mask and white overalls.

He, or she, comes back a few minutes later, purposely ignoring us as he, or she, disappears behind the swinging doors again. Rarely have I felt so helpless.

A few minutes later, the red light is switched off. Finally. We can hear voices in the anteroom. A nurse comes out and tells us cheerfully that it is all over. Everything is all right. Alyosha will be coming out of the anesthetic in a few minutes. Then he will be taken to his room.

At just after half past five, the nurses wheel him out. Even though he is still drunk with the effects of the anesthetic, he recognizes the sound of my voice and the feel of my hand, which he squeezes tightly. Help him, someone. Help him.

The waiting game once more . . .

87   All's well. There are two things that make me shake my head in bewilderment. The first is that Alyosha never complains, the second that he feels no pain. Now he merely has to learn the art of patience as he spends the next three weeks flat on his back, staring at the ceiling of his hospital room.

88   Kyōko telephones me from the prefectural capital and asks me to get to the hospital as soon as possible. Something has gone wrong. The bone grafted into Alyosha's neck has sprung loose. The operation must be done all over again. We are back to square one.

Urayama explains everything when I get to the hospital. "I know it doesn't help you, but this is only the second time that a bone graft of this sort has failed," he shakes his head sadly. "I've no choice but to open up Alyosha's neck again and put in another piece of his hipbone. The only advantage is that this time we should be able to chisel away a deeper notch for the graft and straighten out the second bone from the top a bit more."

Somehow we have to tell Alyosha. Having been on his back for two weeks, he is already counting the days until he can get up. How difficult it is to break bad news gently. For the first time since the accident occurred, he breaks into tears. As we try to comfort him, he smiles.

"Leave me alone for a bit. I want to have a good cry. Then I'll feel better."

We do as he asks. And he is true to his word.

The operation is fixed for January 27, my thirty-eighth birthday. Four more hours of helpless waiting. Again the pale figure being wheeled out of the operating room. Again the squeeze of a cool hand. Is it I who comfort him, or he who comforts me?

89   Finally Alyosha is up and walking. Hobbling would be a better word for it. His legs are so thin. Yet, at the same time, he has got so fat, just lying on his back in his hospital bed. We stuck a map of the world on the ceiling, and he used to stare at it for hours on end.

"Būchan, is there any sea between the bottom of Spain and the north of Africa?"

I told him there was.

"Bother!" he said. There was silence for a while, then, "How about between Egypt and that bit above Saudi Arabia?"

I explained that a canal had been dug there some time ago. He sounded disappointed. Again he studied the map.

"Well, there isn't any sea between North and South America, so that's where I'll build my canal."

Again I had to throw cold water—if that is the right phrase—on his enthusiasm. Again he muttered "Bother!"

"Well, I want to do something useful for people. And if they've dug all the canals worth digging, then I'll build a bridge. Between Siberia and Alaska. Nobody's done that yet. I know."

And today I am allowed to take him downstairs. Very slowly, very gently. He wants to go to the cafe where I've been eating the past month or so. As we step out into the dazzling spring sunlight, he breathes in deeply and smiles happily.

"Sixty-two days!" he exclaims. "The first sunlight for sixty-two days."

And because he is now mobile and able to look after himself, we no longer have to be with him 24 hours a day. I go home for only the fourth night in two and a half months. How long the days have

become in our absence. It is light until well after six in the evening.
I hear a nightingale (*uguisu*) calling. The plum blossoms are out.
The Oni valley is its beautiful self. The past several months are a
nightmare that we want to forget.

And yet we cannot forget. Both Kyōko and I have been through
too much. We are almost strangers to one another, meeting like the
stars of Tanabata on the 7th of July:

Kono yoru mo	Tonight too,
tsuma no hada furenu	I cannot feel my loved one's skin—
tanabata ya	Tanabata.

Oh, to be able to master the art of poetic allusion!

90 Coincidence again. The father of the boy who committed
suicide in his car down in Inekari was able to use his son's life insurance policy to rebuild his house. Aso Harumi's father-in-law has
rebuilt his house, too, with the money that he got for his wife's
sexual indiscretion. Now, I hear that the people whose house
burned down in Hirao had intended to move downhill a few hundred yards because their old house was so inconveniently located,
but had shelved the plan temporarily until the spring. And then the
fire occurred. The house was fully insured, so the family can now
afford to build a new house on their own rice field. Arson? Not a
word is breathed about that. It would, perhaps, be the ultimate
insult to the community.

91 Masaki in the early morning limps across the yard in front
of his house. The dew hangs in droplets from the spiders' webs,
piercing diamonds in the heatless sun. I ask him how Mihoko is.

"We've had her moved to a special home. She can move one arm
a little, but no more. One of us always has to be with her. It's really
inconvenient." Masaki looks drained. His eyes are slightly blood-
shot, his cheeks drawn in even more than before. "Hitomi got married, you know. Yes, it was arranged before the accident, and there
seemed to be no point in canceling it."

There is a sudden surge in the grass of the orchard below us,
followed by the sounds of panting and a low growl.

"Those bloody dogs. We managed to get two of them while you were away. The black one and her puppy. Try as we might, though, we couldn't get those other two over there. They were too quick for us. It really is about time I shot them."

For a moment I think he is joking, but the look on his face tells me that he is quite serious.

"We used to eat dog here not so many years ago. It's pretty good boiled in bean paste and soy sauce. Dog meat also cures some kind of illness. I can't remember what, though. Kuro and Roku? I had the Town Council put them away."

And so Alyosha and Maya have lost their best friends. How do I tell them that?

92　In the meantime I continue my desultory negotiations with Wada Hiromi of the local Education Authority. Hospital fees have been crippling. The school insurance partly covers them, of course, but repayments do not come until two months after I have paid the bills. Hiromi has therefore made arrangements with the hospital that they be paid directly by the insurance program. But there are other expenses incurred by our having to travel back and forth between our house in Ōkubo and the prefectural capital, and these Hiromi is less ready to grant us. To pay us our expenses is to admit a degree of responsibility for the accident. Hiromi is prepared to work only within a framework of regulations that do not admit responsibility. We begin to suspect that his cooperation is merely a ploy to string us along until it is time for us to leave the country. Then it will be too late for us to achieve anything.

I drop in at the post office on my way to the hospital, and Michiya asks how things are. "The PTA went to see Hiromi, you know, soon after the accident last summer. We told him that in our opinion the school's pool facilities were not satisfactory. Hiromi said he'd look into the matter, but we've heard nothing from him since. We told him to handle your case efficiently. Are you satisfied that he is doing so?"

I explain that we are fed up with the way the local Education Authority refuses to accept responsibility for an accident that took place during school hours and under instruction. We've never even had an apology for the accident—presumably because that would be tantamount to an admission of guilt. But both Kyōko and I feel that if the town had said at the start how sorry it was, we wouldn't be feeling so angry and frustrated now. All we are left with is the unpleasantness of legal action.

Michiya is sympathetic. In fact, he is the only one who remains sympathetic when I mention the word lawsuit. Even Inoshige and Katsuhisa look slightly embarrassed when they hear that word.

"Why don't you try to get the media to work on your behalf? You've got the contacts, haven't you? You should use them, you know. It might help because in this country bureaucrats are very afraid of the press. And if there's anything the PTA can do, let me know. I'll be frank with you, though, Būchan. Men like Chitose don't believe much of what they've heard you say, but if you can show them there is something in it for *them* as well as for you, they'll rally around and help. You can be sure of that."

The real trouble is that Kyōko and I are not really sure what we want. We are convinced that we have to fight. That is a matter of principle. Principle is a concept much valued in English society, but it is a term the Japanese don't care for. People don't have "principles" here—at least, not in quite the same sense of the word. They are prepared to let individually held opinions yield to public opinion, and public opinion, of course, is molded by authority. In the eyes of the local people, we are "selfish" precisely because we stick to our "principles," but if our action can change the present system of swimming and diving, if it can prevent any more accidents like this one from happening (and we keep on hearing of similar cases—some worse, but most not so bad), then we feel that it will be worth all the effort. All the same, to have "principles" is to invite conflict, and that is not acceptable in a society that values harmony above all else.

93   Alyosha is not the only one of our problems. Since we have started making preparations for our return to England, I asked Takeshi this morning if he could return me the money we had originally paid him for the land. He was suddenly evasive and began fiddling around with the insecticide pump at the back of his shed.

"I haven't got any money," he muttered with his back to me. "I want to have a talk. Call the intermediaries. We'll meet this evening."

I replied that I thought it would be rather rude to call together two such busy men as Inoshige and Tatetarō at such short notice. "Anyway, I thought everything had been fixed. Aren't you going to return us the money?"

Hanako had joined us by now and muttered to Takeshi that he ought to pay up when things have been fixed that way. He ignored her and repeated that he had no money. "Call the go-betweens. That's what they're for."

So I phoned up Inoshige, who comes over at lunch and, over five bottles of beer, discusses things with Takeshi, while I sit outside in Masaki's yard, watched warily by the two remaining wild dogs.

"I give up on that man," Inoshige exclaims in exasperation, after Takeshi has driven off in his van. "He's going to pay you, but he's not going to pay you. You've got to accept his conditions. One of his daughters is to be married this month, so he hasn't got that much cash. There's something funny going on."

A long telephone call to Tatetarō soon helps him piece together some of the jigsaw puzzle.

"It's partly to do with his daughter's wedding. You know, the one who works in the police station down in town. Let's face it, weddings are an expensive business. But there's something else. Old Haruzō has been egging Takeshi on recently, telling him he's been cheated by a foreigner. That's why Takeshi is now refusing to give you back all he owes you and is talking of getting the sum reduced. Tatetarō and I are going to talk to Takeshi this evening. I'll let you know what happens."

All evening I wait for a phone call to summon me down to Takeshi's house where the three of them are negotiating without me. Eventually, just before midnight, as we prepare to go to bed, the lights of a car briefly illuminate the upstairs windows. I go downstairs. It is Tatetarō and Inoshige. Neither of them is very talkative, and each looks serious. I open a bottle of wine and eventually Inoshige begins.

"Well, you're probably very angry with me, Būchan, and you've got every right to be. But, I can assure you, it's been a trying evening. The short answer to it all is that Takeshi is only going to give you back four hundred thousand yen, instead of the four hundred and fifty thousand we agreed on last summer. That means I've accepted less than I should have done. But what I want to say is that I'd already intended to give you a going-away gift when you leave. Instead of that, I'm going to give you the fifty thousand yen that I failed to get out of Yamaguchi. I'm sorry, and I hope you won't be too angry with me."

Inoshige finishes and takes another gulp of wine, downing it as though it were *sake*. Poor Inoshige. So kind, so typical of him, to try to cover other people's failings.

"I've never known anything like it," says Tatetarō, who has an upset stomach and is, somewhat reluctantly, drinking tea. "Takeshi is my cousin. He's got some good points, of course, but when it comes to money, he's really stingy. Do you know, at one stage he refused to hand back even three hundred thousand yen. We argued with him and finally Haruzō, who was there too, sided with us. Once he'd heard all the ins and outs of the story, he turned to Takeshi and told him he was completely in the wrong."

"Takeshi even began muttering about this being an international affair," adds Inoshige, helped by the wine to regain his usual eloquence. "So I told him in no uncertain terms that in that case he was the Japanese representative. He'd better do his best to show Japan in a good light if he really was so worried about what Būchan would say when he got back to England."

"Yes, and then Takeshi looked all mournful. You know the way he does sometimes. And he said Būchan would probably not write him any letters when he got home. Or did we think he would?"

"We told him not to be so stupid," says Inoshige. "If he wanted letters from Būchan, then he ought to do as he'd promised him. I don't understand that man."

"Neither do I," sighs Tatetarō, "He's a *quiz*." This word he brings out in English.

"Yes. If you understand what's going on in Takeshi's mind, you get a free trip to Hawaii. Like on those TV programs."

"Anyway, that's the last time I help out my cousin. I'm never going to act as his go-between again. If you ask me, it's because Takeshi has never acted as go-between for others that he behaves in such a selfish way."

The subject of *sewa*, acting on behalf of others, is an intriguing one. People in the valley seem incapable of acting on their own and so call on someone else to act as their go-between. There are two types of *sewanin*, intermediaries. One is the professional—like Haruzō, for example, who makes a living out of acting as go-between in business transactions. He will take something like 10 percent of the sum involved. Once Inoshige and Terukichi decided to buy some forest mountain land over on the other side of the town. The deal was concluded in a single evening, with neither Inoshige nor Terukichi seeing the land they were purchasing, and the sale price was fixed at eight million yen. Inoshige then offered the broker (the English word is used) 200,000 yen for his services, but the broker was disgusted at such a low fee. Inoshige argued that the deal, after all, had been concluded in a single evening without the broker's doing anything more than introducing the buyer to the seller. Surely, the normal 10 percent figure was a bit too high? The broker refused to accept anything less. Inoshige and Terukichi both got annoyed, and the deal fell through.

The other kind of intermediary gets nothing tangible for his pains. Men like Tatetarō act as *sewanin* out of goodwill because they are asked to do so. Tatetarō admits that the system can be very tiresome because people use it to try and get their own way. Down in Suzuka village, for example, there is one man who is very difficult to get along with. At least, that's what people generally say. But Tatetarō himself has always got along very well with him over the years. And so, when the villagers wanted to buy a piece of this man's land in order to widen the road, they immediately asked Tatetarō to act as go-between. They felt that he was the only person who would be likely to get the man's permission. It turned out they were right. In Tatetarō's opinion, this is the typical *konjō*, country mind, at work. Make use of someone if it suits your own purposes.

94 *The willow trees bow down to earth as the spring rain softly falls.* Plum blossoms scatter to the ground.

95 Frogs crossing the road at night in the rain. First casualties of the year. All that winter hibernation wasted.

96   If Yamaguchi Takeshi is a quiz, then so are the workings of bureaucracy. A long time ago, Takeshi's uncle, Hiromi, said that he would try to lengthen the coverage of the school insurance plan from two to five years. We have now discovered that the insurance has *always* been valid for five years from the date of an accident. When I ask Hiromi about this, he apologizes and says that we must have misunderstood him. He never meant to say anything of the sort.

But Hiromi also at one stage offered us a loan from his own pocket to help pay for our hospital bills, until we were reimbursed by the insurance program. Then he made "special arrangements" for the program to pay the hospital directly. Now we learn that there has *always* been provision for the payments to be sent directly to a hospital, so that people need not go through the tortuous method of payment and reimbursement that we experienced initially.

For some reason that neither of us can work out, the initial report from the town's Central Hospital to the local Education Authority said that Alyosha had a contusion and sprain, rather than a compressed fracture of the neck. Hiromi uses this report to justify the local Education Authority's attitude that Alyosha's accident was not serious.

Much more seriously, newspaper investigations have now revealed that there is considerable discrepancy between Baba's account of the accident and the tale told by Alyosha and his classmates. Alyosha says that on the day of the accident they had all been swimming relay races for some time when Baba got them out of the water and told them to dive. He gave no demonstration dives, even though it was the first day ever for some of the younger children, and told the children either to sit or to stand on the edge of the pool. Those who had "confidence" were told to stand and dive. This they did and completed three dives; on the fourth one Alyosha hit his head.

According to the report sent in to the local Education Authority by the headmaster, Hageyama, his deputy headmistress, Kaku, and the teacher, Baba, the children were taught to dive in four *stages*, not in four dives, as Alyosha and his friends contend. At each stage—sitting on the overflow, sitting on the side of the pool, kneeling on the side of the pool, and finally standing on the side of the pool—the children were made to dive between eight and ten times. This means that Alyosha's accident occurred after he had dived approximately 30 times.

Two short articles in the Asahi newspaper are enough to goad—finally—the Town Council into action. One afternoon, Inoshige suddenly appears, accompanied by Gotō Chitose—Aso's "cheek-by-jowl" lover and head of the school PTA.

"Būchan, I'm sorry to bother you, but we've been asked by Wada Hiromi to find out what you're proposing to do about Alyosha's accident. I mean, if the Town Council gave you something toward all your expenses, would you be prepared to back down from your demand that they accept responsibility?" He pauses, looking at me slightly embarrassed, knowing that I know that he has been dragged into this affair by Hiromi because of our friendship; knowing that I know that because of our friendship I can hardly refuse. "If the Town Council refuses to give you anything, are you really going to sue them in court?"

I reply to the last question in the affirmative. Very firmly. Inoshige and Chitose go away, only to return an hour or so later, asking us to go and meet Hiromi and his superiors down in the council offices. Inoshige has been drinking and rambles on about how we shouldn't expect anything to come of the meeting. Hiromi will probably only repeat what he has told me before. "But listen," he pleads, "at least, listen to them, please."

We go down to the town and are ushered into the mayor's office. Hiromi informs us that the committee of the local Education Authority has been meeting right up to the time of our arrival. He is now glad to report that the committee members have agreed to present us with an unstated amount of money because they feel sorry for Alyosha. Hiromi emphasizes that this money is not to be seen as "compensation," and that the sum is to be given not because we have requested a reimbursement of our expenses, but because Hiromi himself has asked the committee to agree to it.

Pause.

What are we supposed to say?

"Thank you very much."

Pause.

"Are we permitted to ask how much the committee is going to give us out of its goodwill?" We, too, are learning the phraseology of harmony.

"Well, there was a case of a child being paralyzed a few years back—not because of a swimming accident—and the Town Council gave the parents four hundred thousand yen then. But things have changed a bit since then. How about five hundred thousand yen?"

But there is a catch. We will be expected to sign a document to the effect that this is the end of the matter as far as my relations with the local Education Authority are concerned, and that I promise never to make any further demands of the Town Council, either personally or through a court of law. And all for a mere $2,000.

We ask for time to consider Hiromi's proposal and go home. How tired we both are of negotiating! I dream of negotiations, reliving in restless sleep the verbal duels of the day. What will I do? What *can* I do? The school insurance plan has been set up precisely to cover the loophole in the education system. Even though a child is compelled by law to leave the care of his or her family and attend school, no school is responsible for any accident that may occur to children in its "care." Precisely because there is school insurance, the authorities need not accept responsibility. The trouble is that the insurance plan is inadequate as it stands; its levels of compensation are pitifully low. It seems to me, therefore, that if the education authorities wish to avoid, or are not—for one reason or another—prepared to accept, responsibility for children in their care, then they ought to provide proper, realistic coverage.

When Inoshige appears the next morning, this time accompanied by Michiya, I tell him that we will sign the document, provided that it includes a clause whereby the Town Council agrees to address itself to the task of creating an adequate school insurance plan. Alyosha is to be the last victim in the sacrifice of responsibility. If we achieve this aim—if children, together with their parents, do not have to go through the kind of upsets in the future that we have been through this past year—then Alyosha's accident will have been "worthwhile."

"I admire you, Būchan. You've really thought things out, and we must strike while the iron is hot," Michiya says. "But you realize, of course, that the Town Council will never agree to a clause demanding that it *succeed* in its efforts to change the plan. Only that it will *try* to change it. And that may prove a bit meaningless. Let's see what happens, though."

And so we go down to the town once more.

"Poor Hiromi is really in hot water. He's had the committee members on call for most of the past three days. And he's got everyone, from the mayor down, available until midnight if the need arises." Michiya appears to know all about the backstage maneuvering that has been going on. "Without doubt, the committee has complained that Hiromi has been pressing for too much compensation. Compensation, sickness money! Call it what you will! They'll be accusing him of asking so much because you and he live in the same valley. And yet Hiromi's immediate senior has always made a point of stressing that you should be grateful to Hiromi for working so hard on your behalf because you both live in the same valley. Poor Hiromi! He can't win."

"Chitose seems to be coming around, too," says Inoshige. "He finally recognizes that the problem is not just yours, Būchan, but one common to all parents whose children go to the North Oni Primary School."

"It's what I always told you. The only way I could begin to make him understand it all was by pointing out that the amount of 'sickness money' offered would set a precedent. The higher the amount paid, the more it will be to everyone's advantage in the future. Chitose understands that sort of logic. So the PTA puts pressure on the Town Council, pretending to represent everyone's interests. But its *honshiki*, its real preoccupation, is as always with personal profit." Michiya gives one of his freckled grins. "The Town Council, of course, realizes this. That's why it never bothered to contact the PTA early on. Anything to avoid a backlash."

And so we reach the council offices. Michiya explains to Hiromi and the others that I wish to have a special clause written into the agreement requiring the Town Council to work toward creating an adequate school insurance plan. Hiromi replies that it would not do for a foreigner to tell the Japanese Government what it should do. He is prepared, however, to draw up a separate document between the Town Council and the PTA. Having just listened to Michiya's exposition of the workings of the PTA's collective mind, I realize that my idea will never work. Somehow I have little faith that the PTA will stand by my idea and force the Town Council to keep its promise. Moreover, Alyosha still has to go through one more major operation. It would be madness to sign away all responsibility for him now. I ask for time to consider the matter. Hiromi refuses to grant me time; the document has to be signed then and there.

It is an awful moment. I feel so helpless. I am betraying my friends, asserting my principles before all else and breaking the golden rule of anthropology—that I be "at one" with the people I study.

I walk out of the room without signing. At home *where no one can see me, I give myself to grief.*

97   Home for a night from the hospital, where Alyosha is recovering well from his third and last operation. There is nothing more that Dr. Urayama can do. He has placed a second bone graft at the back of Alyosha's neck and wired together the first and second bones there. This means that the top four bones now form a single piece of solid bone.

"He won't be able to turn his neck from side to side much," Urayama explains, as we sit in his office late in the afternoon, after he has finished seeing dozens of patients at the clinic. "But he's young and he's strong. Things should turn out all right, provided he doesn't do all those sports like football and fencing that he likes so much. I'm sure things will turn out well in the end. Come on, let's go and have a drink."

And with that he takes me off to have a Japanese meal with him and the clinic's administrator, along with half a dozen nurses. After dinner, we make a tour of the city's more expensive bars.

"You know," the administrator confides after we have all downed several whiskies to go on top of the *sake* we consumed at dinner. "Urayama *sensei* was in a cold sweat when he did that second operation on Alyosha. I can tell you now, but at the time we weren't sure whether your boy would pull through. He's a marvelous surgeon."

That certainly is true. We find it hard to believe that one of the three best spinal surgeons in the world should happen to live and work in the prefectural capital, so close to where I chose to do fieldwork, so far from the center of Japan.

Urayama himself, red-faced and splendidly drunk, is singing a popular song on a minute stage. An automatic camera films him in action as he struggles to keep in tune with the recorded orchestra music. As he falls wearily into his seat, amidst a chorus of applause and compliments from the two hostesses beside him, he looks at me hard.

"But I'll tell you something from a medical point of view. It's absurd to make children dive into water that is less than four feet deep. I don't care if the Ministry of Education keeps the water shallow to stop children from drowning, as you say. It's madness to make them dive. Utter madness!"

98   Today is Father's Day—a matter that is much discussed at Takayuki's *sake* shop as Inoshige and I share a few bottles of beer at the counter. The two men indulge in numerous—mainly repetitious—jokes about how their wives will have to give them plenty of "breast" in bed tonight. This is a play on the homonym *chichi*, whose sound can mean either breast or father.

99   Regretfully, after long deliberation, we find that we have no alternative but to sue the town's Education Authority for damages. Rarely have I felt so sick, frustrated, and angry. What annoys me most of all is the fact that I have been unable to discover whether the deception that has taken place over the circumstances of Alyosha's accident was initiated by Hiromi, or the headmaster of the primary school, or Alyosha's swimming teacher. It doesn't say much for my detective work that it has taken me so long to piece together this puzzle of lies and half-truths. Is the anthropologist to end up as no more than a glorified newspaper reporter or a Columbo without the shabby raincoat? My intuition tells me that it is the headmaster who is responsible for the cover-up, that it is he who fabricated the story about Baba teaching the children to dive in four stages, rather than four times. I like to think that Baba is too young, too innocent to betray the children in his care. But that is merely intuition. Unlike Columbo, I'll never know for sure. That is the difference between fiction and fact.

But now that we have brought a lawsuit, we find that we have gained one or two allies among our friends here. In general, the Japanese are very prejudiced against the idea of appealing to law, and the country people in particular still firmly believe that things should somehow be settled amicably. Many men no longer greet me with the warmth they once reserved for me. But now also old grudges break to the surface, and we hear from other parents how their children have been treated. Ryūichi was pushed into the pool by one of the teachers the year before last. He hit his head on the bottom and complained of headaches for weeks. When the parents protested, they were told not to make such a fuss about nothing. This was the attitude taken, too, at a different primary school in town where a boy hit his head on the bottom of a stainless steel swimming pool. The fact that it was made of stainless steel, and not concrete, saved the boy from anything worse than a twisted neck.

Aso Harumi's son, Yoshio, was accidentally hit on the head with a sickle by the same teacher, Baba, when the children were cutting the grass along the edge of the playground, and Yoshio began fooling around. Baba raised his hand and slapped the boy, forgetting that he was still holding his sickle. The gash was large enough that Yoshio had to have several stitches. Baba just apologized, in tears.

Others who take our side include Katō Tamaki, the stubborn old man who got drunk at Akihito's funeral, and even Takeshi, who muttered something about our presumably having thought things out carefully before coming to a decision. "Hiromi's my uncle and that makes things difficult for me," he said, "but I feel sorry for Alyosha. I hope things go well for you."

I suspect that the media's sympathetic reporting of the case has helped influence some people. Other acquaintances from town actually congratulate us for sticking to it, although somehow I feel that congratulations is hardly the right word to use.

"We could never have done what you've done," said one of Kyō-ko's friends, indicating that there would have been too much pressure from the network of her personal relationships. "It's about time somebody said something outright, instead of complaining all the time behind people's backs." What really annoyed this particular friend was the fact that the headmaster of her daughter's primary school in the center of town called all the children together and gave the following speech:

"Today we are gathered together here to open the pool for the summer. This is a joyous occasion, but I'd like to remind you of the dangers of swimming and diving. Last year, as you may have heard, there was an unpleasant accident when a foreign boy called Alyosha Moeran paid no attention to what his teacher told him. He dived into the pool just as he pleased and broke his neck as a result."

Katsuhisa admits that he has heard something similar on the grapevine at the high school where he is still, albeit reluctantly, teaching. "There was an outing earlier this year for all the headmasters of the town's primary schools," he tells me. "That would have given Hageyama the perfect opportunity to spread false rumors. Whether he actually did so, or not, I don't know. But you can judge for yourself, no doubt."

Unfortunately, the headmaster has made his mark closer to home as well. The PTA committee met with the school staff for one of its end-of-term get-togethers. Katsuhisa for once decided to put in an appearance.

"You'll probably not believe it, but Gotō Chitose got up and said that the PTA stood behind the school in the Moeran case, and that one shouldn't allow a lawsuit to interfere with one's loyalty and indebtedness to one's children's teachers. The teachers needed all the support they could get. Then Hageyama told the committee members not to believe too much of what they had been reading in the papers. The media were very good at lying. It's all right," Katsuhisa says, patting me on the shoulder, as I begin to seethe with anger. "Hiromi then stood up and said that, as the father of Alyosha's closest friend, he was in a difficult position, but surely it was not for the PTA to stand behind either one side or the other. That would be to prejudge the issue. Chitose tried to reinforce his argument by saying that you, Būchan, had not consulted him before filing your petition for damages." Once again, individual pique is transferred and framed as a group attitude.

"The way I see it," Katsuhisa goes on, working the blunt end of his toothpick around in his ear, "people in the Oni valley are worried about two things. First of all, no foreigner should be allowed to get his own way. And second, no foreigner should be allowed to take away so much money from the Town Council. You see, the outsider complex [*yoso no mono*] prevails at all times. People like Hageyama and Chitose will do anything to damage your reputation."

This is not the first time the subject of my reputation has cropped up in recent weeks. Tomorrow Daisuke's son, Fujio, is getting married, and I have been invited. But today Inoshige lets slip that Daisuke is in fact worried about somebody saying something during the *sake*-drinking session when the bride is introduced to the villagers of Amagase. To save Daisuke, Reiko, Fujio, his bride, and all the others any embarrassment, I excuse myself from the wedding party. My withdrawal from valley life is now almost complete. What a strange process of seeming assimilation and rejection fieldwork has proved to be.

So I have a "bad reputation," and that is upsetting. But there is a valley proverb that provides some consolation. Reputations based on rumor have a life span of 45 days; then they are forgotten. The fact that I have any kind of reputation, of course, is an indication of my own increased social status. Only those in positions of authority make enemies. The more important they become, the more enemies they are likely to make. Nobody bears a grudge against the poor and lowly. In the same way, perhaps, you can tell an anthropologist's academic standing by the vehemence with which his theories are criticized.

In general, though, people here care as much about the death of a child living next door as about the grazed knees of their own son or daughter. It's been said before, but that is the way things are.

I00   Women in the country do their best to cover their faces so as not to get suntanned as they work in the fields. A white face signifies that a woman does not have to work hard outside the house. Hence it is seen as a sign of status that accrues from a certain leisure. Yuki is a good example of this sentiment.

Women in the city, on the other hand, do their best to get suntanned. There it is seen as a sign of leisure and social status if a woman can afford the time to sunbathe and burn her skin brown.

I0I   Alyosha telephoned from the hospital last night to say that he has been given permission to come back home. Today, for the last time, we take the beautiful mountain road to the prefectural capital. We say farewell to the staff of Urayama's clinic and drive

back to the Oni valley. Here we are, once more, all four of us together in our tumbledown house. Maya chuckles to himself and
sings Mattōya Yumi songs all afternoon. In the evening, as he relaxes in the iron bathtub, he calls out to me as I split wood for the
fire: "How nice to be all together again. It makes even baths that
much more fun!"

And Alyosha has kept a promise he made himself six weeks ago
when he had his third operation: that he would be home in time for
Kyōko's birthday tomorrow.

102   Today we all gave evidence in a court that was brought
up to Ōkubo because of Alyosha's condition. The hearing produced some new pieces of evidence. In the first place, Baba has
admitted that he never got into the pool at any time because he
wears contact lenses and cannot see without them. Second, we have
now discovered that Alyosha dived into an area of the pool where
the maximum depth was 83 cm—not 93 cm as reported to the local
Education Authority. We have also heard that on the day of the
accident the pump that kept the pool full of water was apparently
not working. As the children splashed around, the water depth de-
creased by seven or eight centimeters. By the time Hageyama,
Kaku, and Baba got together to measure the pool, the pump had
been repaired and the water was at its proper, official depth.

I don't know. I just don't know. Suspicion is the seed of alien-
ation and trust the perfect foil for deceit.

103   There is no time to do anything except pack. Sixty-four
boxes of books, clothes, pots, a kickwheel, a koto, and an old pachinko machine that we bought off a roadside vendor somewhere
between the town and the prefectural capital. The bedding, furniture, and children's toys we give away.

Hanako comes up one afternoon just after everything has been
taken off in a truck by the shipping company. She hands Kyōko an
envelope into which she has neatly folded five 10,000-yen bills. She
apologizes for Takeshi's behavior over the past year and begs us to
accept what is rightfully ours. After some discussion in which we
try to return the money, Hanako bursts into tears. Reluctantly, we

do as she asks. Then she tells us how she has managed to grow successfully some of the beetroot seed that Kyōko brought with us from England. She has now passed new seed to friends and neighbors. I can see that beetroot, along with dill, *yomogi* bread, and a single brick-laid stone wall, will confuse social archaeologists in centuries to come.

O-bon comes around once again. Once again I put on my cotton robe and clogs and go down to dance with my fellow villagers. There have been three more deaths in Yashiki during the past 12 months—Tōsuke's mother, Haruzō's ninety-three-year-old father, and the Yamadas' young son, who was killed in a car accident the other day. Even though the Yamadas now live down in the town, they maintain their family home here in Yashiki. It is in the temple in Inekari that the boy's ashes are kept.

And so we dance in the midsummer evening, that slow dance of death that turns into celebration, as we move from first one house to the next, before finishing up at the Yamadas'. At each stop we are entertained with food and drink, and as the alcohol takes effect, the singing gets louder and louder and the dancing more vigorous. Michiya, Takayuki, and Haruo act as main singers, once again huddling together under the porch light to read the words of the song from the crumpled sheet of paper that they share among them.

> Last night Mr. Night Crawler
> Fell from the second floor—
> Pretended to be a cat
> And went "meow, meow."

> How funny last night
> Zassan's night crawling—
> Still feeling his way around
> When the dawn came on.

We join in the choruses, smacking our round summer fans against the palms of our hands as we move rhythmically forward, then backward, circling forever clockwise around the front yard of the house, our faces glistening from exertion in the heat of the summer's evening.

> If you're going to dance,
> Then dance till you're thirty,

> And when you're over thirty,
> Let your children do the dancing.
>
> And if your voice fails,
> Then lick a horse's ass—
> From the horse's ass
> A voice is bound to come.

Finally, we are too tired to go on. The *sake* and beer have reduced us to exhaustion. We split up, taking our leave of one another, and walk home under the stars. Katsuhisa accompanies me across the stepping stones of the stream and up through the rice fields below his house. Then he leaves me, and I walk on up the hill alone, at each shadowy residence startled by the barking of a dog. Even at our own house, the two wild dogs sheltering next door fail to recognize my footsteps for a moment and growl in the night. It is only my foreigner's voice that quiets them.

And so the ancestors have come back once more, and it is this occasion that we have chosen for our leave-taking. On the Monday evening, the ancestors are escorted back to the temple, and then the Yashiki villagers gather for a summer party at the primary school, with draft beer, singing, dancing, and fireworks. We say goodbye, moving slowly from one trestle table to the next, greeting, thanking, and then parting from all of those who have been so kind to us over the past four years—Daisuke and Reiko; Michiya and his wife; Jirō, Kumao, Buntarō, and Tōsuke and their families. Goodbye, goodbye. From some it is easier to part than from others, and some of the women—Misako, Ayako, and Misae—find it hard to hold back their tears. The men, on the other hand, make their farewells so matter-of-fact. Katsuhisa, Inoshige, one after the other they say goodbye. Like the wind in the trees, we have come and now we go. But our friends are as unmoved as the trees that rear above this valley. It is their valley, not mine; their life, not mine.

There is a crackling sound over the loudspeaker as a scratched record is played. Everyone lines up to form a huge circle in the center of the playground as the music begins.

> This is the place where we were born,
> Valley of the blinding sunshine.

I cannot resist one last look at the house. It is as empty and deserted as when I first came here more than three and a half years ago, perched on its steep embankment, silhouetted against the sky. Around it the stillness of the pear orchards and cedar plantations. The pines stand lonely on Mount Toyama's peak. *A cloud breaks free into the open sky.* Down in the valley I can see the fireworks going off—flashes of light and color, followed by a whoosh of sound. Masaki's house is still shut and deserted. Outside the two wild dogs lie in the yard, watching me warily. They, too, never did quite learn to trust me completely. But there is the thump-thump-thump of their tails on the dusty earth as I say goodbye.

Afterword

People have often taken the trouble to ask: "So what happened to Alyosha? Is he all right?" To this many have added as an afterthought: "It must have been awful for you all."

They are right, of course. It was awful—for each of us in different ways. But wounds heal, if only imperfectly, and all of us have had our different ways of coping with their aftereffects, even though in the end Kyōko and I separated and remarried. It's hard to believe that Alyosha could have grown into a towering lad of six foot six, or that he would end up trained as a stonemason. (Will this help him build his bridge from Siberia to Alaska?) Maya, though well over six feet tall, has had the thoughtfulness to remain just shorter than his dad. He is a musician now and lives along the farther reaches of Tokyo Bay. Occasionally the two boys meet and start chattering at once in their local Kyushu dialect—which can sound pretty offbeat in places like the London Underground.

As for Alyosha's injury, well, we don't talk about it much these days. After all, it can't be very pleasant for him to be reminded constantly that he may not be as right as the rain that sometimes falls on his head. So he leads a pretty normal life now. As anticipated, he has some difficulty in turning his neck from side to side, but he has learned to compensate for this loss of movement by revolving his upper body at the same time. The scar he tends to cover with a scarf of some sort. Otherwise, he's what the doctors call a "walking miracle," and the X-rays taken before and after his operations are now used in case studies presented to students at the National Spinal Injuries Centre in Stoke Mandeville Hospital. Rather remarkably, and apparently quite without precedent, the slice of hipbone grafted onto the second,

third, and fourth bones of the boy's neck has actually grown as
Alyosha himself has grown. As they say in Japanese, in our mis-
fortune we have been most fortunate.

Other matters have also worked out well. After a seemingly
endless exchange of documents and examination of witnesses, a
local prefectural court found in our favor and ordered the city
government to pay Alyosha damages of a little over thirty million
yen. At the same time, however, the presiding judges saw fit to
castigate Japan's Ministry of Education for its failure to ensure
proper safety measures in primary school swimming classes—
thereby encouraging the local government authorities to appeal
to a higher court on the grounds that it was only doing as ordered by the Ministry of Education. The case dragged on. We
had to provide more documentation of this and that; the same
people were called to the witness stand to give the same evidence
(which, in some cases, turned out to be different). Eventually, in
1987, our lawyers advised us to come to an out-of-court settle-
ment (*wakai* in Japanese). We agreed because we also learned
that the Ministry of Education had changed its regulations re-
garding aquatic safety. From that same year on, diving has been
forbidden in all primary school swimming pools throughout
Japan. Whoopee!

I have a suspicion that, in the long run, this might prove to be my
single contribution to the culture that during my life as an anthropologist I have spent so much time trying to "explain." A small
step for Bū, perhaps, but a giant leap for Japanese children . . .
provided, of course, that they don't follow the instructions given
to Alyosha by his teacher on that fateful day so long ago and leap
too high.

Hong Kong, 1997